Julia 1.0 Programming Cookbook

Over 100 numerical and distributed computing recipes for your daily data science workflow

Bogumił Kamiński
Przemysław Szufel

BIRMINGHAM - MUMBAI

Julia 1.0 Programming Cookbook

Commissioning Editor: Richa Tripathi
Acquisition Editor: Alok Dhuri
Content Development Editor: Zeeyan Pinheiro
Technical Editor: Gaurav Gala
Copy Editor: Safis Editing
Project Coordinator: Vaidehi Sawant
Proofreader: Safis Editing
Indexer: Rekha Nair
Graphics: Alishon Mendonsa
Production Coordinator: Deepika Naik

First published: November 2018

Production reference: 1281118

Published by Packt Publishing Ltd.
Livery Place
35 Livery Street
Birmingham
B3 2PB, UK.

ISBN 978-1-78899-836-9

www.packtpub.com

To the memory of my mother for setting me on a journey to explore science.

– Bogumił Kamiński

I would like to thank my wonderful wife Bożena for her support and understanding during the writing of this book and my daughters Zofia and Maria for bringing inspiration to each day of my life.

– Przemysław Szufel

We would like to thank our friend Timothy (Timek) Harrell for proofreading an initial version of this text and for valuable language and technical feedback.

– Bogumił Kamiński and Przemysław Szufel

`mapt.io`

Mapt is an online digital library that gives you full access to over 5,000 books and videos, as well as industry leading tools to help you plan your personal development and advance your career. For more information, please visit our website.

Why subscribe?

- Spend less time learning and more time coding with practical eBooks and Videos from over 4,000 industry professionals

- Improve your learning with Skill Plans built especially for you

- Get a free eBook or video every month

- Mapt is fully searchable

- Copy and paste, print, and bookmark content

Packt.com

Did you know that Packt offers eBook versions of every book published, with PDF and ePub files available? You can upgrade to the eBook version at `www.packt.com` and as a print book customer, you are entitled to a discount on the eBook copy. Get in touch with us at `customercare@packtpub.com` for more details.

At `www.packt.com`, you can also read a collection of free technical articles, sign up for a range of free newsletters, and receive exclusive discounts and offers on Packt books and eBooks.

Contributors

About the authors

Bogumił Kamiński (GitHub username: bkamins) is an associate professor and head of the Decision Support and Analysis Unit at the SGH Warsaw School of Economics, as well as adjunct professor at the data science laboratory, Ryerson University, Toronto. He is co-editor of the Central European Journal of Economic Modeling and Econometrics, and of the Multiple Criteria Decision Making journal. His scientific interests center on operational research and computational social science. He has authored over 50 research articles on simulation, optimization, and prediction methods. He also has 15+ years' experience in the deployment of large-scale advanced analytics solutions for industry and public administration.

Przemysław Szufel (GitHub username: pszufe, web: szufel.pl) is an assistant professor in the Decision Support and Analysis Unit at the SGH Warsaw School of Economics. His current research focuses on distributed systems and methods for the execution of large-scale simulations for numerical experiments and optimization. He is working on asynchronous algorithms for the parallel execution of large-scale computations in the cloud and distributed computational environments. He has authored, and co-authored, several open source tools for high-performance and numerical simulation.

About the reviewer

Jalem Raj Rohit is an IIT Jodhpur graduate with a keen interest in recommender systems, machine learning, and serverless and distributed systems. Raj currently works as a data scientist at GEP, prior to which he worked at GEP and Kayako. He contributes to open source projects in Python, Go, and Julia. He also speaks at tech conferences on serverless engineering and machine learning.

Packt is searching for authors like you

If you're interested in becoming an author for Packt, please visit authors.packtpub.com and apply today. We have worked with thousands of developers and tech professionals, just like you, to help them share their insight with the global tech community. You can make a general application, apply for a specific hot topic that we are recruiting an author for, or submit your own idea.

Table of Contents

Preface

The Julia programming language, with its dynamic nature and high performance, reduces the time that needs to be taken for the development of computational models with easy-to-maintain computational code. *Julia 1.0 Programming Cookbook* will be your solution-based guide, and will take you through different programming aspects with Julia.

Starting with the new features of Julia 1.0, each recipe addresses a specific problem, along with a discussion that explains the solution and offers insight into how it works. You will work with the powerful Julia tools and data structures, along with the most popular Julia packages. You will learn how to create vectors, handle variables, and work with functions. You will be introduced to various recipes for numerical computing, distributed computing, and achieving high performance. You'll see how to optimize data science programs with parallel computing and memory allocation. Moving forward, we will look into more advanced concepts, such as metaprogramming and functional programming. Finally, you will learn how to tackle issues while working with databases and data processing, and will learn about data science problems, data modeling, data analysis, data manipulation, parallel processing, and cloud computing with Julia.

By the end of the book, you will have the skills you need to work more effectively with your data.

Who this book is for

The target audience of this book is data scientists or programmers that want to improve their skills in working with the Julia programming language.

It is recommended that the user has a little experience with Julia or intermediate-level experience with other programming languages such as Python, R, or MATLAB.

What this book covers

Chapter 1, *Installing and Setting Up Julia*, introduces the use of the Julia command line and the setup of the entire Julia computational infrastructure, including building Julia, optimizing performance, and configuring Julia for the cloud.

Chapter 2, *Data Structures and Algorithms*, contains practical examples of how custom algorithms can be implemented, while also taking advantage of the built-in functionality.

Chapter 3, *Data Engineering in Julia*, explains that working with data requires good understanding of streams and data sources. In this chapter, the reader will learn how to write data to IO streams with Julia and how to handle web transfers.

Chapter 4, *Numerical Computing with Julia*, contains recipes showing how computing tasks can be performed in the Julia language. Each recipe implements a relatively simple and standard algorithm to show a specific feature of the language. Therefore, the reader can concentrate on the implementation issues.

Chapter 5, *Variables, Types, and Functions*, presents topics related to variables and their scoping, Julia type systems and processing functions, and exceptions in Julia.

Chapter 6, *Metaprogramming and Advanced Typing*, presents various advanced programming topics in Julia.

Chapter 7, *Handling Analytical Data*, presents the `DataFrames.jl` package, providing a rich set of functionalities for working with them—manipulating rows and columns, handling categorical and missing data, and various standard transformations of tables (filtering, sorting, joins, wide-long transformation, and tabulation).

Chapter 8, *Julia Workflow*, explains the recommended workflow and shows how to build it using modules.

Chapter 9, *Data Science*, explains that Julia provides great support for various numerical and data science tasks. It allows us to define and optimize models in a very flexible solver-agnostic way. Julia also contains a huge toolbox for visualizing data and machine learning.

Chapter 10, *Distributed Computing*, shows how to use Julia for parallel and distributed computing tasks. An important feature of Julia is the ability to scale up computations across many processes, threads, and up to distributed computational clusters.

To get the most out of this book

Some understanding of Julia would be a bonus.

In this book, we use many Julia packages. Here, we provide an installation script for those packages.

This script can be also found in the GitHub repository in the `cookbookconf.jl` file.

All packages are installed and pinned in a concrete version that ensures that they will work correctly with the recipes given in the book. More information about managing packages can be found in the *Managing Packages* recipe in `Chapter 1`, *Installing and Setting Up Julia*.

If you do not pin the packages to the required version, they might still work, but it is possible that newer versions of some packages introduce non-compatible API changes, in which case the codes of the recipes might need small alterations to make them run.

We have divided packages into three groups:

- Packages that do not depend on external software
- Packages that can optionally depend on an external Anaconda Python installation
- Packages that require external software to be run.

For each package group, we provide an installation script that installs exactly the same version that we have used in the book.

All the packages listed are installed by calling the following function:

```
using Pkg

function addandpin(spec)
    Pkg.add(PackageSpec(; spec...))
    Pkg.pin(spec.name)
end
```

Packages that do not depend on external software can be installed with the following commands:

```
pkg1 = [(name="StatsBase", version="0.26.0"),
        (name="TimeZones", version="0.8.1"),
        (name="BSON", version="0.2.1"),
        (name="Revise", version="0.7.12"),
        (name="Distributions", version="0.16.4"),
        (name="Clp", version="0.5.0"),
```

```
                (name="HTTP", version="0.7.1"),
                (name="Gumbo", version="0.5.1"),
                (name="StringEncodings", version="0.3.1"),
                (name="ZMQ", version="1.0.0"),
                (name="CodecZlib", version="0.5.0"),
                (name="JSON", version="0.19.0"),
                (name="BenchmarkTools", version="0.4.1"),
                (name="JuliaWebAPI", version="0.5.0"),
                (name="FileIO", version="1.0.2"),
                (name="ProfileView", version="0.4.0"),
                (name="StaticArrays", version="0.8.3"),
                (name="ForwardDiff", version="0.9.0"),
                (name="Optim", version="0.17.1"),
                (name="JuMP", version="0.18.4"),
                (name="JLD2", version="0.1.2"),
                (name="XLSX", version="0.4.2"),
                (name="Cbc", version="0.4.2"),
                (name="DataFrames", version="0.14.1"),
                (name="CSV", version="0.4.3"),
                (name="DataFramesMeta", version="0.4.0"),
                (name="Feather", version="0.5.0"),
                (name="FreqTables", version="0.3.0"),
                (name="OnlineStats", version="0.19.1"),
                (name="MySQL", version="0.7.0"),
                (name="Cascadia", version="0.4.0"),
                (name="UnicodePlots", version="0.3.1"),
                (name="ParallelDataTransfer", version="0.5.0")]]

    foreach(addandpin, pkg1)
```

Packages that can optionally depend on an external Python Anaconda installation (refer to the *Calling Python from Julia* recipe in `Chapter 8, `*Julia Workflow,* for details) can be installed with the following commands:

```
    pkg2 = [(name="Conda", version="1.0.2"),
            (name="PyCall", version="1.18.4"),
            (name="PyPlot", version="2.6.3"),
            (name="Plots", version="0.20.5"),
            (name="StatPlots", version="0.8.1")]

    foreach(addandpin, pkg2)
```

Some packages require external software to be installed. This includes the
RCall.jl, JDBC.jl, LibPQ.jl and Gurobi.jl packages. Before installing those
packages, make sure that the required software is installed on your system. For
the RCall.jl package, check the *Calling R from Julia* recipe in Chapter 8, *Julia Workflow*,
for JDBC.jl and LibPQ.jl, check the *Working with databases in Julia* recipe, and
for Gurobi.jl, check the *Optimization using JuMP* recipe; both recipes can be found
in Chapter 9, *Data Science*. Once you make sure that all software dependencies are
installed, you can use the following commands:

```
pkg3 = [(name="RCall", version="0.12.1"),
        (name="JDBC", version="0.4.0"),
        (name="LibPQ", version="0.5.0"),
        (name="Gurobi", version="0.5.3")]

foreach(addandpin, pkg3)
```

Download the example code files

The example code files are organized in folders representing chapters and recipes. For each
recipe, there is a commands.txt file that contains commands that should be typed-in by the
reader. Every entry in this file is prepended by an appropriate prompt (example, $,
julia>) to make sure that the user knows in which environment the command should be
executed (typically the OS shell, the Julia command line). Most recipes also contain
additional files, for example, source codes of Julia programs. A full list of files along with
their contents is given in the *Getting ready* section of every recipe.

You can download the example code files for this book from your account at
www.packt.com.If you purchased this book elsewhere, you can
visit www.packt.com/support and register to have the files emailed directly to you.

You can download the code files by following these steps:

1. Log in or register at www.packt.com.
2. Select the **SUPPORT** tab.
3. Click on **Code Downloads & Errata**.
4. Enter the name of the book in the **Search** box and follow the onscreen
   instructions.

Once the file is downloaded, please make sure that you unzip or extract the folder using the latest version of:

- WinRAR/7-Zip for Windows
- Zipeg/iZip/UnRarX for Mac
- 7-Zip/PeaZip for Linux

The code bundle for the book is also hosted on GitHub at `https://github.com/PacktPublishing/Julia-1.0-Programming-Cookbook`. We also have other code bundles from our rich catalog of books and videos available at `https://github.com/PacktPublishing/`. Check them out!

Download the color images

We also provide a PDF file that has color images of the screenshots/diagrams used in this book. You can download it `https://www.packtpub.com/sites/default/files/downloads/9781788998369_ColorImages.pdf`.

Conventions used

There are a number of text conventions used throughout this book.

`CodeInText`: Indicates code words in text, database table names, folder names, filenames, file extensions, path names, dummy URLs, user input, and Twitter handles. Here is an example: "Mount the downloaded `WebStorm-10*.dmg` disk image file as another disk in your system."

A block of code is set as follows:

```
html, body, #map {
 height: 100%;
 margin: 0;
 padding: 0
}
```

For each block of code, we explain how it should be used (for example, maybe it should be pasted into a file or executed on the console).

Any command-line input is written in bold and the command-line output is written in normal font:

```
julia> collect(1:5)
5-element Array{Int64,1}:
 1
 2
 3
 4
 5

julia> sin(1)
0.8414709848078965

julia>
```

Code that is executed in an OS shell (for Linux or Windows) is indicated with the $ sign (for Windows, this will be C:\). You should write commands that follow this sign (without the sign itself). For example, this command would give information about files in a current working directory:

```
$ ls
```

All single commands passed to the Julia command line are prepended with the julia> prompt marker. For example, this is a minimal Julia session:

```
$ julia --banner=no
julia> 1+2
3

julia> exit()

$
```

We have started Julia from the OS shell using the julia command. Then, we have entered 1+2 in the Julia command line and Julia printed 3. Finally, we have entered exit() in Julia to terminate the the Julia command-line session and go back to the shell (so we have the shell $ prompt in the last line of the output). Please note that for the aforementioned blocks of code, separate, instructions might be given that might also include copying and pasting them to the console.

In several recipes, we also discuss non-standard prompts in the Julia command line (for example, package manager mode or shell mode). They are explained in the relevant recipes.

All examples in this book have been tested on Linux Ubuntu 18.04 LTS and Windows 10. Please note that users of other Linux distributions will need to update their scripts (for example, Linux distributions from the Red Hat family use yum instead of apt). Most Linux-related commands should also work on macOS; however, they have not been tested on this OS.

Bold: Indicates a new term, an important word, or words that you see on screen. For example, words in menus or dialog boxes appear in the text like this. Here is an example: "Select **System info** from the **Administration** panel."

 Warnings or important notes appear like this.

 Tips and tricks appear like this.

Sections

In this book, you will find several headings that appear frequently (*Getting ready, How to do it..., How it works..., There's more...,* and *See also*).

To give clear instructions on how to complete a recipe, use these sections as follows:

Getting ready

This section tells you what to expect in the recipe and describes how to set up any software or any preliminary settings required for the recipe.

How to do it...

This section contains the steps required to follow the recipe.

How it works...

This section usually consists of a detailed explanation of what happened in the previous section.

There's more...

This section consists of additional information about the recipe in order to make you more knowledgeable about the recipe.

See also

This section provides helpful links to other useful information for the recipe.

Get in touch

Feedback from our readers is always welcome.

General feedback: If you have questions about any aspect of this book, mention the book title in the subject of your message and email us at customercare@packtpub.com.

Errata: Although we have taken every care to ensure the accuracy of our content, mistakes do happen. If you have found a mistake in this book, we would be grateful if you would report this to us. Please visit www.packt.com/submit-errata, selecting your book, clicking on the Errata Submission Form link, and entering the details.

Piracy: If you come across any illegal copies of our works in any form on the internet, we would be grateful if you would provide us with the location address or website name. Please contact us at copyright@packt.com with a link to the material.

If you are interested in becoming an author: If there is a topic that you have expertise in and you are interested in either writing or contributing to a book, please visit authors.packtpub.com.

Reviews

Please leave a review. Once you have read and used this book, why not leave a review on the site that you purchased it from? Potential readers can then see and use your unbiased opinion to make purchase decisions, we at Packt can understand what you think about our products, and our authors can see your feedback on their book. Thank you!

For more information about Packt, please visit packt.com.

Installing and Setting Up Julia 1

In this chapter, we present recipes covering the following topics:

- Installation issues:
    - How to install Julia in different environments
    - How to compile your own Julia binaries
    - How to use Julia in the cloud in **Amazon Web Services** (**AWS**) using Cloud9
- Basic usage of Julia:
    - The various ways you can customize the start-up of Julia
    - How to set up Julia to work with multiple cores
    - How to perform the standard steps comprising a daily workflow using the Julia command line (the Julia language shell also referred to as the **Julia REPL**)
    - How to display computational results in Julia
    - How to manage packages
- More advanced configurations of Julia usage:
    - How to launch Julia in Jupyter Notebook
    - How to use Julia with JupyterLab
    - How to connect to Jupyter Notebook in Terminal-only cloud environments

Introduction

A key condition for successfully working with any programming language is the careful configuration of the development environment. Julia, being an open source language, offers integration with several popular tools. This means that developers have a number of alternatives at hand when setting up the complete Julia toolbox.

The first decision to be made is the choice of Julia distribution. Available options include binary and source code forms. For non-typical hardware configurations, or when one wishes to use all the latest compiler features, Julia source code can be downloaded. Another decision concerns which compiler to use in order to build Julia (GCC or Intel) and whether to link Julia against Intel's mathematical libraries.

The second decision lies in the choice of IDE. Julia can be integrated with various editors, with Atom plus the Juno plugin being the most popular choice. Yet another option is to use a browser-based Julia IDE—Jupyter Notebook, JupyterLab, or Cloud9.

In this chapter, we discuss all the preceding options and show how to set up the complete Julia programmer's environment, along with the most important technical tips and recommendations.

Installing Julia from binaries

The goal of this recipe is to present how to install and configure the Julia environment with the development toolbox. We show basic installation instructions for Linux and Windows.

Getting ready

In this recipe, we present how to install and configure Julia on Windows and Linux.

All Linux examples in this book have been tested on Linux Ubuntu 18.04.1 LTS and Windows 10. All Linux Ubuntu commands have been run as the user ubuntu. Please note that users of other Linux distributions will need to update their scripts (for example, Linux distributions from the Red Hat family use yum instead of apt).

For Windows examples in this book, we use Windows 10 Professional.

In the GitHub repository for this recipe you will find the commands.txt file that contains the presented sequence of shell commands.

How to do it...

For most users, the recommended way to start with Julia is to use a binary version.

In this section, we present the following options:

- *Installing Julia on Linux Ubuntu*
- *Installing Julia on Windows*

Installing Julia on Linux Ubuntu

Installing the binary release is the easiest way to proceed with Julia on Linux. Here, we show how to install Julia on Ubuntu, although the steps will be very similar for other Linux distributions.

Before the installation and use of Julia, we recommend installing a standard set of build tools for the Linux platform. Although this is not required for running Julia itself, several Julia package installers assume that the standard build tools set is present on the operating system. Hence, run the following commands in bash:

```
$ sudo apt update
$ sudo apt -y install build-essential
```

In order to install Julia, simply download the binary archive from `julialang.org`, uncompress it, and finally create a symbolic link named **Julia**. These steps are shown in the following three bash commands (we assume that these commands are run in the `/home/ubuntu` folder):

```
$ wget
https://julialang-s3.julialang.org/bin/linux/x64/1.0/julia-1.0.1-linux-x86_64.tar.gz
$ tar xvfz julia-1.0.1-linux-x86_64.tar.gz
$ sudo ln -s /home/ubuntu/julia-1.0.1/bin/julia /usr/local/bin/julia
```

Please note that the last command creates a symbolic link to the Julia binaries. After this installation, it is sufficient to run the `julia` command in the OS shell to start working with Julia.

Please note that on the Julia web page (`https://julialang.org/downloads/`), a newer version of the installer could be available. You can update the preceding script accordingly by simply updating the filename. Additionally, *nightly build* Julia versions are available on the preceding website. These versions are only recommended for testing new language features.

Installing Julia on Windows

The most convenient way to install Julia on Windows is by using the binary version installer available from the JuliaLang website.

The following steps are required to install Julia on a Windows system:

1. Download the **Windows Self-Extracting Archive (.exe)** from `https://julialang.org/downloads/`. It is recommended to select the **64-bit** version.
2. Run the downloaded `*.exe` file to unpack Julia. We recommend extracting Julia into a directory path that does not contain any spaces, for example, `C:\Julia-1.0.1`.
3. After a successful installation, a Julia shortcut will be added to your start menu—at this point, you can select the shortcut to see whether Julia loads correctly.
4. Add `julia.exe` to your system path, as follows:
    1. Open Windows Explorer, right-click on the **This PC** computer icon, and select **Properties**.
    2. Click **Advanced system settings** and go to **Environment Variables....**
    3. Select the `Path` variable and click **Edit....**
    4. To the variable value, add `C:\Julia-1.0.1\bin` (in this instruction, we assume that Julia has been installed to `C:\Julia-1.0.1`). Please note that, depending on your Windows version, there is either one `Path` value per line or a semicolon `;` is used to separate values in the `Path` list.
    5. Click **OK** to confirm. Now, Julia can be run anywhere from the console.

When adding `julia.exe` to your system path, please note that there are two variable groups on this screen, **User variables** and **System variables**. We recommend using **User variables**. Please note that adding `julia.exe` to the system `Path` makes it possible for other tools, such as Juno, to automatically locate Julia (Juno also allows for manual Julia path configuration—this can be found in the option marked **Packages | Julia client | Settings**).

For the most convenient workflow, we recommend installing the ConEmu terminal emulator for Windows users.

The steps to install ConEmu on your Windows system are as follows:

1. Go to the ConEmu website (`http://conemu.github.io/`) and click the **Download** link. Select **Download ConEmu Stable Installer**.
2. Once you download the `*.exe` file, run it to install ConEmu. Select the 64-bit version in the installer; other settings can keep their default values.
3. Once ConEmu is installed, a new link in the start menu and on the desktop will be created.
4. During the first application run, ConEmu asks about color settings—just stay with the defaults. Run ConEmu, type `julia`, and press *Enter,* and you should see a Julia prompt.

There's more...

Those users who want to try Julia without the installation process should try JuliaBox.

JuliaBox is a ready-made pre-installed Julia environment accessible from the web browser. It is available at `https://juliabox.com/`. You can use this version to play with a preconfigured and installed version of the Julia environment. Julia is available in a web browser via the Jupyter Notebook environment. The website is free to use, though it does require registration. JuliaBox comes with a set of pre-configured popular Julia libraries and is therefore ready for immediate use. This is an ideal solution for people wanting to try out the language or for using Julia inside a classroom.

See also

Excellent documentation on how to install Julia on various systems can be found on the JuliaLang website: `https://julialang.org/downloads/platform.html`.

Julia IDEs

Integrated Desktop Environments (**IDEs**) are integrated tools that provide a complete environment for software development and testing. IDEs provide visual support for the development process, including syntax highlighting, interactive code editing, and visual debugging.

Getting ready

Before installing an IDE, you should have Julia installed (either from binaries or source), following the instructions given in previous recipes.

 In the GitHub repository for this recipe, you will find the `SublimeText.txt` file that contains configuration for Sublime Text described in this recipe. The configuration process of other IDEs described in this recipe is completely done with a point and click interface.

How to do it...

The three most popular Julia IDEs are Juno, Microsoft Visual Studio Code, and Sublime Text. In subsequent sections, we discuss the installation process for each particular IDE.

Juno

Juno is the recommended IDE for Julia development. The Juno IDE is available at `http://junolab.org/`. However, Juno runs as a plugin to Atom (`https://atom.io/`). Hence, in order to install Juno, you need to take the following steps:

1. Make sure that you have installed Julia and added it to the command path (following the instructions given in previous sections).
2. Download and install Atom, available at `https://atom.io/`.
3. Once the installation is complete, Atom will start automatically.
4. Press *Ctrl* + , (*Ctrl* key + *comma* key) to open the Atom settings screen.
5. Select the **Install** tab.
6. In the **Search packages** field, type `uber-juno` and press *Enter*.
7. You will see the `uber-juno` package developed by JunoLab—click **Install** to install the package.
8. In order to test your installation, click the **Show console** tab on the left.

Please note that when being run for the first time from Atom, Julia takes longer to start. This happens because Juno is installed along with several other packages that are being compiled before their first use.

Microsoft Visual Studio Code

Note that at the time of publishing this book the Microsoft Visual Studio Code does not yet support Julia 1.0. However, since we believe that this support will be available very soon, we provide the instructions below.

The Microsoft Visual Studio Code editor can be obtained from `https://code.visualstudio.com/`. Simply download the installer executable and install using the default settings. After launching Visual Studio Code, perform the following steps:

1. Click **Extensions** tab (or press *Ctrl + Shift + X*).

2. In the search box, type `julia`. You will see **Julia Language Support** on the list. Click the green **Install** button to start the installation.

3. Click **File | New File** to create a new, empty file.

4. Click **File | Save As...** to save the newly created file. In the **Save As...** type drop-down list, select **Julia** (please note that the file type list might not be sorted alphabetically and Julia type might be at the bottom of the list).

5. Open the Terminal tab and issue the `julia` command.

After following these steps, you will have a Julia file open in the editor and an active Julia Terminal. Pressing *Ctrl + Enter* will now send the currently highlighted code line to the Terminal to execute it.

Sublime Text

Another option for the IDE is utilizing the functionality of Sublime Text:

1. If you are using Sublime Text, then add the package named `Julia` through **Package Control**.

2. Next, the simplest thing to add is a custom build system for Julia (**Tools | Build System | New Build System**):

```
{
    "cmd": ["ConEmu64", "/cmd", "julia -i", "$file"],
    "selector": "source.julia"
}
```

3. Now, you can execute an opened Julia script by pressing *Ctrl + B* in the console in interactive mode (–i switch).

The preceding example assumes that ConEmu64 and julia are defined in the search path.

The only inconvenience of this method is that if there is an error in the Julia script, the console will be immediately terminated (a cleaner way to test your scripts is to keep your Terminal with Julia open) and use the include command, as explained in the recipe *Useful options for interaction with Julia* in this chapter.

See also

For integration with other editors and IDEs, take a look at the https://github.com/JuliaEditorSupport project.

Julia support for text editors

On some computational environments, no desktop is available and so users may want to use Julia in a text-only mode.

Getting ready

Before installing Julia support for text editors, you should have Julia preinstalled (either from binaries or source), in accordance with the instructions given in previous recipes.

 In the GitHub repository for this recipe, you will find the commands.txt file that contains the presented sequence of shell commands.

How to do it...

The three most popular text editors used by Julia developers include Nano, Vim, and Emacs. Here, we provide some hints on how to configure Julia with these popular text-mode editors. All the following examples have been tested with Ubuntu 18.0.4.1 LTS.

Configuring Julia with Nano

Nano is a popular Linux text editor for beginners. By default, nano does not provide syntax highlighting for Julia. However, this can easily be remedied by adding appropriate lines to the .nanorc configuration file, which should be located in the user's home directory. The following commands will update the .nanorc file with the appropriate syntax coloring for Julia. Firstly, download syntax highlighting for Julia (https://stackoverflow.com/questions/35188420/syntax-highlighting-support-for-julia-in-nano):

```
$ wget -P ~/
https://raw.githubusercontent.com/Naereen/nanorc/master/julia.nanorc
```

Secondly, add highlighting to the nano configuration file, using the bash command, as follows:

```
$ echo include \"~/julia.nanorc\" >> ~/.nanorc
```

Configuring Julia with Vim

In order to configure Julia for Vim, you need to use the files available at the git://github.com/JuliaEditorSupport/julia-vim.git project. All you need to do for this is to copy them to the Vim configuration folder. On a Linux platform, this can be achieved by running the following commands:

```
git clone git://github.com/JuliaEditorSupport/julia-vim.git
mkdir -p ~/.vim
cp -R julia-vim/* ~/.vim
```

Once julia-vim is installed, one interesting feature is the support for LaTeX-style special characters. Try running vim file.jl and type \alpha, then press the *Tab* key. You will observe the text changing to the corresponding α character.

Further information and other useful options can be found on the julia-vim project website at git://github.com/JuliaEditorSupport/julia-vim.git.

Configuring Julia with Emacs

Since Emacs is not present by default in Ubuntu, the following instruction assumes that it has been installed by the `sudo apt install emacs25` command. In order to configure Emacs support for Julia, you need to activate the `julia-mode` mode. This can be achieved with the following bash commands:

```
wget -P ~/julia-emacs/
https://raw.githubusercontent.com/JuliaEditorSupport/julia-emacs/master/jul
ia-mode.el
echo "(add-to-list 'load-path \"~/julia-emacs\")" >> ~/.emacs
echo "(require 'julia-mode)" >> ~/.emacs
```

See also

For integration with other editors and IDEs, take a look at the Julia Editor Support project, which is available at `https://github.com/JuliaEditorSupport`.

Building Julia from sources on Linux

Building Julia allows you to test the latest developments and includes bug fixes. Moreover, when Julia is compiled, it is optimized for the hardware that the compilation is performed on. Consequently, building Julia from source code is the recommended option for those production environments where performance is strongly affected by platform-specific features. These instructions will also be valuable for those Julia users who would like to check out and experiment with the latest source versions from the Julia Git repository.

In the following examples, we show how to install and build a stable version of Julia 1.0.1.

Getting ready

All the following examples have been tested on Ubuntu 18.04.1 LTS.

Here is a list of steps to be followed:

1. Open the console and install all the prerequisites. Please refer to the following script (run each shell command shown as follows):

   ```
   $ sudo apt update
   $ sudo apt install --yes build-essential python-minimal gfortran m4
   cmake pkg-config libssl-dev
   ```

2. Download the source code (run each shell command shown as follows; we assume that the commands are run in your home folder):

```
$ git clone git://github.com/JuliaLang/julia.git
$ cd julia
$ git checkout v1.0.1
```

 In the GitHub repository for this recipe you will find the commands.txt file that contains the presented sequence of shell commands.

How to do it...

In this section, we describe how to build Julia in three particular variations:

- With open source mathematical libraries
- With Intel's **Math Kernel Library** (**MKL**), but without Intel LIBM (Math Library)—this scenario requires registration on Intel's website
- With Intel's Math Kernel Library (MKL) and with Intel LIBM (Math Library)—a commercial license from Intel is required

The libraries from Intel (MKL and LIBM) provide an implementation for a number of mathematical operations optimized for Intel's processor architecture. In particular, the Intel MKL library contains optimized routines for BLAS, LAPACK, ScaLAPACK, sparse solvers, fast Fourier transforms, and vector math (for more details see https://software.intel.com/en-us/mkl). On the other hand, the Intel LIBM library provides highly optimized scalar math functions that serve as direct replacements for the standard C calls—this includes optimized versions of standard math library functions, such as exp, log, sin, and cos). More information on Intel LIBM can be found at https://software.intel.com/en-us/articles/implement-the-libm-math-library.

Before running each of the recipes, please make sure that you are inside the folder where you ran the checkout command for Julia (see the *Getting ready* section).

Option 1 – build Julia without Intel's MKL

Once you have followed the steps in the *Getting ready* section and Julia has been checked out from the Git repository, perform the following steps:

1. In order to build Julia, simply run the following bash shell command:

    ```
    $ make -j $((`nproc`-1)) 1>build_log.txt 2>build_error.txt
    ```

    The build logs will be available in the `build_log.txt` and `build_error.txt` files.

2. Once the Julia environment has been built, you can run the `./julia` command and use `versioninfo()` to check your installation:

    ```
    julia> versioninfo()
    Julia Version 1.0.1
    Commit 0d713926f8* (2018-09-29 19:05 UTC)
    Platform Info:
      OS: Linux (x86_64-linux-gnu)
      CPU: Intel(R) Xeon(R) Platinum 8124M CPU @ 3.00GHz
      WORD_SIZE: 64
      LIBM: libopenlibm
      LLVM: libLLVM-6.0.0 (ORCJIT, skylake)
    ```

Option 2 – build Julia with Intel MKL (without Intel LIBM)

Once you have followed the steps in the *Getting ready* section and Julia has been checked out from the Git repository, perform the following the steps:

1. The MKL library is freely available from Intel. In order to get access to Intel MKL, you need to submit a form on Intel's website at `https://software.intel.com/en-us/mkl`.

2. Once the form has been completed, you receive an MKL download link (please note that the actual filenames may be different in the library version you obtain).

3. Execute the following commands to install MKL:

```
$ cd ~
# Get link from MKL website
$ wget http://registrationcenter-download.intel.com/[go to Intel
MKL web site to get link]/l_mkl_2019.0.117.tgz
$ tar zxvf l_mkl_2019.0.117.tgz
$ cd l_mkl_2019.0.117
$ sudo bash install.sh
```

4. Once the Intel MKL library is installed, you can build Julia (run each shell command as shown):

```
cd ~/julia
echo "USEICC = 0" >> Make.user
echo "USEIFC = 0" >> Make.user
echo "USE_INTEL_MKL = 1" >> Make.user
echo "USE_INTEL_LIBM = 0" >> Make.user

source /opt/intel/bin/compilervars.sh intel64

make -j $((`nproc`-1)) 1>build_log.txt 2>build_error.txt
```

The build logs will be available in the build_log.txt and build_error.txt files.

5. Once Julia is successfully built, run the ./julia command to start it.

6. Use versioninfo() to check the status of Julia. Information about the MKL status is available from the ENV["MKL_INTERFACE_LAYER"] system variable. Take a look at a sample screen, as follows:

```
julia> versioninfo()
Julia Version 1.0.1
Commit 0d713926f8* (2018-09-29 19:05 UTC)
Platform Info:
  OS: Linux (x86_64-linux-gnu)
  CPU: Intel(R) Xeon(R) Platinum 8124M CPU @ 3.00GHz
  WORD_SIZE: 64
  LIBM: libopenlibm
  LLVM: libLLVM-6.0.0 (ORCJIT, skylake)

julia> ENV["MKL_INTERFACE_LAYER"]
"ILP64"
```

Please note that if you build Julia with MKL, whenever you start a new Linux session you need to tell Julia where the Intel compilers are so that it can properly find and use the MKL libraries. This is done by executing the following bash command:

```
$ source /opt/intel/bin/compilervars.sh intel64
```

The preceding command needs to be executed each time prior to launching the `julia` process in a new environment.

Option 3 – build Julia with Intel MKL and with Intel LIBM

Once you have followed the steps in the *Getting ready* section and Julia has been checked out from the Git repository, perform the following steps:

1. Acquire an Intel Parallel Studio XE (https://software.intel.com/en-us/c-compilers/ipsxe) license, which entitles you to use the Intel C++ compilers (https://software.intel.com/en-us/c-compilers) along with the Intel Math Library (Intel LIBM, available at https://software.intel.com/en-us/node/522653).

2. Once you acquire the license, together with a download link from Intel, download and install the software by running the shell commands given as follows (please note that the actual filenames may be different in the library version you obtain):

```
$ cd ~
# Get the link from Intel C++ compilers website
$ wget http://[go to Intel to get
link]/parallel_studio_xe_2018_update3_professional_edition.tgz
$ tar zxvf parallel_studio_xe_2018_update3_professional_edition.tgz
$ cd parallel_studio_xe_2018_update3_professional_edition
$ sudo bash install.sh
```

3. Select the MKL among the installation options in Intel Parallel Studio XE.
4. Build Julia (run each shell command as shown):

```
cd ~/julia
echo "USEICC = 0" >> Make.user
echo "USEIFC = 0" >> Make.user
echo "USE_INTEL_MKL = 1" >> Make.user
echo "USE_INTEL_LIBM = 1" >> Make.user

source /opt/intel/bin/compilervars.sh intel64

make -j $((`nproc`-1)) 1>build_log.txt 2>build_error.txt
```

The build logs will be available in the build_log.txt and build_error.txt files.

5. Once Julia has been compiled, you can start it with the ./julia command and use the versioninfo() command—the LIBM parameter should point to libimf.

Please note that if you build Julia with MKL/LIBM, when you start a new Linux session, you need to tell Julia where Intel compilers are so it can properly find and use MKL/LIBM libraries:

```
$ source /opt/intel/bin/compilervars.sh intel64
```

The preceding command needs to be executed each time before launching the julia process in a new environment (hence, one might want to add that command to the ~/.profile start-up file).

How it works...

For the highest performance, it is recommended to compile Julia with the Linux Intel MKL (Intel MKL is available at https://software.intel.com/en-us/mkl) drivers, which are available for free from Intel. The numerical performance can also be enhanced by using the Intel Math Library (Intel LIBM is available at https://software.intel.com/en-us/node/522653). However, LIBM can only be obtained with the Intel C++ compilers (see https://software.intel.com/en-us/c-compilers), which are free for academic and open source use but paid otherwise. Therefore, some users might be interested in building Julia with MKL, but without LIBM.

Please note that in all the scenarios outlined, we use GNU compilers rather than Intel compilers—even when using Intel's MKL and LIBM libraries. If you want to use Intel's compilers, you need to set the appropriate options in the `Make.user` file (that is, change `USEICC = 0` and `USEIFC = 0` to `USEICC = 1` and `USEIFC = 1`). However, Intel compilers are currently not supported by Julia compiler scripts (see `https://github.com/JuliaLang/julia/issues/23407`).

There's more...

Once Julia is installed on your system, it can be run by giving the full path to the Julia executable (for example, `~/julia/julia`). This is not always convenient—many users simply want to type `julia` to get Julia running:

```
$ sudo ln -s /home/ubuntu/julia/usr/bin/julia /usr/local/bin/julia
```

The preceding path assumes that you installed Julia as the `ubuntu` user in your `home` folder. If you have installed Julia to a different location, please update the path accordingly.

See also

If you want to build Julia in a supercomputing environment (for example, Cray), please follow the online tutorial written by one of the authors of this book, available at `https://github.com/pszufe/Building_Julia_On_Cray_and_Clusters`.

Running Julia inside the Cloud9 IDE in the AWS cloud

Cloud9 is an integrated programming environment that can be run inside a web browser. We will demonstrate how to configure this environment for programming with Julia. The web page of Cloud9 can be reached at `https://aws.amazon.com/cloud9/`.

Getting ready

In order to use Cloud9, you must have an active **Amazon Web Services** (**AWS**) account and log in to the AWS management console.

Cloud9 can create a new EC2 instance running Amazon Linux or can connect to any existing Linux server that allows SSH connections and has Node.js installed. In order to start working with Julia on Cloud9, complete the following steps:

1. Prepare a Linux machine with Julia installed (you can follow the instructions in the previous sections).
2. Install Node.js. In Ubuntu 18.04.1 LTS, for example, the only step needed is to run `sudo apt install nodejs`.
3. Make sure that your server is accepting external SSH connections. For an AWS EC2 instance, you need to configure the instance security group to accept SSH connections from `0.0.0.0/0`—in order to do this, click on the EC2 instance in the AWS console, select **Security Groups** | **Inbound** | **Edit,** and add a new rule that accepts all traffic.

> In the GitHub repository for this recipe, you will find the `JuliaRunner.run` file that contains the configuration for the AWS Cloud9.

How to do it...

Once you have prepared a server with Julia and Node.js, you can take the following steps to use Cloud9:

1. In the AWS console, go to the Cloud9 service and create a new environment.
2. Select the **Connect and run in remote server (SSH)** option.
3. For the username, type `ubuntu` if you use Ubuntu Linux, or `ec2-user` if you are running Amazon Linux, CentOS, or Red Hat (please note that this recipe has been tested with Ubuntu).
4. Provide the hostname (public DNS) of your EC2 instance.
5. Configure SSH authorization.
6. In the **Environment settings** screen, select **Copy key to clipboard** to copy the key.
7. Open an SSH connection to your remote server in a Terminal window.
8. Execute the `nano ~/.ssh/authorized_keys` command to edit the file.
9. Create an empty line and paste the public key content that you have just copied.
10. Press *Ctrl + X* and confirm the changes with *Y* to exit.

11. Now, you are ready to click the **Next step** button in the Cloud9 console. Cloud9 will connect to your server and automatically install all the required software. After a few minutes, you will see your Cloud9 IDE. By default, Cloud9 does not support running programs in Julia.

12. Go to the **Run** menu and select **Run with** | **New runner**. Type the following contents:

```
{
"cmd" : ["julia", "$file", "$args"],
"info" : "Started $project_path$file_name",
"selector" : "source.jl"
}
```

13. Save the file as `JuliaRunner.run`.

14. Now, pressing the **Run** button will run your Julia `*.jl` file.

Please make sure that the `Cloud9` folder points to `/.c9/runners`.

How it works...

The Cloud9 environment runs in your web browser. The browser opens a REST connection back to Cloud9's server, which in turn opens an SSH connection to your Linux instance (see the following diagram). This functionality will, in fact, run with any Linux server that accepts incoming connections from Cloud9 (more details on configuring other Linux servers with Cloud9 can be found at `https://docs.aws.amazon.com/cloud9/latest/user-guide/ssh-settings.html`):

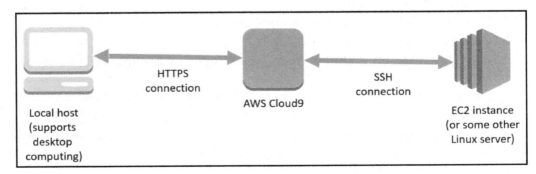

Please note that this means that the EC2 instance supporting Cloud9 should allow incoming connections from the AWS Cloud9 infrastructure. In production environments, we recommend limiting traffic to the EC2 instance (via `SecurityGroup`) to the IP ranges defined for Cloud9. Detailed instructions can be found in Cloud9's documentation: `https:/ /docs.aws.amazon.com/cloud9/latest/user-guide/ip-ranges.html`.

See also

The Cloud9 environment is being continuously updated by AWS; new features are being added frequently. For the latest documentation, we recommend looking at AWS Cloud9's user guide, available at `https://docs.aws.amazon.com/cloud9/latest/user-guide/`. In particular, it is worth looking at `https://docs.aws.amazon.com/cloud9/latest/user-guide/get-started.html`.

How to customize Julia on startup

Julia has multiple parameters that can be used to tune its behavior during startup. In this recipe, we explain three ways in which you can change them:

- Using command line options
- Using scripts run at startup
- Using environment variables

Also, we discuss several important and non-obvious use cases.

Getting ready

Before we begin, make sure that you have the Julia executable in your search path, as explained in the *Installing Julia from binaries* recipe. Also, create a `hello.jl` file in your working directory, containing the following line:

```
println("Hello " * join(ARGS, ", "))
```

We will later run this file on Julia startup.

 In the GitHub repository for this recipe, you will find
the `commands.txt` file that contains the presented sequence of shell and
Julia commands, the `hello.jl` file described above and
the `startup.jl` file that is discussed in the recipe.

Now, open your favorite terminal to execute commands.

How to do it...

In this recipe, we will show various options for controlling how the `julia` process is started: running scripts on startup, running a single command, and configuring a startup script for Julia installation. They are discussed in the consecutive subsections.

Running a script on Julia startup

We want to run the `hello.jl` file on Julia startup while passing some switches and arguments to it.

In order to execute it, write the command following $ in your OS shell and press *Enter*:

```
$ julia -i hello.jl Al Bo Cyd
Hello Al, Bo, Cyd
   _       _ _(_)_     |  Documentation: https://docs.julialang.org
  (_)     | (_) (_)    |
   _ _   _| |_  __ _   |  Type "?" for help, "]?" for Pkg help.
  | | | | | | |/ _` |  |
  | | |_| | | | (_| |  |  Version 1.0.2 (2018-11-08)
 _/ |\__'_|_|_|\__'_|  |  Official https://julialang.org/ release
|__/                   |
julia>
```

Notice that we remain in the Julia command line after the script finishes its execution because we have passed through the `-i` switch. The Al, Bo, and Cyd arguments got passed as the ARGS variable to the printing command contained in the `hello.jl` file.

Now, press *Ctrl + D* or write `exit()` and press *Enter* to exit Julia and go back to the shell prompt.

Running a single Julia command on startup

If we just want to run a single command, we can use the −e switch.

Write the command following $ in your shell:

```
$ julia -e "println(factorial(10))"
3628800
$
```

In this example code, we have calculated 10! and printed the result to standard output. Notice that Julia exited immediately back to the shell because we did not pass the −i switch.

Running a script every time Julia starts

If there are commands that you repeatedly pass to Julia after startup, you can automate this process by creating a startup file.

First, put the following statements in the ~/.julia/config/startup.jl file, using your favorite editor:

```
using Random
ENV["JULIA_EDITOR"] = "vim"
println("Setup successful")
```

Now, start Julia from the OS shell:

```
$ julia --banner=no
Setup successful
julia> RandomDevice()
RandomDevice(UInt128[0x0000000000000000000000000153e4040])

julia>
```

We can see that the startup script was automatically executed as it has printed a greeting message and we have access to the RandomDevice constructor that is defined in the Random module. Without the specifier using Random, trying to execute the RandomDevice() expression in the Julia command line would throw an UndefVarError exception. Additionally, we used the --banner=no switch to suppress printing the Julia banner on startup.

How it works...

There are four methods you can use to parameterize the booting of Julia:

- By setting startup switches
- By passing a startup file
- By defining the ~/.julia/config/startup.jl file
- By setting environment variables

The general structure of running Julia from the command line is this:

```
$ julia [switches] -- [programfile] [args...]
```

The simplest way to control Julia startup is to pass switches to it. You can get the full list of switches by running the following in the console:

```
$ julia --help
```

In the previous examples, we have used three switches: -i, -e, and --banner=no.

The first of these switches (-i) keeps Julia in interactive mode after executing the commands. If we did not use the -i switch then Julia would terminate immediately after finishing the passed commands.

You can pass Julia a file to execute directly or a command to run following the -e switch. The latter option is useful if you want to execute a short expression. However, if we want to start some commands repeatedly every time Julia starts, we can save them in the ~/.julia/config/startup.jl file. It will be run every time Julia starts unless you set the --startup-file=no command line switch.

In the preceding path, ~ is your home directory. Under Linux, this should simply work. Under Windows, you can check its location by running homedir() in the Julia command line (typically, it will be the C:\Users\[username] directory).

What are some useful things to put into ~/.julia/config/startup.jl?

In the recipe, we put the using Random statement in ~/.julia/config/startup.jl to load the Random package by default, since we routinely need it in our daily work. The second command, ENV["JULIA_EDITOR"]="vim", specifies a default editor used by Julia. Use of the editor in Julia is explained in the *Useful options for interaction with Julia* recipe.

There's more...

The full list of environment variables that are scanned by Julia is described at `https://docs.julialang.org/en/v1.0/manual/environment-variables/`. They can all be set in the shell and then are read by Julia. In Julia, environment variables can be accessed and changed via the `ENV` dictionary.

See also

- The use of an external editor in Julia is described in the *Useful options for interaction with Julia* recipe.
- An explanation of how to work with packages is given in the *Managing packages* recipe.
- A more advanced topic is passing commands on startup to multiple processes. It is described in the *Setting up Julia to use multiple cores* recipe.

Setting up Julia to use multiple cores

Current computers have multiple cores installed. In this recipe, we explain how to start Julia so that we can utilize them. There are two basic ways you can use multiple cores: via multithreading and multiprocessing (visit `https://www.backblaze.com/blog/whats-the-diff-programs-processes-and-threads/` and `https://en.wikipedia.org/wiki/Thread_(computing)#Threads_vs._processes`, where you can find a basic explanation of the differences between these two approaches). The major difference is that processes have separate state information, whereas multiple threads within a process share process state as well as memory and other resources. Both options are discussed in this recipe.

Getting ready

In order to test how multiprocessing works, prepare two simple files that display a text message in the console. When running parallelization tests, we will see messages generated by those scripts appear asynchronously.

Create a `hello.jl` file in your working directory, containing the following code:

```
println("Hello " * join(ARGS, ", "))
```

And create `hello2.jl` with the following code:

```
println("Hello " * join(ARGS, ", "))
sleep(1)
```

 In the GitHub repository for this recipe, you will find the `commands.txt` file that contains the presented sequence of shell and Julia commands and the `hello.jl` and `hello2.jl` files described above.

Now, open your favorite terminal to execute the commands.

How to do it...

We will first explain how to start Julia using multiple processes. In the second part of the recipe, we will set up Julia to use multiple threads.

Multiple processes

In order to start several Julia processes, perform the following steps:

1. Specify the number of required worker processes using the –p option on Julia startup.
2. Then, check the number of workers in Julia by using the `nworkers()` function from the `Distributed` package.
3. Run the command following $ in your OS shell, then import the `Distributed` package and write `nworkers()` while in Julia, and then use `exit()` to go back to the shell:

```
$ julia --banner=no -p 2

julia> using Distributed

julia> nworkers()
2

julia> exit()

$
```

If you want to execute some script on every worker on startup, you can do it using the −L option.

4. Run the hello.jl and hello2.jl scripts (the steps to start Julia and exit it are the same as in the preceding steps):

```
$ julia --banner=no -p auto -L hello.jl
Hello !
 From worker 4: Hello !
 From worker 5: Hello !
julia> From worker 2: Hello !
 From worker 3: Hello !
julia> exit()

$ julia --banner=no -p auto -L hello2.jl
Hello !
 From worker 4: Hello !
 From worker 5: Hello !
 From worker 2: Hello !
 From worker 3: Hello !
julia> exit()

$
```

We can see that when the −L option is passed, then Julia stays in command line after executing the script (as opposed to running a script normally, where we have to pass the −i option to remain in REPL). The difference in behavior between hello.jl and hello2.jl is explained in the *How it works...* section.

Multiple threads

Julia can be run in a multithreaded mode. This mode is achieved via the JULIA_NUM_THREADS system environment parameter. One should perform the following steps:

1. To start Julia with the number of threads equal to the number of cores in your machine, you have to set the environment variable JULIA_NUM_THREADS first

2. Check how many threads Julia is using with the Threads.nthreads() function

Running the preceding steps is handled differently on Linux and Windows.

Here is a list of steps to be followed:

1. If you are using **bash** on Linux, run the following commands:

```
$ export JULIA_NUM_THREADS=`nproc`
$ julia -e "println(Threads.nthreads())"
4
$
```

2. If you are using **cmd** on Windows, run the following commands:

```
C:\> set JULIA_NUM_THREADS=%NUMBER_OF_PROCESSORS%
C:\> julia -e "println(Threads.nthreads())"
 4
C:\>
```

Observe that we have not used the -i option in either case, so the process terminated immediately.

How it works...

A switch, -p {N|auto}, tells Julia to spin up N additional worker processes on startup. The auto option in the -p switch starts as many workers as you have cores on your machine, so julia -p auto is equivalent to:

- julia -p `nproc` on Linux
- julia -p %NUMBER_OF_PROCESSORS% on Windows

It is important to understand that when you start N workers, where N is greater than 1, then Julia will spin up N+1 processes. You can check it using the nprocs() function—one master process and N worker processes. If N is equal to 1, then only one process is started.

We can see here that hello.jl was executed on the master process and on all of the worker processes. Additionally, observe that the execution was asynchronous. In this case, workers 4 and 5 printed their message before the Julia prompt was printed by the master process, but workers 2 and 3 executed their print method after it. By adding a sleep(1) statement in hello2.jl, we make the master process wait for one second, which is sufficient time for all workers to run their println command.

As you have seen, in order to start Julia with multiple threads, you have to set the environment variable JULIA_NUM_THREADS. It is used by Julia to determine how many threads it should use. This value—in order to have any effect—must be set before Julia is started. This means that you can access it via the ENV["JULIA_NUM_THREADS"] option but changing it when Julia is running will not add or remove threads. Therefore, before running Julia you have to type the following in a terminal session:

- export JULIA_NUM_THREADS=[number of threads] on Linux or if you use **bash** on Windows
- set JULIA_NUM_THREADS=[number of threads] on Windows if you use the standard shell

There's more...

You can also add processes after Julia has started using the addprocs function. We are running the following code on Windows with two drives, C: and D:, present. Julia is started in the D:\ directory:

```
D:\> julia --banner=no -p 2 -L hello2.jl
Hello
 From worker 3: Hello
 From worker 2: Hello
julia> pwd()
"D:\\"

julia> using Distributed

julia> pmap(i -> (i, myid(), pwd()), 1:nworkers())
2-element Array{Tuple{Int64,Int64,String},1}:
 (1, 2, "D:\\")
 (2, 3, "D:\\")

julia> cd("C:\\")

julia> pwd()
"C:\\"

julia> addprocs(2)
2-element Array{Int64,1}:
 4
 5

julia> pmap(i -> (i,myid(),pwd()), 1:nworkers())
4-element Array{Tuple{Int64,Int64,String},1}:
```

```
(1, 3, "D:\\")
(2, 2, "D:\\")
(3, 5, "C:\\")
(4, 4, "C:\\")
```

In particular, we see that each worker has its own working directory, which is initially set to the working directory of the master Julia process when it is started. Also, addprocs does not execute the script that was specified by the -L switch on Julia startup.

Additionally, we can see the simple use of the pmap and myid functions. The first one is a parallelized version of the map function. The second returns the identification number of a process that it is run on.

As we explained earlier, it is not possible to add threads to a running Julia process. The number of threads has to be specified before Julia is started.

Deciding between using multiple processes and multiple threads is not a simple decision. A rule of thumb is to use threads if there is a need for data sharing and frequent communication between tasks running in parallel.

See also

More details about how to work with multiple processes and multiple threads are explained in the *Multithreading in Julia* and *Distributed computing with Julia* recipes in Chapter 10, *Distributed Computing*.

Useful options for interaction with Julia

Julia has powerful functionalities built into its console that make your daily workflow more efficient. In this recipe, we will investigate some useful options in an interactive session.

Getting ready

Create an example.jl file containing this:

```
println("An example was run!")
```

We will run this script in this recipe.

In the GitHub repository for this recipe you will find the `commands.txt` file that contains the presented sequence of shell and Julia commands and the `example.jl` file described above.

Now open your favorite terminal to execute the commands.

How to do it...

We will learn how to work interactively with Julia by going through the following steps:

1. Start the Julia command line.
2. Execute two commands in the Julia command line:

   ```
   julia> x = 10 # just a test command
   10

   julia> @edit sin(1.0)
   ```

   After running these commands, an editor with the location of a code section containing the `sin` function opens. We explained earlier how to choose the editor that Julia uses in the *How to customize Julia on startup* recipe.

3. Close the editor to get back to Julia.
4. Now press *Ctrl + L*. You will notice that the screen was redrawn and the output from previous commands was cleared.

   Now, let us check if `example.jl` is in our current working directory.

5. Press *;* key and the prompt in Julia should change to this:

   ```
   shell>
   ```

6. Type `ls` if you are on Linux or `dir` in Windows, to execute the shell command. You should get a list of files in your current working directory and after this command, Julia comes back to a standard prompt. When you are sure you have the `example.jl` file in your working directory, we can continue.

7. Start by typing `inc` in the Julia console:

   ```
   julia> inc
   ```

8. Press *Tab*. Julia will autocomplete it to `include`, a built-in function in Julia:

   ```
   julia> include
   ```

9. Next, continue by entering the text `("exa` in the Julia console:

   ```
   julia> include("exa
   ```

10. Press *Tab* again to get the following:

    ```
    julia> include("example.jl"
    ```

11. Finally, type `)` and hit *Enter*. Running `include` will execute the commands given in the `example.jl` file. At this point, you would probably like to understand what function the `include` command performs.

12. Press *?* in Julia REPL to switch to `help` mode. The prompt will change to the following:

    ```
    help?>
    ```

13. Start writing the command you want to check by pressing `in`:

    ```
    help?> in
    ```

14. Next, press *Tab* twice to get the following:

    ```
    help?> in
    in include_string indexin indmax init_worker interrupt inv invoke
    include ind2chr indexpids indmin insert! intersect invdigamma
    invperm
    include_dependency ind2sub indices info instances intersect! invmod
    help?> in
    ```

    This time we see that there are multiple commands matching the `in` pattern and Julia lists them all (this is the reason that the *Tab* key had to be pressed twice).

15. Press `c` and press *Tab*—now there is only one feasible completion that is filled.

16. Press *Enter* to get the following:

    ```
    help?> include
    search: include include_string include_dependency

      include(path::AbstractString)

      Evaluate the contents of the input source file in the global
    scope of the
    ```

```
    containing module. Every module (except those defined with
baremodule) has its
    own 1-argument definition of include, which evaluates the file in
that module.
    Returns the result of the last evaluated expression of the input
file. During
    including, a task-local include path is set to the directory
containing the file.
    Nested calls to include will search relative to that path. This
function is
    typically used to load source interactively, or to combine files
in packages that
    are broken into multiple source files.

    Use Base.include to evaluate a file into another module.
```

And we understand exactly what include does. Now, what if we wanted to run the x = 10 command again (this is mostly useful for longer and complex commands in practice)?

17. Press *Ctrl + R* to switch Julia into reverse search mode and type x = to get the following:

    (reverse-i-search)`x =': x = 10

18. Press *Enter* to have the command you found inserted into the Julia prompt:

    julia> x = 10

19. Press *Enter* to execute the command. Alternatively, we could use arrow up/down or page up/down to traverse the command history.

20. Finally, to terminate Julia, you can either press *Ctrl + D* or run the exit() function.

How it works...

Julia REPL offers you several modes, of which the most commonly used are these:

- **Julian**: For the execution of Julia code (this is the default).
- **Help**: Started by pressing the *?* key. As you proceed, you will find instructions on how to use this mode.
- **Shell**: Started by pressing the *;* key. In this mode, you can quickly execute a shell command without leaving Julia.

- **Package manager**: Started by pressing the *]* key. In this mode, you can manage packages installed in your system.
- Backward search mode, which you can enter using *Ctrl + R*.

You can find more details about options for interacting with Julia in all those modes at https://docs.julialang.org/en/v1.0/stdlib/REPL/.

As you can observe, Julia is smart enough to perform tab completion in a context-sensitive manner—it understands if you are entering a command or a filename. Command history search is also very useful in interactive work.

In the *How to customize Julia on startup* recipe, we explained how to set up the editor. In this recipe, we saw how you can use the @edit macro to open the location of the definition of the sin function in your chosen editor. Julia recognizes the following editors: Vim, Emacs, gedit, textmate, mate, kate, Sublime Text, atom, Notepad++, and Visual Studio Code. Importantly, @edit recognizes the types of arguments you pass to a function and will show an appropriate method if your chosen editor supports line search on startup (otherwise, an appropriate file will be opened and the line number of the function at hand will be printed in the Julia command line).

There's more...

Apart from the @edit macro, you can use the @less macro or the edit and less functions to see the source code of the function you wish to use (please consult the Julia help guide to understand the detailed differences between them).

If we only want to know the location of a method definition without displaying it, we can use the @which macro:

```
julia> @which sin(1.0)
sin(x::T) where T<:Union{Float32, Float64} in Base.Math at
special/trig.jl:30
```

See also

The *How to customize Julia on startup* recipe explains how to use the startup.jl file and how to choose the default Julia editor.

Displaying computation results in Julia

In this recipe, we discuss how to control when Julia displays the results of computations. It is an important part of the standard behavior of Julia code that people often find unclear in their first encounter with the Julia ecosystem. In particular, there are differences in how Julia programs display computation results when running in the console and in script modes, which we explain in this recipe.

Getting ready

Make sure you have the PyPlot package installed by entering using PyPlot in the Julia command line. If it is not installed (an error message will be printed), then run the following command to add it:

```
julia> using Pkg; Pkg.add("PyPlot")
```

More details about package management are described in the *Managing packages* recipe in this chapter.

Then, create the display.jl file in your working directory:

```
using PyPlot, Random

function f()
    Random.seed!(1)
    r = rand(50)
    @show sum(r)
    display(transpose(r))
    print(transpose(r))
    plot(r)
end

f()
```

 In the GitHub repository for this recipe, you will find the commands.txt file that contains the presented sequence of shell and Julia commands, the display.jl file described above and the display2.jl file described in the recipe.

Now open your favorite terminal to execute the commands.

How to do it...

In the following steps, we will explain how the output of Julia depends on the context in which a command is invoked:

1. Start the Julia command line and run `display.jl` in interactive mode:

```
julia> include("display.jl")
sum(r) = 23.134209483707394
 1x50 LinearAlgebra.Transpose{Float64,Array{Float64,1}}:
 0.236033 0.346517 0.312707 0.00790928 0.488613 0.210968 0.951916
... 0.417039 0.144566 0.622403 0.872334 0.524975 0.241591 0.884837
 [0.236033 0.346517 0.312707 0.00790928 0.488613 0.210968 0.951916
0.999905 0.251662 0.986666 0.555751 0.437108 0.424718 0.773223
0.28119 0.209472 0.251379 0.0203749 0.287702 0.859512 0.0769509
0.640396 0.873544 0.278582 0.751313 0.644883 0.0778264 0.848185
0.0856352 0.553206 0.46335 0.185821 0.111981 0.976312 0.0516146
0.53803 0.455692 0.279395 0.178246 0.548983 0.370971 0.894166
0.648054 0.417039 0.144566 0.622403 0.872334 0.524975 0.241591
0.884837]
 1-element Array{PyCall.PyObject,1}:
 PyObject <matplotlib.lines.Line2D object at 0x0000000026314198>
```

Apart from the printed value presented earlier, a plot window will open as shown in the following figure:

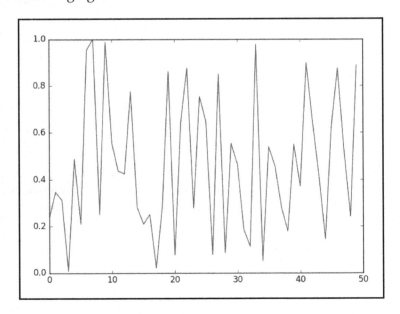

2. Now, exit Julia and run the script in non-interactive mode from the OS shell:

```
$ julia display.jl
 sum(r) = 23.134209483707394
 1×50 LinearAlgebra.Transpose{Float64,Array{Float64,1}}:
 0.236033 0.346517 0.312707 0.00790928 0.488613 0.210968 0.951916
0.999905 0.251662 0.986666 0.555751 0.437108 0.424718 0.773223
0.28119 0.209472 0.251379 0.0203749 0.287702 0.859512 0.0769509
0.640396 0.873544 0.278582 0.751313 0.644883 0.0778264 0.848185
0.0856352
 0.553206 0.46335 0.185821 0.111981 0.976312 0.0516146 0.53803
0.455692 0.279395 0.178246 0.548983 0.370971 0.894166 0.648054
0.417039 0.144566 0.622403 0.872334 0.524975 0.241591
0.884837[0.236033 0.346517 0.312707 0.00790928 0.488613 0.210968
0.951916 0.999905 0.251662 0.986666 0.555751 0.437108 0.424718
0.773223 0.28119 0.209472 0.251379 0.0203749 0.287702 0.859512
0.0769509 0.640396 0.873544 0.278582 0.751313 0.644883 0.0778264
0.848185 0.0856352 0.553206 0.46335 0.185821 0.111981 0.976312
0.0516146 0.53803 0.455692 0.279395 0.178246 0.548983 0.370971
0.894166 0.648054 0.417039 0.144566 0.622403 0.872334 0.524975
0.241591 0.884837]
```

In this case, nothing is plotted. Additionally, observe that the display function, in this case, produced a different output than in interactive mode and no newline was inserted after the result (so the output of the print function is visually merged).

3. Now, add show() after plot(r) in the display.jl file and name it display2.jl:

```
using PyPlot, Random

function f()
    Random.seed!(1)
    r = rand(50)
    @show sum(r)
    display(transpose(r))
    print(transpose(r))
    plot(r)
    show()
end

f()
```

4. Run the updated file as a script:

```
$ julia display2.jl
```

This time the plot is shown and Julia is suspended until the plot dialog is closed.

How it works...

In Julia, the `display` function is aware of the context in which it is called. This means that depending on what context is passed to this function, you may obtain a different result. For instance, an image passed to the `display` in the Julia console usually opens a new window with a plot, but in Jupyter Notebook it might embed it in a notebook. Similarly, many objects in the Julia console are displayed as plain text but in Jupyter Notebook they are converted to a nicely formatted HTML. In short, `display(x)` typically uses the richest supported multimedia output for x in a given context, with plain text `stdout` output as a fallback.

In particular, the `display` function is used by default in the Julia console when a command is executed, for example:

```
julia> transpose(1:100)
1×100 LinearAlgebra.Transpose{Int64,UnitRange{Int64}}:
 1 2 3 4 5 6 7 8 9 10 11 ... 93 94 95 96 97 98 99 100
```

In this case, the output is adjusted to the size of the Terminal. However, as we saw in the previous example if `display` is run in a script in non-interactive mode, no adjustment of the output to the size of the device is performed.

An additional issue that is commonly required in practice is suppressing the display of an expression value in the Julia console. This is easily achieved by adding `;` at the end of the command, for example:

```
julia> rand(100, 100);

julia>
```

And nothing is printed (otherwise, the screen would be flooded by a large matrix).

Finally, in the script in this recipe, we were able to examine the use of the `@show` macro, which is useful for debugging, as it prints the expression along with its value.

At the end of this recipe, we observed that the `PyPlot` package can alter its behavior based on whether it is run in interactive mode or not. Each custom package might have similar specific conditions for handling output to a variety of devices. Being aware of this, it is best to consult the documentation relating to a given package to understand the defaults.

If you are developing your own code that needs to be sensitive to the Julia mode (REPL or script) in which it is invoked, there is a handy `isinteractive` function. This function allows you to dynamically check the Julia interpreter mode at runtime.

There's more...

An in-depth explanation of how display management in Julia works is given at `https://docs.julialang.org/en/v1.0/manual/types/#man-custom-pretty-printing-1`.

See also

In the *Defining your own types - linked list* recipe in `Chapter 6`, *Metaprogramming and Advanced Typing*, we explain how to specify custom printing for user-defined types.

Managing packages

Julia has a built-in package manager that allows you to fully control the combination of packages that your project can use.

In this recipe, we explain the fundamentals of how to manage packages in a default (global) project. In the *Managing project dependencies* recipe in `Chapter 8`, *Julia Workflow*, we discuss how you can customize which packages you use in your local project repositories.

Getting ready

In this recipe, we will use the Julia command line. Make sure that your computer is connected to the internet.

 In the GitHub repository for this recipe, you will find the `commands.txt` file that contains the presented sequence of shell and Julia commands.

Now open your favorite terminal to execute the commands.

How to do it...

Here is a list of steps to be followed:

1. Go to the Julia command line:

   ```
   julia>
   ```

2. Press] to switch to the package manager mode:

   ```
   (v1.0) pkg>
   ```

3. We can check the initial status of packages using the status command:

   ```
   (v1.0) pkg> status
       Status `~/.julia/environments/v1.0/Project.toml`
   ```

   We can see that we currently have a clean environment with no additional packages installed.

4. To add the BenchmarkTools package, use the add command:

   ```
   (v1.0) pkg> add BenchmarkTools
       Cloning default registries into /home/ubuntu/.julia/registries
       Cloning registry General from
   "https://github.com/JuliaRegistries/General.git"
     Updating registry at `~/.julia/registries/General`
     Updating git-repo
   `https://github.com/JuliaRegistries/General.git`
     Resolving package versions...
     Installed BenchmarkTools — v0.4.1
     Installed JSON ———————————— v0.19.0
     Updating `~/.julia/environments/v1.0/Project.toml`
     [6e4b80f9] + BenchmarkTools v0.4.1
     Updating `~/.julia/environments/v1.0/Manifest.toml`
     [6e4b80f9] + BenchmarkTools v0.4.1
     [682c06a0] + JSON v0.19.0
     [2a0f44e3] + Base64
     [ade2ca70] + Dates
     [8ba89e20] + Distributed
     [b77e0a4c] + InteractiveUtils
     [76f85450] + LibGit2
     [8f399da3] + Libdl
     [37e2e46d] + LinearAlgebra
     [56ddb016] + Logging
     [d6f4376e] + Markdown
     [a63ad114] + Mmap
     [44cfe95a] + Pkg
   ```

```
[de0858da] + Printf
[3fa0cd96] + REPL
[9a3f8284] + Random
[ea8e919c] + SHA
[9e88b42a] + Serialization
[6462fe0b] + Sockets
[2f01184e] + SparseArrays
[10745b16] + Statistics
[8dfed614] + Test
[cf7118a7] + UUIDs
[4ec0a83e] + Unicode
```

5. Now, use the status command to see the versions of your installed packages:

```
(v1.0) pkg> status
    Status `~/.julia/environments/v1.0/Project.toml`
[6e4b80f9] BenchmarkTools v0.4.1
```

Notice that only the BenchmarkTools package is visible, although more packages have been installed by Julia. They reside in the package repository but are not visible to the user unless explicitly installed. Those packages are dependencies of the BenchmarkTools package (directly or via recursive dependency).

6. After installing a package, we precompile the installed packages:

```
(v1.0) pkg> precompile
Precompiling project...
Precompiling BenchmarkTools
[ Info: Precompiling BenchmarkTools [6e4b80f9-
dd63-53aa-95a3-0cdb28fa8baf]
```

7. Exit the package manager mode by pressing the *Backspace* key:

```
(v1.0) pkg>

julia>
```

8. Now, we can check that the package can be loaded and used:

```
julia> using BenchmarkTools

julia> @btime rand()
  4.487 ns (0 allocations: 0 bytes)
0.07253910317708079
```

9. Finally, install the BSON package version v0.2.0 (this is not the latest version of this package, as as of writing of the book the currently released version is v0.2.1). Switch to the PackageManager mode by pressing] and then type:

```
(v1.0) pkg> add BSON@v0.2.0
[output is omitted]
```

Now you have version 0.2.0 of the BSON package installed

10. Often you want to keep the version of some package fixed to avoid its update by the Julia Package Manager, when its new version is released. You can achieve it with the pin command as follows

```
(v1.0) pkg> pin BSON
[output is omitted]
```

11. If you decide that you want to allow the Julia Package Manager to update some package that was pinned you can do it using the free command:

```
(v1.0) pkg> free BSON
[output is omitted]
```

The process of installing a specified version of some package (step 9 of the recipe) and pinning it (step 10) might be useful for you when you will need to install the exact versions of the packages that we use in this book, as in the future new releases of the packages might introduce breaking changes. The full list of packages used in this book along with their required versions is given in the *To get the most out of this book* section in the Preface of this book.

How it works...

For each environment, Julia keeps information about the required packages and their versions in the Project.toml and Manifest.toml files. For the global default environment, they are placed in the ~/.julia/environments/v1.0/ folder. The first file contains a list of installed packages along with their UUIDs (see https://en.wikipedia.org/wiki/Universally_unique_identifier or https://www.itu.int/ITU-T/studygroups/com17/oid.html). The second file describes detailed dependencies of the project with exact versions of the packages used.

In this recipe, we have only made use of the basic commands of the package manager. In most cases, this is all a regular user needs to know. There are many more commands available, which you can find using the `help` command in package manager mode. Some of the potentially useful commands are as follows:

- `add`: installs the indicated package
- `rm`: removes the indicated package
- `up`: updates the indicated package to a different version
- `develop`: Clones the full package repository locally for development (useful in circumstances such as when wanting to use the latest `master` version of the package)
- `up`: Updates packages in the manifest (be warned that updating packages in your project might lead to incompatibilities with old code, so use this with caution)
- `build`: Runs the build script for packages (useful as sometimes installing packages fails to correctly build them, for example, due to external dependencies that have to be configured)
- `pin`: Pins the version of packages (ensures that a given package version is not changed by using other commands)
- `free`: Undoes a `pin`, `develop`, or stops tracking a repository

There's more...

All the commands we have described are also available programmatically using functions from the `Pkg.jl` package. For instance, running `Pkg.add("BenchmarkTools")` would install the package the same way as writing `add BenchmarkTools` in package manager mode in the Julia console. In order to use those functions, you have to load the `Pkg` package using `using Pkg` first.

In addition, it is important to know that many packages are preinstalled with Julia and thus do not require installation and can be directly loaded with the `using` command. Here is a selection of some of the more important ones, along with a brief description of their functionality:

- `Dates`: Works with date and time features
- `DelimitedFiles`: Basic loading and writing of delimited files
- `Distributed`: Multiprocessing
- `LinearAlgebra`: Various operations on matrices

- Logging: Support for logging
- Pkg: Package manager
- Random: Random number generation
- Serialization: Support for serialization/deserialization of Julia objects
- SparseArrays: Support for non-dense arrays
- Statistics: Basic statistical functions
- Test: Support for writing unit tests

Extensive coverage of these packages is given in the standard library section of the Julia manual, which can be accessed at https://docs.julialang.org/en/v1.0/.

See also

The true power of the Julia package manager is realized when you need to have different versions of packages for your different projects on the same machine. In the *Managing project dependencies* recipe in Chapter 8, *Julia Workflow,* we discuss how you can achieve this.

Configuring Julia in Jupyter Notebook

Jupyter Notebook is a *de facto* standard for exploratory data science analysis. In this recipe, we show how to configure Jupyter with Julia.

Getting ready

Before installing Jupyter Notebook, perform the following steps:

1. Prepare a Linux machine with Julia installed (you can follow the instructions in the *Installing Julia from binaries* recipe).

2. Open a Julia console.

3. Install the IJulia package. Press] in the Julia REPL to go to the Julia package manager and execute the add IJulia command:

```
(v1.0) pkg> add IJulia
```

In the GitHub repository for this recipe, you will find the commands.txt file that contains the presented sequence of shell and Julia commands.

How to do it...

Once IJulia is installed, there are two options for running Jupyter Notebook:

- Running Jupyter Notebook from within the Julia console

- Running Jupyter Notebook from bash

Running Jupyter Notebook from within the Julia environment

Simply start the Julia console and run the following commands:

```
julia> using IJulia

julia> notebook()
```

A web browser window will open with Jupyter, where you can start to work with Julia. In order to stop the Jupyter Notebook server, go back to the console and press *Ctrl + C*.

Running Jupyter Notebook outside of the Julia environment

In order to run Jupyter Notebook outside of Julia, firstly make sure that you have installed IJulia (see the *Getting ready* section). Once IJulia is installed, perform the following steps:

1. Execute the shell command (this assumes that you used the default setting for the Julia packages folder; in particular the hsaaN part of the path below might be different; in such case please look-up the correct path in the ~/.julia/packages/Conda/ folder):

```
$ ~/.julia/packages/Conda/hsaaN/deps/usr/bin/jupyter notebook
```

Please note that the preceding command in Windows will look different:

```
C:\>
%userprofile%\.julia\packages\Conda\hsaaN\deps\usr\Scripts\jupyter-
notebook
```

2. Look for console output similar to what is shown here:

```
Copy/paste this URL into your browser when you connect for the
first time,
to login with a token:
http://localhost:8888/?token=b86b66b81a62d4be1ae34e7d6bd006a8ba5cb9
37e74b99cf
```

3. Paste the link (in the preceding output marked with bold font) into your browser's address bar.

How it works...

Jupyter Notebook runs a local web server on port 8888. Once it is started, you can simply connect to it via a web browser. It is also possible to run such environments on a different machine than that used to access the notebook—please check the *Jupyter in the cloud* recipe for more details.

There's more...

Please note that for some packages, Julia installation might have conflicts with Windows security settings and thus prevent installation. In particular, **IE Enhanced Security Configuration** should be turned off (the default setting on Windows Server environments is on). In order to turn it off, open **Server Manager** and click **Local Server,** which is located on the left. In the right column, you will see the option **IE Enhanced Security Configuration.** Click on it to turn it off.

Another possible problem can be with the installation of IJulia, since it sometimes conflicts with an existing Python installation due to IJulia attempting to fetch and install a minimal Python environment itself. In such cases, if you get an error, run the following:

```
ENV["JUPYTER"] = "[path to your jupyter program]"
using Pkg
Pkg.build("IJulia")
```

You will have to manually find the `[path to your jupyter program]`. For example, on my Windows system with Anaconda installed, the path will be `"C:\\Program Files\\Anaconda\\Scripts\\jupyter-notebook.exe"`. Note that we need to use two backslashes of the Julia string to represent a single backslash in a path. If you have provided a proper path, the build should finish successfully.

See also

The most recent documentation can be found on `IJulia`'s website (`https://github.com/JuliaLang/IJulia.jl`). It is worth checking, as some details of the process described earlier may change.

Configuring Julia to work with JupyterLab

JupyterLab is a new, extended version of Jupyter Notebook. Before installing it, make sure that you have successfully completed the *Configuring Julia in Jupyter Notebook* tutorial. Running JupyterLab requires Python to be installed. We strongly recommend Python Anaconda as the standard execution environment.

Getting ready

The configuration of JupyterLab requires having `IJulia` configured on your system:

1. Prepare a Linux or Windows machine with Julia installed.

2. Follow the *Configuring Julia in Jupyter Notebook* tutorial and install `IJulia`.

 In the GitHub repository for this recipe, you will find the `commands.txt` file that contains the presented sequence of shell and Julia commands.

How to do it...

By default, Julia does not include JupyterLab. However, it is possible to add JupyterLab by using the `Conda.jl` package. We will show, step-by-step, how to add JupyterLab to a Julia installation and run it from bash:

1. Press the *]* key to go to the Julia package manager and install the `Conda.jl` package:

   ```
   (v1.0) pkg> add Conda
   ```

2. Use `Conda` to add JupyterLab to Julia's installation:

   ```
   julia> using Conda

   julia> Conda.add("jupyterlab")
   ```

3. Once JupyterLab is installed, exit Julia and run it from the command line:

   ```
   $ ~/.julia/packages/Conda/hsaaN/deps/usr/bin/jupyter lab
   ```

4. Please note that the preceding command in Windows will look different:

   ```
   C:\>%userprofile%\.julia\packages\Conda\hsaaN\deps\usr
   \Scripts\jupyter-lab
   ```

5. If the preceding command did not automatically start the web browser, do it manually and look for console output similar to this:

   ```
   Copy/paste this URL into your browser when you connect for the
   first time,
   to login with a token:
   http://localhost:8888/?token=b86b66b81a62d4be1ae34e7d6bd006a8ba5cb9
   37e74b99cf
   ```

6. Paste the link (in the preceding output marked with bold font) into your browser's address bar.

Once you have followed the preceding steps, you should see in the browser a screen similar to the one shown here (please note that since Python is installed with `IJulia.jl`, it is also available alongside Julia):

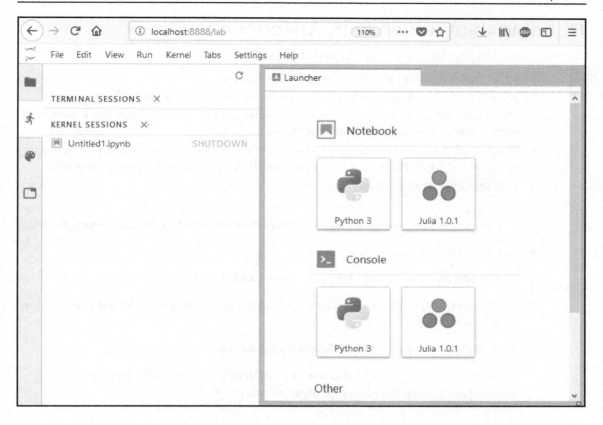

How it works...

JupyterLab is an extension of Jupyter Notebook and hence it works in a very similar fashion. JupyterLab runs a local web server on port 8888 (the same port that would have been used by Jupyter Notebook). Once it is started, you can simply connect to it via a web browser. It is also possible to run such environments on a separate machine. Please check the *Configuring Julia with Jupyter Notebook headless cloud environments* recipe for more details (that recipe is valid for both Jupyter Notebook and JupyterLab).

There's more...

Yet another option is to use JupyterLab from a completely external Anaconda installation. Since the installation process differs for Linux and Windows, we present both versions.

Running JupyterLab with Anaconda on Linux

In order to install JupyterLab on Linux, perform the following steps:

1. Go to the Anaconda for Linux download website (`https://www.anaconda.com/download/#linux`) and find the current download link for the 64-bit Python 3 version (usually it can be done in a web browser by right-clicking the **Download** button and selecting **Copy link location**).

2. Download Anaconda Python. Please note that depending on the time when you perform the installation, the exact link might look different—new Anaconda versions are being released frequently:

```
$ wget
https://repo.anaconda.com/archive/Anaconda3-5.3.0-Linux-x86_64.sh
```

3. Run the Anaconda installer:

```
$ sudo bash Anaconda3-5.3.0-Linux-x86_64.sh
```

4. Now, you can launch JupyterLab (we assume that you have selected the standard install locations):

```
$ /home/ubuntu/anaconda3/bin/jupyter lab
```

5. If the preceding command did not automatically start the web browser, do it manually and look for console output similar to this:

```
[I 11:07:55.625 LabApp] The Jupyter Notebook is running at:
[I 11:07:55.625 LabApp]
http://localhost:8888/?token=c3756ac2013d780af16b0401d67ab017c5e4a1
7cc9bc7924
[I 11:07:55.625 LabApp] Use Control-C to stop this server and shut
down all kernels (twice to skip confirmation).
[W 11:07:55.625 LabApp] No web browser found: could not locate
runnable browser.
```

6. Paste the link (in the preceding log marked with bold font) your browser's address bar.

Please note that if you follow the preceding steps (including the installation of the `IJulia.jl` package), once you open the JupyterLab welcome screen, you should see Python 3 as well as Julia Notebook execution kernels.

Running JupyterLab with Anaconda on Windows

In the following steps, we describe how to run JupyterLab with Anaconda on Windows:

1. Go to the Anaconda for Windows download website (`https://www.anaconda.com/download/#windows`) and find the current download link for the 64-bit Python 3 version. Download the `*.exe` installation file to your computer.

2. Run the installer. Here, we assume that you are installing it to the default folder, which on Windows is `C:\ProgramData\Anaconda3\`.

> If you decide to install to a different location, make sure that the path contains no spaces.

3. Once Anaconda 3 is installed, simply run `jupyter-lab.exe`:

   C:\> C:\ProgramData\Anaconda3\Scripts\jupyter-lab.exe

4. If the preceding command did not automatically start the web browser, do it manually and look for console output similar to this:

   ```
   Copy/paste this URL into your browser when you connect for the
   first time,  to login with a token:
   http://localhost:8888/?token=7f211507e188ecfc22e2858b195c8de915c7c2
   21f012ee86
   ```

5. Paste the link (in the preceding log marked with bold font) into your browser's address bar.

Please note that if you follow the preceding steps (including the installation of the `IJulia.jl` package), once you open the JupyterLab welcome screen, you should see Python 3 as well as Julia Notebook execution kernels.

See also

The JupyterLab project is developing rapidly, so it is worth checking the latest news on the project's website (`https://github.com/jupyterlab/jupyterlab`).

Configuring Julia with Jupyter Notebook in Terminal-only cloud environments

In this recipe, we show how to configure Jupyter (both JupyterLab and Jupyter Notebook) for use in Terminal-only environments on a Linux platform (that is, environments that do not provide any graphical desktop interface). For these remote environments, running Jupyter Notebook is trickier. For illustrative purposes, we will use the AWS Cloud.

Getting ready

Before you start, you need to have a Linux machine with `IJulia` and either Jupyter Notebook or JupyterLab installed:

1. Prepare a Linux machine (for example, an AWS EC2 instance) with Julia installed, and Jupyter Notebook or JupyterLab (you can follow the instructions in the previous recipes).

2. Make sure that you can open an SSH connection to your Linux machine. If this is an instance of Linux on the AWS Cloud, you can follow the instructions given at `https://docs.aws.amazon.com/AWSEC2/latest/UserGuide/AccessingInstancesLinux.html`. In particular, you need to know the server's address, login name (in the examples we use `ubuntu`, which is the default username on Ubuntu Linux), and have the private key file (in the examples, we name it `keyname.pem`, and the user's password could be used instead of the key file).

Please note that for Windows 10, there is no default SSH client. Hence, this recipe has been tested with the SSH client included with Git for Windows tools, available at `https://git-scm.com/download/win/`. Once Git for Windows is installed, the SSH executable by default can be found at `C:\Program Files\Git\usr\bin\ssh.exe`.

Please note that on `*ux` environments (for example, Linux, OS X) the key file, `keyfile.pem`, which is used for connection should be readable only to the local user. If you just downloaded it from AWS, you need to execute the

`$ chmod 400 keyfile.pem` command before running the `ssh` command to open the SSH connection.

In the GitHub repository for this recipe, you will find the `commands.txt` file that contains the presented sequence of shell and Julia commands.

How to do it...

A general scenario for working with Jupyter Notebook/JupyterLab on a remote machine consists of the following three steps:

1. Set up the SSH tunnel on port `8888`
2. Start JupyterLab on the remote machine
3. Find the link in the launch log and copy it to the browser on the local machine

We discuss each step in detail and consider alternative configurations for Jupyter Notebook and JupyterLab:

1. Connect to the Linux machine from your desktop computer (local machine). While opening the SSH connection, set up a tunnel on port `8888`. In place of `[enter_hostname_here]`, provide the appropriate hostname (for example, in the AWS Cloud, the hostname could look like this: `ec2-18-188-4-172.us-east-2.compute.amazonaws.com`):

   ```
   $ ssh -i path/to/keyfile.pem -L8888:127.0.0.1:8888
   ubuntu@[enter_hostname_here]
   ```

2. Once the connection has been set up, run your Jupyter Notebook or JupyterLab on the remote machine. Execute the command shown (this assumes that the `IJulia` package is installed on your machine along with instructions from the previous recipes and you used the default setting for the Julia `packages` folder):

```
$ ~/.julia/packages/Conda/hsaaN/deps/usr/bin/jupyter lab
```

Please note that the Windows version of the preceding command is the following:

```
C:\>
%userprofile%\.julia\packages\Conda\hsaaN\deps\usr\Scripts\jupyter-
lab
```

You can also use either Jupyter Lab or Jupyter Notebook command versions (see the instructions from the previous recipe).

 Please note that, depending on your Julia and Anaconda configuration, the executable `jupyter` file could be in a different location. On Linux environments, you can search for it with the `$ find ~/ -name "jupyter"` command. This assumes the search is run in your local home folder.

3. Look for console output similar to this:

```
Copy/paste this URL into your browser when you connect for the
first time,to login with a token:
http://localhost:8888/?token=b86b66b81a62d4be1ae34e7d6bd006a8ba5cb9
37e74b99cf
```

4. Paste the link marked with bold to your browser on your **local machine** (not the remote server).

If you have properly configured the SSH tunnel, you should see Jupyter Notebook/JupyterLab running on the remote server in the browser on the local machine. Please note that the environment will be available for only as long as the SSH connection is open. If you close the SSH connection, you will lose access to your Jupyter Notebook or JupyterLab.

How it works...

Using Jupyter Notebook via the internet requires setting up an SSH tunnel to the server. This is the option we present in this tutorial. Please note that on a local network, you can connect directly to the server without SSH tunneling.

In the preceding scenario, the command-line argument -L 8888:127.0.0.1:8888 tells ssh to open a secure tunnel over SSH from your machine to port 8888 on the target machine in the cloud (as shown in the following diagram):

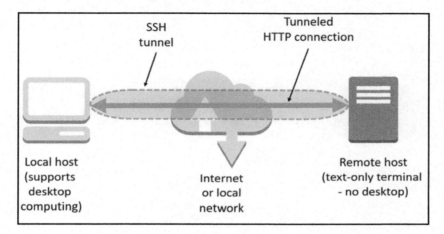

There's more...

Yet another option for running IJulia on a text-only Terminal remote machine is to use a detached mode for the Jupyter environment. However, in order to obtain access to Jupyter Notebook, a token key is required. Please see the following example:

```
julia> using IJulia

julia> notebook(detached=true)

julia> run(`$(IJulia.notebook_cmd[1]) notebook list`)
Currently running servers:
http://localhost:8888/?token=2bb8421e3bba78c8c551a8af1f22460bb4bb3fdc5a0986
bb
```

Now, you can simply copy and paste the preceding link into your web browser.

See also

More information on SSH tunneling can be found at https://www.ssh.com/ssh/tunneling/example.

Data Structures and Algorithms 2

In this chapter, we will cover the following recipes:

- Finding the index of a random minimum element
- Fast matrix multiplication
- Implementing a custom pseudo-random number generator
- Parsing Git logs with regular expressions
- Non-standard ways to sort your data
- Creating a function preimage—understanding how dictionaries and sets work
- Working with UTF-8 strings

Introduction

Julia is shipped with a vast array of utility functions built into the core language and its standard libraries. Also, because of its speed, it is very well suited for the implementation of custom algorithms (as opposed to many other high-level languages, where users compose the analysis solely by using predefined algorithms from installed packages).

In this chapter, we show practical examples of how such custom algorithms can be implemented, while also taking advantage of the inbuilt functionality. The range of recipes shows that you can often implement your own low-level algorithm that is much faster than using standard functions (the recipe for finding the index of a random minimum element in an array) and that you can easily modify how standard operations work by overriding them with custom behavior (the matrix multiplication optimization recipe). Finally, we discuss in the recipes how the most frequently used data structures and operations can be effectively used, concentrating on dictionaries, sets, sorting, and string processing.

Finding the index of a random minimum element in an array

In many applications, you need to find the index of the minimum element of some array. The built-in `argmin` function is designed to perform this task—it returns the index of the minimum element in a collection. However, if there are multiple minimal elements, then the first one will be returned. There are situations when we need to get all indices of a minimal element or a single index is chosen uniformly at random from this set. In this recipe, we discuss how you can implement such a function.

Getting ready

Make sure that you have the `StatsBase.jl` and `BenchmarkTools.jl` packages installed.

You can add them by running the following commands in the Julia command line:

```
julia> using Pkg; Pkg.add("StatsBase"); Pkg.add("BenchmarkTools")
```

 In the GitHub repository for this recipe you will find the `commands.txt` file that contains the presented sequence of shell and Julia commands and the `randargmin2.jl` file that contains the source code of a function defined in this recipe.

Now open your favorite terminal to execute commands.

How to do it...

In this recipe, we compare two functions that find all indices of minimal elements in an array. One is simple, but slower; the other is more elaborate, but faster. We compare their outputs and execution speeds:

1. Define a function that finds all indices of minimal elements in an array. Here is how it can be defined:

```
julia> function allargmin(a)
           m = minimum(a)
           filter(i -> a[i] == m, eachindex(a))
       end
allargmin (generic function with 1 method)
```

2. Test in the Julia command line that it produces the expected results:

```
julia> allargmin([1,2,3,1,2,3])
2-element Array{Int64,1}:
 1
 4
```

The result is correct.

3. Define an initial version of the function, finding a random index of a minimum element:

```
julia> randargmin1(a) = rand(allargmin(a))
randargmin1 (generic function with 1 method)
```

4. Using `include("randargmin2.jl")` command execute the following code, that you can find in the `randargmin2.jl` file. The function defined in it finds a random index of a minimum element of an array in a single pass:

```
function randargmin2(a)
    indices = eachindex(a)
    y = iterate(indices)
    y === nothing && throw(ArgumentError("collection must be non-
    empty"))
    (idx, state) = y
    minval = a[idx]
    bestidx = idx
    bestcount = 1
    y = iterate(indices, state)
    while y !== nothing
        (idx, state) = y
        curval = a[idx]
        if isless(curval, minval)
            minval = curval
            bestidx = idx
            bestcount = 1
        elseif isequal(curval, minval)
            bestcount += 1
            rand() * bestcount < 1 && (bestidx = idx)
        end
        y = iterate(indices, state)
    end
    bestidx
end
```

5. Check both functions produce the same distributions of results in the Julia command line:

```julia
julia> using StatsBase

julia> x = [1, 2, 3, 1, 2, 3, 1, 1]
8-element Array{Int64,1}:
 1
 2
 3
 1
 2
 3
 1
 1

julia> countmap([randargmin1(x) for i in 1:10^6])
Dict{Int64,Int64} with 4 entries:
  7 => 250201
  4 => 249437
  8 => 249902
  1 => 250460

julia> countmap([randargmin2(x) for i in 1:10^6])
Dict{Int64,Int64} with 4 entries:
  7 => 249511
  4 => 250550
  8 => 251003
  1 => 248936
```

You might get slightly different results due to the random nature of the test. In general, you can expect the second version of our function to be faster and use less memory.

6. Run the following test in the Julia command line to confirm it:

```julia
julia> x = rand(1:10, 1000);

julia> using BenchmarkTools

julia> @btime randargmin1($x);
  34.056 µs (602 allocations: 18.05 KiB)

julia> @btime randargmin2($x);
  2.022 µs (0 allocations: 0 bytes)
```

How it works...

The key part of this recipe is understanding how the `randargmin2` function works. There are two challenges we face in its implementation. The first is algorithmic—how to choose a random minimal element. The second is on the implementation side—how to make the function work for a maximally wide class of iterators in Julia.

Let's start by explaining the algorithmic part. As you can see from the code, if we encounter a new minimum value, we simply store it. The challenge is what to do if we encounter a minimal element more than once. Assume that we have already seen some element `bestcount` times. A variable `bestidx`, with probability `1/bestcount`, holds each previously encountered minimal index. If we encounter a new index `idx` for which `a[idx]` is equal to the current minimum `minval`, then in the code with probability `1/(bestcount+1)`, we set `bestidx` to this value. This means that this new value has the correct probability of being stored. However, notice that all earlier values have the following probability of being stored: `1/bestcount * bestcount/(bestcount+1)`, which is also equal to `1/(bestcount+1)`. This means that, ultimately, our algorithm properly randomizes the choice of the returned index.

The second challenge is related to the fact that Julia features many different types of collections that can be efficiently accessed using different indexing, for example, linear indexing or Cartesian indexing. Therefore, in our code, we traverse a collection of indices into a, returned by `eachindex(a)`, using an iteration protocol. The protocol is based on the `iterate` function. If we pass an iterable to this function (for example, `iterate(indices)`), it returns a tuple containing the following:

- The first element of the iterable
- A state variable that can be used in subsequent calls

Then, we can iterate over the collection by passing two arguments to `iterate`—a collection and an earlier returned state. Finally, we know that we have reached the end of the collection if `iterate` returns `nothing`.

Note that we have iterated over `eachindex(a)` and not over a, since we needed to work with the indices of collection a rather than the values contained in it.

Also, notice how much faster it is to use an iteration protocol using our algorithm compared to a naive method—no memory is allocated in the process and we pass through the whole collection only once.

There's more...

If you wanted to iterate over the indices and values of a collection, you could use the `pairs` function for that. It is relatively simple to change our implementation of `randargmin2`, so we encourage you to try it.

The second thing to consider is that we use the `isless` and `isequal` functions in tests and not the `<` and `==` functions (which someone moving from R or Python would likely use).

The main reason for this is that `isless` and `isequal` guarantee to always return a `Bool` result while `<` and `==` can return `missing` when one of their arguments is `missing`. Additionally, there are subtle differences between those functions when comparing `0.0` and `-0.0` and `NaN`, as you can see in the following Julia command line session:

```julia
julia> 0.0 == -0.0, -0.0 < 0.0
(true, false)

julia> isequal(0.0, -0.0), isless(-0.0, 0.0)
(false, true)

julia> NaN == NaN, NaN < NaN
(false, false)

julia> isequal(NaN, NaN), isless(NaN, NaN)
(true, false)
```

And we can see that `<` and `==` do not define a proper order on floats.

See also

The iteration protocol is one of the cornerstones of Julia language design. Therefore, we strongly recommend that you read about its details in the documentation: https://docs.julialang.org/en/v1.0/manual/interfaces/#man-interface-iteration-1.

Fast matrix multiplication

Performing computations on matrices are one of the fundamental operations in numerical computing. In particular, if we want to multiply an $n \times m$ matrix by an $m \times p$ matrix, this operation has $O(nmp)$ complexity, producing an $n \times p$ matrix. Therefore, if we want to multiply several matrices in a chain, the cost of this operation depends on the sequence in which we perform the multiplications.

For example, assume that we have the following matrices:

- A having dimensions 10 x 40
- B having dimensions 40 x 10
- C having dimensions 10 x 50

And, we want to compute A*B*C. We can perform the computation either like this, (A*B)*C, or like this, A*(B*C). The cost of the first approach is proportional to 10*40*10+10*10*50=9000. The cost of the second approach is 40*10*50+10*40*50=40000. It is therefore evident that the order of operations has a significant influence on performance.

In this recipe, we implement a procedure that performs multiplication of matrices in an order that minimizes the computational cost of the operation.

Getting ready

In this recipe, we will use a dynamic programming algorithm that finds the optimal order of multiplications. Before we proceed to how the solution is implemented, take a quick look at our brief description to check your understanding of what this algorithm does.

You can find its detailed outline at https://en.wikipedia.org/wiki/Matrix_chain_multiplication or here: Cormen, Thomas H; Leiserson, Charles E; Rivest, Ronald L; Stein, Clifford (2001): *Introduction to Algorithms, Second Edition*. MIT Press and McGraw-Hill. pp. 331–338. The general idea of the algorithm is the following. Assume that we want to multiply matrices $A_1, A_2, \ldots, A_n$. Let $f(i, j)$ be a function that returns a minimal cost of multiplying matrices from A_i to A_j.

Hence, our objective is to find $f(1, n)$. Clearly, we have the following relationships:

- Performing no multiplications has zero cost, thus: $f(i, i) = 0$.
- The minimal cost of multiplying matrices from i to j can be found by considering all possible outermost points of multiplication, so:
$f(i, j) = \min_{i \leq k < j}\{f(i, k) + f(k - 1, j) + d(i, 1)d(k, 2)d(j, 2)\}$, where by $d(i, s)$,
we denote the sth dimension of the matrix i.

In this recipe, we will use those formulas to find an optimal order of matrix multiplication. Observe that in order to perform the actual multiplication, we must know the value of $f(i, j)$ as well as the value of k for which the expression in the recurrence relation was minimal.

Make sure that you have the `BenchmarkTools.jl` package installed. If it is missing then you should add it by running `using Pkg; Pkg.add("BenchmarkTools")` in the Julia command line.

In the GitHub repository for this recipe, you will find the `commands.txt` file that contains the presented sequence of shell and Julia commands and the `fastmatmul.jl` file that contains the source code of functions defined in this recipe.

Now open your favorite terminal to execute commands.

How to do it...

In this recipe, we first define functions that provide the fast matrix multiplication functionality. Next, we test their results and performance:

1. Define the functions `fastmatmul`, `solvemul` and `domul` in the Julia console by executing `fastmatmul.jl` file using `include("fastmatmul.jl")` command in the Julia command line:

```
# take a sequence of matrices and multiply them in an optimal order
function fastmatmul(args::AbstractMatrix...)
    length(args) ≤ 1 && return *(args...)
    sizes = size.(args)
    if !all(sizes[i][2] == sizes[i+1][1] for i in
1:length(sizes)-1)
        throw(ArgumentError("matrix dimensions mismatch"))
    end
    partcost = Dict{Tuple{Int,Int}, Tuple{Int, Int}}()
    from, to = 1, length(sizes)
    solvemul(sizes, partcost, from, to)
```

```
            domul(args, partcost, from, to)
end

# find the optimal sequence of multiplications
function solvemul(sizes, partcost, from, to)
    if from == to
        partcost[(from, to)] = (0, from)
        return
    end
    mincost = typemax(Int)
    minj = -1
    for j in from:to-1
        haskey(partcost, (from, j)) || solvemul(sizes, partcost,
from, j)
        haskey(partcost, (j+1, to)) || solvemul(sizes, partcost,
j+1, to)
        curcost = sizes[from][1]*sizes[j][2]*sizes[to][2] +
                    partcost[(from, j)][1] + partcost[(j+1, to)][1]
        if curcost < mincost
            minj = j
            mincost = curcost
        end
    end
    partcost[(from, to)] = (mincost, minj)
end

# perform the multiplication given precomputed information
# about the optimal multiplication order
function domul(args, partcost, from, to)
    from == to && return args[from]
    from+1 == to && return args[from]*args[to]
    j = partcost[(from, to)][2]
    domul(args, partcost, from, j) * domul(args, partcost, j+1, to)
end
```

2. Check how our functions work. We will multiply 20 matrices interchangeably, having dimensions 5 x 5000 and 5000 x 5, as follows:

```
julia> using BenchmarkTools

julia> A = ones(5, 5000);

julia> B = ones(5000, 5);

julia> @btime *(repeat([A,B], outer=10)...);
  1.219 ms (33 allocations: 1.72 MiB)
```

```
julia> @btime fastmatmul(repeat([A,B], outer=10)...);
  706.329 µs (102 allocations: 54.23 KiB)
```

We can see that with the optimal order, the computations are almost twice as fast, even though we have the extra overhead of finding the optimal sequence of multiplications.

How it works...

In the recipe, we define three functions:

- fastmatmul: A wrapper function to be called by the user
- solvemul: A helper function that finds the optimal order of multiplications
- domul: A function that takes the result of solvemul and performs the actual multiplication in an optimal order

A pivotal data structure in our example is the partcost dictionary. It represents the f function defined in the *How it works...* section. The keys of this dictionary are represented by a tuple (i, j), indicating from which matrix to which matrix we want to perform the multiplication. The value assigned to the key (i, j) is also a tuple holding two values: the minimum cost of computing the multiplications, and the value of the optimal point of multiplication (it is k, minimizing the expression given in the recurrence relation in the *How it works...* section). We need to store the value of k because later in domul, it is used to actually perform the multiplications.

It is important to note that we use the partcost dictionary as a **memoization** (see https:/ /github.com/JuliaCollections/Memoize.jl
or https://en.wikipedia.org/wiki/Memoization) data structure, to avoid computing $f(i, j)$ multiple times for the same values of i and j.

Two additional things to take heed of are these:

- In the fastmatmul function, we first check that the dimensions of the multiplied matrices will allow the multiplication to be performed.
- In the solvemul function, for simplicity, we assume that the cost of the product is less than the maximum value of Int. For this reason, we initialize the mincost variable to typemax(Int).

There's more...

In practice, we might want to define our fast matrix multiplication as `macro`, which takes a standard matrix multiplication expression and modifies it to be a fast one. This `macro` can be implemented in the following way:

```julia
julia> macro fastmatmul(ex::Expr)
           ex.head == :call || throw(ArgumentError("expression must be
           a call"))
           ex.args[1] == :(*) || throw(ArgumentError("only
           multiplication is allowed"))
           new_ex = deepcopy(ex)
           new_ex.args[1] = :fastmatmul
           esc(new_ex)
       end
```

When you evaluate the preceding code check how this macro works:

```julia
julia> @fastmatmul ones(2,3)*ones(3,4)*ones(4,5)
2×5 Array{Float64,2}:
 12.0 12.0 12.0 12.0 12.0
 12.0 12.0 12.0 12.0 12.0
```

A thing to notice about the implementation of this `macro` is that we perform a `deepcopy` of `ex` inside it. The reason is that `ex` might be used for some other purposes (outside of `macro`), so we want to avoid modifying it directly. Also we return the value of the call to the `esc` function from the macro in order to prevent the macro hygiene pass from modifying variables embedded in `new_ex`.

As an additional note, it is worth remembering that under finite precision multiplication of floats, changing the order of operations might slightly alter the results, so it is not guaranteed that `*` and `fastmatmul` produce exactly the same result (it will be only approximately identical).

See also

More details about metaprogramming in Julia can be found in the *Metaprogramming* recipe in `Chapter 6`, *Metaprogramming and Advanced Typing*.

Implementing a custom pseudo-random number generator

In many situations in Julia, you might want to extend some abstract type defined in the base language. In this recipe, we will show how you can implement a simple pseudo-random number generator extending AbstractRNG.

Getting ready

In order to create your own pseudo-random number generator, you have to define a concrete type that is a subtype of the AbstractRNG abstract type and which implements methods for the seed!, rand, and rng_native_52 functions. In this recipe, we will show how you can achieve this.

The generator we will implement is called **64-bit Xorshift**. It was proposed by George Marsaglia in the paper, *Xorshift RNGs*, published in the *Journal of Statistical Software, Vol 8 (2003), Issue 14*.

Before running this recipe, make sure that you have the StatsBase.jl and BenchmarkTools.jl packages installed. If it is missing make sure that you have it by running the following commands:

```julia
julia> using Pkg

julia> Pkg.add("BenchmarkTools")

julia> Pkg.add("StatsBase")
```

in the Julia command line.

 In the GitHub repository for this recipe, you will find the commands.txt file that contains the presented sequence of shell and Julia commands.

Now open your favorite terminal to execute commands.

How to do it...

In order to define our own pseudo-random number generator, you should go through the following steps in the Julia console:

1. Load the `Random` module:

   ```julia
   julia> using Random
   ```

2. Define the `Xorhift` type, which is a subtype of `AbstractRNG`:

   ```julia
   julia> mutable struct Xorshift <: AbstractRNG
              state::UInt64
          end

   julia> Xorshift() = Xorshift(rand(RandomDevice(), UInt64))
   Xorshift
   ```

3. Define custom methods for working with the newly created type:

   ```julia
   julia> Random.seed!(r::Xorshift, seed::UInt64 =
   rand(RandomDevice(), UInt64)) = r.state = seed

   julia> function xorshift_rand(r::Xorshift)
              state = r.state
              state ⊻= state << 13
              state ⊻= state >> 7
              state ⊻= state << 17
              r.state = state
          end
   xorshift_rand (generic function with 1 method)

   julia> const XorshiftSamplers = Union{map(T->Random.SamplerType{T},
       [Bool, UInt32, Int32, UInt64, Int64])...}
   Union{SamplerType{Bool}, SamplerType{Int32}, SamplerType{Int64},
   SamplerType{UInt32}, SamplerType{UInt64}}

   julia> Base.rand(r::Xorshift, sampler::XorshiftSamplers) =
   xorshift_rand(r) % sampler[]

   julia> Random.rng_native_52(::Xorshift) = UInt64
   ```

4. Finally, we do a simple test, to see if our generator works as expected and generates approximately uniform distributions:

   ```julia
   julia> using StatsBase

   julia> r = Xorshift(0x0139408dcbbf7a44)
   ```

```
    Xorshift(0x0139408dcbbf7a44)

julia> countmap(rand(r, 1:10, 10^8))
Dict{Int64,Int64} with 10 entries:
  7 => 9996777
  4 => 9997119
  9 => 10004173
  10 => 9998711
  2 => 10000084
  3 => 9998660
  5 => 10002696
  8 => 10001941
  6 => 9996874
  1 => 10002965

julia> const X = zeros(Int, 5, 5)
5×5 Array{Int64,2}:
 0 0 0 0 0
 0 0 0 0 0
 0 0 0 0 0
 0 0 0 0 0
 0 0 0 0 0

julia> foreach(i -> X[rand(r, 1:5), rand(r, 1:5)] += 1, 1:10^7)

julia> 25 * X / 10^7
5×5 Array{Float64,2}:
 0.99838   0.99897   1.00105   0.99999   1.00083
 1.00029   0.998483  0.999677  0.99849   0.999127
 1.00189   1.00288   0.998112  1.0006    0.997885
 0.999413  0.999378  1.00081   0.997613  1.00225
 0.99996   1.00161   1.00097   0.998367  1.00298
```

And we can see that both the results of countmap and foreach are approximately uniform.

How it works...

Julia provides two built-in random number generators. The first is MersenneTwister, which is a popular pseudo-random number generator. The second is RandomDevice, which uses operating system entropy to generate random numbers. They are defined in the Random.jl package from the standard library, which exports many useful functions for working with them, for example, rand, randn, randexp, and shuffle.

The design of methods from the `Random` module does not restrict the user to the predefined random number generators. In fact, they all accept an object of `AbstractRNG` type, making it easy to define your own random number generator. All you need to do is define a type that is an `AbstractRNG` subtype and define methods for three functions:

- `Random.seed!`: Allows the user to set the seed of the random number generator
- `rand`: Produces a single pseudo-random value
- `rng_native_52`: Tells Julia the type of native random value produced by the sampler

The parts of the code that deserve highlighting are the following:

- The default constructor of `Xorshift` type requires a seed. In order to provide a method of random seeding of our type, we create an outer constructor, taking no arguments and taking a random value generated by the `RandomDevice` generator as the seed.
- We create methods for the functions defined in the `Base` and `Random` modules. Therefore, in order to add methods to existing functions, we prepend the function names with the module name, for example, `Random.seed!` or `Base.rand`. If we omitted this step, new functions would be defined in the current module, thus hiding the ones imported from the `Random` and `Base` modules.
- We can see from the definition of `XorshiftSamplers` that in Julia we are able to programmatically create type signatures, in this case, a `Union` of `SamplerType` types. The type `SamplerType` is an internal type of the `Random` module; therefore, we have to qualify access to it. Its role is very simple—it defines what types of random values our generator can produce. We have specified that we want Boolean, signed and unsigned 32-bit and 64-bit integers. Generation of floating-point values is ensured automatically by the `rng_native_52` function.
- You might wonder what the `sampler[]` statement does. It is translated to a `getindex(sampler)` call, so in other words, it is a kind of 0-dimensional array access operator. If we check the source code of this function by writing `@edit getindex(Random.SamplerType{Int}())`, then we find out that it returns the type of the sampler.

- We use the `countmap` function from the `StatsBase.jl` package, which creates a dictionary of counts of elements in the collection. Next, we use the `foreach` function from `Base`, which is also worth knowing. It works similarly to `map` but does not collect the result. Typically, we use it when we are only interested in the side-effect of the iteration, as in our example.

There's more...

You might wonder why Julia needs `SamplerType` in the `rand` function. In order to understand this, consider how a `UInt128` value could be generated. We see that we need two `UInt64` values to create it. Therefore, under our preceding definitions, if we want to generate such a number, we get an error:

```
julia> rand(Xorshift(), UInt128)
ERROR: ArgumentError: Sampler for this object is not defined
```

We have to define a method that handles `UInt128` values explicitly. Here is how you can do it:

```
julia> function Base.rand(r::Xorshift,
sampler::Random.SamplerType{UInt128})
           r1 = rand(r, UInt64)
           r2 = rand(r, UInt64)
           (UInt128(r1) << 64) | r2
       end
```

Now, we can generate the desired random values, for example:

```
julia> rand(Xorshift(), UInt128)
0x1088e2ff5b8875d343f434adaa6871f8
```

Finally, you might wonder why we should even bother replacing `MersenneTwister` with `Xorshift` in the code. There are two reasons. One is practical—sometimes we need to reproduce external results that used the `Xorshift` pseudo-random number generator. The other is speed—it is almost twice as fast:

```
julia> using BenchmarkTools

julia> r = Xorshift()
Xorshift(0x77baaba677d18be7)

julia> @benchmark rand()
BenchmarkTools.Trial:
 memory estimate: 0 bytes
```

```
 allocs estimate: 0
 --------------
 minimum time: 6.064 ns (0.00% GC)
 median time: 7.464 ns (0.00% GC)
 mean time: 7.467 ns (0.00% GC)
 maximum time: 25.660 ns (0.00% GC)
 --------------
 samples: 10000
 evals/sample: 1000

julia> @benchmark rand($r)
BenchmarkTools.Trial:
 memory estimate: 0 bytes
 allocs estimate: 0
 --------------
 minimum time: 3.732 ns (0.00% GC)
 median time: 4.199 ns (0.00% GC)
 mean time: 4.392 ns (0.00% GC)
 maximum time: 56.917 ns (0.00% GC)
 --------------
 samples: 10000
 evals/sample: 1000
```

The downside is that Xorshift has a shorter period and slightly worse statistical properties.

See also

It is also possible to create a random number generator that fetches randomness from an external source. If you are interested in this, you can refer to https://www.random.org/. How to fetch data from the internet is described in the *Fetching data from the internet* recipe in Chapter 4, *Data Engineering in Julia*.

If you are interested in a more advanced way of creating cross-tabulations than the countmap function offers, then it is worth checking out the Freqtables.jl package.

Parsing Git logs with regular expressions

One of the very common tasks in data science is parsing logs produced by some application. In this recipe, we will write a simple snippet that presents how we can analyze the contributions of committers to the Git repository.

Getting ready

In order to run this recipe, you need to have the `DataFrames.jl` and `DataFramesMeta.jl` packages installed. If they are missing run the following commands to add them:

```julia
julia> using Pkg

julia> Pkg.add("DataFrames")

julia> Pkg.add("DataFramesMeta")
```

Also, you need to have Git installed. You can get it from `https://git-scm.com/`.

When you run the `git log --stat` command on a repository, it prints output that looks similar to this:

```
$ git log --stat
commit 14f30ad448a5d38be38c7b0e7274f0f7b0a951ee (HEAD -> master,
upstream/master)
Author: Bogumił Kamiński <bkamins@sgh.waw.pl>
Date: Mon Jun 18 21:40:46 2018 +0200

    Allow aggregate to use column number for aggregation (#1426)

 src/groupeddataframe/grouping.jl | 6 +++---
 test/data.jl | 8 ++++++++
 2 files changed, 11 insertions(+), 3 deletions(-)

commit b791af16eb0555f237eff1132125be6fcdf76947
Author: Nick Eubank <nickeubank@users.noreply.github.com>
Date: Mon Jun 18 14:38:51 2018 -0500

    add indicator keyword to join (#1424)

 src/abstractdataframe/join.jl | 59 ++++++++++++++++++++++++++++++++++++++++++++++------
----
 test/join.jl | 25 +++++++++++++++++++
 2 files changed, 71 insertions(+), 13 deletions(-)
```

You can observe that for each commit, we have some information about the author of the commit and about insertions and deletions (if they are present). We want to extract information about the activity of each contributor to the repository and present it in an aggregated form.

In the GitHub repository for this recipe, you will find
the commands.txt file that contains the presented sequence of shell and
Julia commands and the parselog.jl file that contains the source code
of functions defined in this recipe.

Now open your favorite terminal to execute commands.

How to do it...

Here is a list of steps to be followed:

1. Execute the parselog.jl file using include("parselog.jl") command in
   the Julia command line in order to define the following functions that analyze the
   Git repository:

```julia
using DataFrames, DataFramesMeta

function parselog(lines)
    author = r"^Author: ([^<]*) <"
    insc = r"^.+changed, ([0-9]+) insertion"
    delc = r"^.+changed.*, ([0-9]+) deletion"
    authordata = DataFrame(author=String[], action=String[],
    count=Int[])
    curauthor = ""
    for line in lines
        m = match(author, line)
        m === nothing || (curauthor = m[1])
        m = match(insc, line)
        m === nothing || push!(authordata,
                                (curauthor, "insertion", parse(Int,
                                 m[1])))
        m = match(delc, line)
        m === nothing || push!(authordata,
                                (curauthor, "deletion", parse(Int,
                                 m[1])))
    end
    authorstats = @by(authordata, [:author, :action],
    count=sum(:count))
    unstack(authorstats, :action, :count)
end

function gitstats(dir)
    if isdir(dir)
        println("\nAnalyzing")
        cd(dir) do
```

```
            try
                res = read(`git log --stat`, String)
                lines = split(res, ['\r', '\n'], keepempty=false)
                df = parselog(lines)
                df.all = coalesce.(df.deletion, 0) .+
                        coalesce.(df.insertion, 0)
                display(sort!(df, :all, rev=true))
            catch
                error("Running git log failed")
            end
        end
    else
        error("$dir is not a directory")
    end
end
```

2. Test the defined functions, using the following commands. While in the Package Manager mode check out the DataFrames.jl package for development:

```
(v1.0) pkg> dev DataFrames
[the output is omitted]
```

In this way, we have a full copy of the Git repository of this package downloaded to your local storage.

3. Now, switch back to the Julia mode and analyze this repository it:

```
julia> gitstats(joinpath(DEPOT_PATH[1], "dev/DataFrames"))
```

```
Analyzing
133×4 DataFrame
| Row | author           | deletion | insertion | all    |
|     | String           | Int64    | Int64     | Int64  |
|-----|------------------|----------|-----------|--------|
|  1  | John Myles White | 31288    | 105657    | 136945 |
|  2  | Cameron Prybol   | 73847    | 3486      | 77333  |
|  3  | Tom Short        | 10039    | 12975     | 23014  |
|  4  | Sean Garborg     | 9991     | 4008      | 13999  |
[the output is trimmed]
```

4. Finally, revert back to the DataFrames.jl package to its released version (remember to switch to the Package Manager mode first):

```
(v1.0) pkg> free DataFrames
[the output is omitted]
```

How it works...

In this code, we define two functions, `parselog` and `gitstats`:

- `parselog` parses a vector of lines of text that is produced by running the `git log --stat` command on the Git repository
- `gitstats` is a wrapper that prepares data for `parselog` to work on

Let's first understand how the `gitstats` function works, since it does the key work involved. We define a regular expression object using the `r` prefix for a string literal. For example, `r"^Author: ([^<]*) <"` extracts a pattern from a line that starts with the `"Author: "` string and later includes a `" <"` string. Additionally, everything between those two strings, if there is a match, should be captured for later processing (this is the contributor's name).

Then, using the `match(author, line)` command, where `author` is a regular expression and `line` is a string, it tries to find the pattern represented by `author` in `line`. If the match fails, then `match` returns `nothing`; otherwise, the returned object can be indexed to retrieve a match.

One issue with this function that may not be obvious is that we need to define a `curauthor` variable outside of the `for` loop. In this way, the value of `curauthor` is remembered over consecutive iterations of the loop.

If we omitted the `curauthor = ""` line in our script then the following line will produce an error:

```
m === nothing || push!(authordata,
                       (curauthor, "insertion", parse(Int, m[1])))
```

The reason is that `curauthor` would be introduced as a local variable inside a loop. Such variables receive a new binding in every iteration of the loop (see `https://docs.julialang.org/en/v1.0/manual/variables-and-scoping/#For-Loops-and-Comprehensions-1`). Observe that a similar loop in Python, for instance, would work without an error.

Here is a smaller example showing the same problem. First, define the following function:

```julia
julia> function f()
           for i in 1:2
               if i == 1
                   j = 1
               else
                   println(j)
```

```
                 end
            end
        end
    f (generic function with 1 method)
```

Now, if we try to run this in the Julia command line, we get an error:

```
julia> f()
ERROR: UndefVarError: j not defined
Stacktrace:
 [1] f() at .\REPL[1]:6
 [2] top-level scope at none:0
```

Going back to our recipe, in the loop, each time we find a line in the log indicating the insertion or deletion of a line, we use the push! function to add a row to the authordata data frame. This operation is cheap and updates the data frame in place, as opposed to the rbind function in R.

Finally, we use the @by macro from the DataFramesMeta.jl package and the unstack function from the DataFrames.jl package to get a nice table summarizing all contributions to the repository.

Moving on to the gitstats function, we see that it takes a path to be analyzed. It makes sure that it is a directory and then *temporarily* switches the current directory of Julia to it using a do block.

Finally, we try to parse the log and report an error if it fails. The way it works is through storing the result of the git command into a string using the read(`git log --stat`, String) function. Notice that using a backtick ` creates a Cmd object that is executed and its result is stored into the res variable. We split the res variable using a \n separator in the split(res, '\n') function call. In general, however, a string coming from an unknown source could have a different line ending ("\n", "\r", or "\r\n"). Therefore, we could work around this via split(res, ['\r', '\n'], keepempty=false).

The final puzzle is how we test our function in the final part of the recipe. The DEPOT_PATH[1] variable contains a location for user depot—a path where, most likely, packages are installed. Then, we construct a path to the DataFrames.jl package checked out for development using the joinpath function.

There's more...

You can work directly with the Git repository via a programmatic API in Julia using the `LibGit2.jl` package. You can read the details about it at `https://docs.julialang.org/en/latest/stdlib/LibGit2/`.

See also

To gain a better understanding of how depots work in Julia, you can take a look at `https://docs.julialang.org/en/v1.0/stdlib/Pkg/`.

More details about using the `DataFrames.jl` and `DataFramesMeta.jl` packages can be found in `Chapter 7`, *Handling Analytical Data*.

Non-standard ways to sort your data

Sorting is one of the basic operations commonly performed when processing data. In this recipe, we will explore several options for how you can perform sorting in non-standard cases. In particular, we will compare the performance of the various options that can be used for sorting.

Getting ready

In this recipe, we want to sort rows of an array of `Float64` numbers by their norms. For our purposes, the norm of a list of values $x_1, x_2, \ldots, x_n$ is defined as $\left(\sum_{i=1}^{n} x_i^2\right)^{1/2}$, that is, the Euclidean norm (see `http://mathworld.wolfram.com/MatrixNorm.html`).

 In the GitHub repository for this recipe you will find the `commands.txt` file that contains the presented sequence of shell and Julia commands.

Now open your favorite terminal to execute commands.

How to do it...

In order to compare different custom sorting strategies, we first create sample test data and then perform the sorting on it as follows:

1. In this recipe, we will use the seed! function from the Random module and the norm function from the LinearAlgebra module, so start by loading them:

```julia
julia> using Random, LinearAlgebra
```

2. Now, generate a random matrix to be sorted:

```julia
julia> Random.seed!(1);

julia> x = rand(1000, 1000);
```

3. Sort its rows by their norm in three separate ways:

```julia
julia> x1 = sortslices(x, by=norm, dims=1);

julia> x2 = sortslices(x, lt=(x,y) -> norm(x) < norm(y), dims=1);

julia> x3 = x[sortperm([norm(view(x, i, :)) for i in 1:size(x, 1)]), :];
```

4. Check that the operation worked correctly in all cases:

```julia
julia> issorted(sum(x1.^2, dims=2))
true

julia> x1 == x2 == x3
true
```

5. Finally, perform a simple performance check of the three options considered:

```julia
julia> @time x1 = sortslices(x, by=norm, dims=1);
  0.120219 seconds (1.06 k allocations: 7.708 MiB)

julia> @time x2 = sortslices(x, lt=(x,y) -> norm(x) < norm(y), dims=1);
  0.314779 seconds (320.44 k allocations: 23.879 MiB, 2.80% gc time)

julia> @time x3 = x[sortperm([norm(view(x, i, :)) for i in 1:size(x, 1)]), :];
  0.071230 seconds (72.70 k allocations: 11.210 MiB)
```

How it works...

A standard use of the sort function in Julia is to sort a vector that is a one-dimensional array, such as [1,2,3].

However, it is good to know that if you want to sort all the rows or columns of a matrix, you can use the sortslices function.

In this recipe, we learned that if we want to use a custom rule of sorting of data, we can do the following:

- Pass the lt keyword argument, which specifies a function comparing pairs of elements
- Pass the by keyword argument, which specifies how data should be transformed before comparison
- Create a permutation vector using the sortperm function, which applied to the original data yields the sorted result

Additionally, we can see that using sortperm was quickest. The reason is that the norm operation is expensive and with sortperm it is performed only once per consecutive row (which is extracted using view to avoid data copying). With the by or lt arguments, norm is called every time the sorting algorithm performs a comparison. Actually, with lt, we can see that it is least efficient and it performs approximately twice as much work as by does.

There's more...

If you want to perform an in-place sorting of your data, then you need to use functions that have the ! suffix in their name, for example, sort!, sortslices!. The details are explained at https://docs.julialang.org/en/v1.0/base/sort/.

See also

If you want to learn how we could perform a more careful comparison of code timings, check out the *Benchmarking code* recipe in Chapter 8, *Julia Workflow*.

Creating a function preimage – understanding how dictionaries and sets work

In this recipe, we will explain in detail how the `Dict` and `Set` types identify keys in Julia.

Getting ready

The example that we will use is the creation of a dictionary that stores a `preimage` function.

Given a function, $f: A \rightarrow B$ and $b \in B$, we will call `preimage` of b a set $\{a \in A : f(a) = b\}$; see the example at `http://mathworld.wolfram.com/Preimage.html`.

In particular, we need to create `preimage` of all possible values of a mapping, $f(x, y) = x/y$, given the domain, $A = \{(x, y) : x, y \in \{-2, -1, 0, 1, 2\}\}$ and the set B defined as an image of A under f, as calculated by Julia.

 In the GitHub repository for this recipe, you will find the `commands.txt` file that contains the presented sequence of shell and Julia commands.

Now open your favorite terminal to execute commands.

How to do it...

We will perform the computations in three steps. Firstly, we create an appropriate data structure that will hold our data, then we will add elements to it, and finally, we will print out its contents to understand which key-value pairs were stored in it:

1. Create a data structure that will hold our `preimage` mapping:

   ```
   julia> preimage = Dict{Float64, Set{Tuple{Float64, Float64}}}()
   Dict{Float64,Set{Tuple{Float64,Float64}}} with 0 entries
   ```

2. Populate the dictionary with mappings for the assumed domain:

```
julia> for x in -2.0:2.0, y in -2.0:2.0
           k = x / y
           v = (x, y)
           if haskey(preimage, k)
               push!(preimage[k], v)
           else
               preimage[k] = Set([v])
           end
       end
```

3. Finally, print the formatted contents of the `preimage` dictionary:

```
julia> for k in sort!(collect(keys(preimage)))
       println(k, ":\t", join(sort!(collect(preimage[k])), ",\t"))
           end
-Inf:  (-2.0, 0.0),   (-1.0, 0.0)
-2.0:  (-2.0, 1.0),   (2.0, -1.0)
-1.0:  (-2.0, 2.0),   (-1.0, 1.0),   (1.0, -1.0),  (2.0, -2.0)
-0.5:  (-1.0, 2.0),   (1.0, -2.0)
-0.0:  (0.0, -2.0),   (0.0, -1.0)
0.0:   (0.0, 1.0),    (0.0, 2.0)
0.5:   (-1.0, -2.0),  (1.0, 2.0)
1.0:   (-2.0, -2.0),  (-1.0, -1.0),  (1.0, 1.0),   (2.0, 2.0)
2.0:   (-2.0, -1.0),  (2.0, 1.0)
Inf:   (1.0, 0.0),    (2.0, 0.0)
NaN:   (0.0, 0.0)
```

How it works...

At the beginning of the recipe, we create a `preimage` dictionary. Observe that its constructor is `Dict{Float64, Set{Tuple{Float64, Float64}}}()`, which means that the dictionary has keys of type `Float64` and its values are a `Set` of tuples consisting of two `Float64` values.

Next, we populate the dictionary by traversing x and y over a range from -2.0 to 2.0, with a step equal to 1.0.

If a certain value of the ratio x/y has already been encountered in the process, we add the tuple (x, y) to a set already stored in the `preimage` dictionary using `push!`. If it is the first time we have encountered this ratio, we create a new set using the `Set` constructor.

In the final part, we perform pretty printing of our data structure. Note that we sort the keys and entries of the `preimage` dictionary. In order to do this, we have to use the `collect` function to transform the underlying object (`keys(preimage)` and `preimage[k]` respectively) to a vector, which then can be sorted in place using `sort!`. Observe that the sort order of `Float64` values is from `-Inf` to `Inf` and `NaN` at the end. This means that `NaN` is considered larger than any other `Float64` value.

There's more...

There are two corner cases with `Float64` that you should be aware of. Firstly, the dictionary (and also set) treats all `NaN` instances as having the same value:

```
julia> f1 = NaN
NaN

julia> f2 = -NaN
NaN

julia> reinterpret(UInt64, f1)
0x7ff8000000000000

julia> reinterpret(UInt64, f2)
0xfff8000000000000

julia> f1 === f2
false

julia> isequal(f1, f2)
true

julia> Set([f1, f2])
Set([NaN])
```

Secondly, Julia distinguishes `0.0` and `-0.0` as being different when selecting unique values in a collection; for example:

```
julia> Set([0.0, -0.0])
Set([0.0, -0.0])
```

The reason is that they have a different underlying representation:

```julia
julia> reinterpret(UInt64, 0.0)
0x0000000000000000

julia> reinterpret(UInt64, -0.0)
0x8000000000000000
```

And this potentially avoids the problem whereby functions might return a different value with 0.0 versus -0.0 arguments, for example:

```julia
julia> 1/0.0
Inf

julia> 1/-0.0
-Inf
```

An identical behavior is exhibited by the unique function, for example:

```julia
julia> unique([-0.0, 0.0, 0.0, -0.0, NaN, -NaN])
3-element Array{Float64,1}:
  -0.0
   0.0
 NaN
```

The underlying reason is that all these functions use isequal when testing for equality.

See also

You can find another example of the application of the Dict type in the *Working with UTF-8 strings* recipe.

Working with UTF-8 strings

Julia supports handling UTF-8 strings. However, the way you work with them is slightly different from such languages as R or Python. In this recipe, you will discover more about the String and SubString types, as well as the correct method of indexing into a string in Julia.

We will learn this by parsing a file containing the word Hello, written in different languages.

Getting ready

In this recipe we will work with text stored in the file `hello.txt` that has the following contents as shown in the following screenshot:

```
Bulgarian Здравейте
Chinese 你好
English Hello
Greek Χαίρετε
Hindi नमस्ते
Japanese こんにちは
Khmer សួស្តី
Korean 여보세요
Polish cześć
Russian Здравствуйте
```

Some terminals, in particular, the standard Windows terminal started by **cmd**, might have problems with displaying some of the characters in this recipe. If you encounter such a problem then we recommend you to either uses Juno, ConEmu (under Windows) or terminal in-built into Vim 8.1.1. We have tested that in these three environments all characters display correctly if you make them use a font that supports an appropriate range of Unicode. Such a font is for example `Consolas`.

In the GitHub repository for this recipe, you will find the `commands.txt` file that contains the presented sequence of shell and Julia commands and the `hello.txt` file that contains texts that we will process in this recipe.

Now open your favorite terminal to execute commands.

How to do it...

Following that, we present the steps to work with a UTF-8 file in Julia:

1. Read the data from the file into Julia:

```
julia> hello = readlines("hello.txt")
```

The preceding command generates the output as follows:

```
julia> readlines("hello.txt")
10-element Array{String,1}:
 "Bulgarian Здравейте"
 "Chinese 你好 "
 "English Hello"
 "Greek Χαίρετε"
 "Hindi नमस्ते "
 "Japanese こんにちは "
 "Khmer សួស្ដី "
 "Korean 여보세요 "
 "Polish cześć"
 "Russian Здравствуйте"
```

2. Create a dictionary mapping the language name to `"Hello"` greeting in this language:

```
julia> hello_dict = Dict(map(x->Pair(x...), split.(hello, ' ')))
```

The preceding command generates the output as follows:

```
julia> hello_dict = Dict(map(x->Pair(x...), split.(hello, ' ')))
Dict{SubString{String},SubString{String}} with 10 entries:
  "Chinese"   => "你好 "
  "English"   => "Hello"
  "Greek"     => "Χαίρετε"
  "Khmer"     => " សួស្ដី "
  "Korean"    => "여보세요 "
  "Hindi"     => " नमस्ते "
  "Japanese"  => "こんにちは "
  "Bulgarian" => "Здравейте"
  "Polish"    => "cześć"
  "Russian"   => "Здравствуйте"
```

3. Extract `"Hello"` greeting in Chinese:

```
julia> chinese = hello_dict["Chinese"]
„你好„
```

4. Finally, investigate the contents of this string in detail:

```
julia> codeunits(chinese)
6-element Base.CodeUnits{UInt8,SubString{String}}:
 0xe4
 0xbd
 0xa0
```

```
0xe5
0xa5
0xbd

julia> ncodeunits(chinese)
6

julia> collect(chinese)
2-element Array{Char,1}:
 ,你,

 ,好,

julia> length(chinese)
2

julia> isvalid.(chinese, 1:ncodeunits(chinese))
6-element BitArray{1}:
  true
 false
 false
  true
 false
 false

julia> thisind.(chinese, 0:ncodeunits(chinese)+1)
8-element Array{Int64,1}:
 0
 1
 1
 1
 4
 4
 4
 7

julia> nextind.(chinese, 0:ncodeunits(chinese))
7-element Array{Int64,1}:
 1
 4
 4
 4
 7
 7
 7

julia> prevind.(chinese, 1:ncodeunits(chinese)+1)
7-element Array{Int64,1}:
```

```
0
1
1
1
4
4
4
```

How it works...

We start with the readlines function, which reads in the file. Each line of the file is represented as a string with the end-of-line mark stripped out.

Creating hello_dict is done in the following steps:

1. We split each entry of the hello vector by a space character delimiter. Note that we are broadcasting the split function using the dot (.) operator.
2. Please note that the split function produces a vector of SubString{String}. This type is similar to view in the array so that we avoid allocating memory anew. The drawback is that our hello_dict now holds the SubString{String} type, which you should be aware of when working with it. You can convert a SubString{String} value to a string if you need to by using a String constructor; for example, String.(split("a b c")) produces Vector{String}.
3. Finally, observe that we map a vector of two element vectors into a dictionary using a Dict constructor that takes a collection of Pair.

In the second part of the recipe, we concentrate on Hello in Chinese, that is, "你好", and we learn the following:

- It consists of six bytes that constitute two characters.
- It is valid to index into this string only with indices equal to 1 (gets the first character) and 4 (gets the second character).
- There are three low-level functions that allow you to move over a string. The first is thisind(s, i) and it finds a valid index of a start of the character, which continues in index i. The second is nextind(s, i), which finds a valid index of a start of the first character beyond index i. The third is prevind(s, i), which finds a valid index of a start of the first character before or at index i. Additionally, observe that thisind and nextind allow i to be equal to 0 and, similarly, thisind and prevind allow i to be equal to ncodeunits(s)+1.

In general, it is not advised to use direct string indexing as it can be tricky to handle. If you want to find an index of the ith character in a string s, somewhat surprisingly, you should use nextind(s, 0, i). This means that to extract a string starting from character i and ending at character j, you should write s[nextind(s, 0, i):nextind(s, 0, j)]. Fortunately, most of the work can usually be done using higher-level functions; for example, regular expressions.

There's more...

Julia will accept invalid UTF-8 strings without a problem. However, it will notify the user that the string is not valid; for example:

```julia
julia> s=String([0xff, 0xff, 0xff])
"\xff\xff\xff"

julia> isvalid(s)
false

julia> collect(s)
3-element Array{Char,1}:
 '\xff'
 '\xff'
 '\xff'
```

Observe that we are iterating through malformed characters, but this cannot be helped in this case:

```julia
julia> s[1]
'\xff': Malformed UTF-8 (category Ma: Malformed, bad data)
```

See also

You can read about the details of handling strings in Julia at https://docs.julialang.org/en/v1.0/manual/strings/.

There are extension packages providing an alternative implementation of strings for Julia. You can find them at https://github.com/JuliaString.

3
Data Engineering in Julia

In this chapter, various recipes for manipulating files and data streams across many formats are presented. The chapter contains the following recipes related to data processing:

- Managing streams, and reading and writing files
- Using `IOBuffer` to efficiently work with in-memory streams
- Fetching data from the internet
- Writing a simple RESTful service
- Working with JSON data
- Working with date and time
- Using object serialization in Julia
- Running Julia as a background process
- Reading and writing Microsoft Excel files
- Handling Feather data
- Reading CSV and FWF files

Introduction

This chapter shows how a Julia process can interact with its operating system environment. We show how to interact with files, and networks and how to access various data types from Julia. The data formats discussed in this chapter include **JSON** (short for **JavaScript Object Notation**), **Julia native object serialization**, **JLD2 (Julia data format)**, **BSON** (short for **Binary JSON**), **Microsoft Excel**, **Feather**, **CSV** (short for **comma-separated values**), and **FWF** (short for **Fixed Width Format**) files. Additionally, we also show how to publish a Julia functions as a RESTful web service.

Managing streams, and reading and writing files

Each process in an operating system can interact with the data available on different devices connected to the operating system. Sample devices include files or network connections. Interaction with devices is done via **streams**. A stream is a logical representation of a data transfer state.

In this recipe, we will show how to interact with the built-in system streams, as well as file streams, in Julia.

Getting ready

The way a program exchanges data with its environment is often called **I/O**, which stands for **input/output**. I/O operations are built into the Julia language. Hence, none of the typical installations is required to run these recipes; simply open the Julia command-line console.

 In the GitHub repository for this recipe, you will find the `commands.txt` file, which contains the presented sequence of shell and Julia commands.

How to do it...

In this example, we will consider two cases—interacting with built-in process streams, and reading and writing text files.

Built-in system streams (stdin, stdout, stderr)

In order to see how Julia can interact with built-in system streams, follow these steps:

1. Create a file called `iotest.jl`, and insert the following content:

```
a = parse(Float64, readline(stdin))
b = parse(Float64, readline(stdin))
println(stdout, "Got values: $a, $b")
if b > a
    println(stderr, "Wrong values: ", b, ">", a)
    exit(1)
end
```

```
println(stdout, "log(", a, "-", b, ")=", log(a-b))
exit(0)
```

2. Test the file. Go to the bash (or in Windows, the command line) and run `julia iotest.jl`, then enter the numbers 4 and 3 (after typing each number, press *Enter*):

```
$ julia iotest.jl
4
3
Got values: 4.0, 3.0
log(4.0-3.0)=0.0
```

3. Create a file, `iotest.txt`, with the following content:

```
4
3
```

4. Run the following commands in Linux Terminal or Windows bash:

```
$ more iotest.txt | julia iotest.jl 1> ioout1.txt 2> ioout2.txt

$ more ioout1.txt
Got values: 4.0, 3.0
log(4.0-3.0)=0.0
$ more ioout2.txt

$
```

Note that the `ioout2.txt` file is empty.

5. Create a file called `iotest2.txt` and insert the following content:

```
3
4
```

6. Run the following commands in Linux Bash or Windows Terminal:

```
$ more iotest2.txt | julia iotest.jl 1> ioout1.txt 2> ioout2.txt
$ more ioout1.txt
Got values: 3.0, 4.0
$ more ioout2.txt
Wrong values: 4.0>3.0
```

Reading and writing files

In order to see how Julia can be used to manipulate files, follow these steps:

1. For this example, open the Julia command line console and execute the following command to start writing to a file:

```julia
julia> f = open("my_data.txt", "w")
IOStream(<file my_data.txt>)
```

2. Now, let's write some information to this file:

```julia
julia> write(f, "first line\nsecond line\n")
23
```

Note that 23 is the number of bytes, written to IOStream, representing the file.

3. It is also possible to use the print and println functions, as follows:

```julia
julia> println(f, "last line")
```

4. Finally, the file should be closed as follows:

```julia
julia> close(f)
```

5. Now, read the data from the file. Reading data is done in a way analogous to writing:

```julia
julia> f = open("my_data.txt", "r")
IOStream(<file my_data.txt>)
```

Please note that when a stream is opened, the default mode is reading, so the "r" parameter is unnecessary. Therefore, we could also use a shorter version, in the form of f = open("my_data.txt").

6. In order to read a single line from a file, use the readline function:

```julia
julia> readline(f)
"first line"

julia> readline(f)
"second line"

julia> readline(f)
"last line"
```

Once all lines have been read, the stream is in an **end-of-file** (EOF) state:

```
julia> eof(f)
true
```

Subsequent reads from a stream in an EOF state will simply return an empty string:

```
julia> readline(f)
""
```

7. Remember to always close an opened stream (or use the do syntax):

```
julia> close(f)
```

8. It is also possible to read the entire file with the read command (here we use the do syntax, which allows you to avoid closing the stream):

```
julia> lines = open("my_data.txt", "r") do f
           readlines(f)
       end
3-element Array{String,1}:
 "first line"
 "second line"
 "last line"
```

9. The read function should be used in place of readlines when the data that should be read is in binary, rather than plain text:

```
julia> data = open("my_data.txt", "r") do f
           read(f)
       end
33-element Array{UInt8,1}:
 0x66
 0x69
    .
    .
    .
 0x65
 0x0a
```

10. Now the data variable contains all bytes within the file. However, converting bytes back to a string is straightforward:

```
julia> text = String(data);
```

Please note that after this operation, the `data` array is empty, since all the bytes have been used to construct `String`. This behavior is caused by the need to avoid a byte-copying operation—the bits from `Array{UInt8,1}` (data object) can be immediately used to construct the `String` object.

11. Since strings are immutable in Julia, the reference to the original bytes is removed:

```julia
julia> length(data)
0
```

12. The bytes-to-string conversion can be skipped by reading in the data directly as a `String` with the following command:

```julia
julia> text = read(f, String);
```

How it works...

I/O is a way for programs to exchange data with their environments. As was discussed at the beginning of this recipe, the interaction of a process with external devices is done via streams, where a stream is a logical representation of a data transfer state.

The following stream types can be considered:

- **Input streams**: Used to *read* data from a given device
- **Output streams**: Used to *write* data to a given device
- **Input-output streams**: Used to simultaneously *read* and *write* data from a given device

Additionally, there are two stream access types:

- **Sequential**: Data is *read/written* sequentially in a certain order (for example, the order of bytes in a file).
- **Random access**: Is *read/written* from/to an arbitrary place in a stream. A `seek` operation is provided by the operating system to place the read/write mark in the appropriate location. This functionality has been achieved in Julia with the `seek` command (for instance, in the preceding examples, `seek(f, 0)` will move the reading to the beginning of the file).

Any process started in an operating system (Windows/Linux/Mac) has three default streams that enable any process to interact with the execution environment:

- Standard input, often abbreviated as **stdin** (in Julia, represented as the built-in `stdin` object), is a stream of the sequential read type.
- Standard output, often abbreviated as **stdout** (in Julia, represented as the built-in `stdout` object), is a stream of the sequential write type.
- Standard error, often abbreviated as **stderr** (in Julia, represented as the built-in `stderr` object), is a stream of the sequential write type.

See the following diagram, outlining the interaction between a process and its environment:

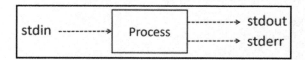

Furthermore, any process can open several input and output streams to system devices (such as files, network connections, and so on). There are usually some system limits on the number of streams that a process can open; for example, in Linux, the default limit for a single process is 1024 simultaneously opened files.

We can interact with a process's streams via bash commands. In particular, the `|` piping operator redirects the output of the first process as the standard input of the second process; the `1>` operator redirects the standard output and `2>` redirects the standard error.

There's more...

In the file operations presented in the preceding recipes, we assumed that the `data` variable is UTF-8 encoded (UTF-8 is the default encoding for strings in Julia). If your file contains non-UTF-8 encoded characters outside of the standard ASCII set, this function will wrongly interpret characters and produce garbage.

If the data in your file is using character encodings other than UTF-8, you should use the `StringEncodings.jl` package. To do this, first, press the *]* key to start the Julia package manager, then enter the following:

```
(v1.0) pkg> add StringEncodings
```

Now, you can use `StringEncodings` to process `data` in any selected encoding. See the example code (the example assumes that `data` is `Windows-1250` encoded):

```
using StringEncodings
data = open("my_data.txt", "r") do f
    read(f)
end;
txt = StringEncodings.decode(data, "Windows-1250")
```

When working with streams, it is very important to remember to close the stream. Sometimes, you might forget to use the `close` function. Hence, Julia provides the `do` syntax, which will automatically close an opened stream—we strongly recommend using it. Consider the following example for writing a file:

```
open("my_data.txt", "w") do f
    write(f, "line\nsecond line")
end
```

In the preceding example, there is no need to close the `f` file; it will be automatically closed once the `end` statement is reached.

See also

If you are new to character encoding issues, have a look at this introduction https://www.w3.org/International/questions/qa-what-is-encoding.

Please also see the next recipe, *Using IOBuffer to efficiently work with in-memory streams*, where we show how to manage `IOBuffer`-based streams.

Using IOBuffer to efficiently work with in-memory streams

In the recipe on *Managing streams, and reading and writing files*, we discussed how you can read and write streams. In this recipe, we will explain how you can create an in-memory stream that allows you to perform fast read and write operations on data using functions operating on streams.

We will show how you can create a simple string builder using an `IOBuffer` object.

Getting ready

In this recipe, we are going to create a function that takes a string and splits it into two substrings, one consisting of even characters in a string, and the other consisting of odd characters.

 In the GitHub repository for this recipe, you will find the `commands.txt` file, which contains the presented sequence of shell and Julia commands.

Now, open your favorite terminal to execute the commands.

How to do it...

You will first define a function that splits the string and then test it on a sample input:

1. Define the following function in the Julia command line:

```
julia> function splitstring(s::AbstractString)
           bufs = [IOBuffer() for i in 1:2]
           idx = 1
           for c in s
               write(bufs[idx], c)
               idx = 3 - idx
           end
           @. String(take!(bufs))
       end
splitstring (generic function with 1 method)
```

2. Check this function with a simple string, as follows:

```
julia> s = join('1':'9', "-")
"1-2-3-4-5-6-7-8-9"

julia> splitstring(s)
2-element Array{String,1}:
 "123456789"
 "--------"
```

How it works...

An instance of `IOBuffer` produces an in-memory stream that is very easy to read, write, and append to. The biggest advantage of using `IOBuffer` is that you can work with it in the same way as a normal stream. In this recipe, we used the `write` function. The only function specific to `IOBuffer` is `take!`, which obtains the contents of an `IOBuffer` object as an array and resets the buffer. In this recipe, we convert this array to `String`.

Two specific constructs in this recipe that also merit some explanation are as follows:

- When we write `idx = 3 - idx`, we make `idx` flip between the `1` and `2` values; this is a common transformation in languages using `1`-based indexing when you want to implement a `switch` variable.
- Using the `@.` macro in `@. String(take!(bufs))` means that we want to broadcast over both of the `String` and `take!` functions, and is equivalent to writing `String.(take!.(bufs))`.

There's more...

There are two natural alternative approaches for implementing our `splitstring` function. One uses `join`, as follows:

```julia
julia> function splitstring1(s::AbstractString)
           bufs = [Char[] for i in 1:2]
           idx = 1
           for c in s
               push!(bufs[idx], c)
               idx = 3 - idx
           end
           join.(bufs)
       end
splitstring1 (generic function with 1 method)
```

The other uses string concatenation, as shown here:

```julia
julia> function splitstring2(s::AbstractString)
           bufs = ["" for i in 1:2]
           idx = 1
           for c in s
               bufs[idx] *= c
               idx = 3 - idx
           end
           bufs
       end
splitstring2 (generic function with 1 method)
```

However, both of them are slower, as you can see in this benchmark (you need to have the `BenchmarkTools.jl` package installed for this code to work; if it is missing, run the following commands using `Pkg; Pkg.add("BenchmarkTools")` to add it):

```julia
julia> using BenchmarkTools

julia> s = "1"^10^4;

julia> @benchmark splitstring($s)
BenchmarkTools.Trial:
  memory estimate: 21.34 KiB
  allocs estimate: 28
  --------------
  minimum time: 195.477 µs (0.00% GC)
  median time: 215.071 µs (0.00% GC)
  mean time: 237.863 µs (4.28% GC)
  maximum time: 48.545 ms (99.56% GC)
  --------------
  samples: 10000
  evals/sample: 1

julia> @benchmark splitstring1($s)
BenchmarkTools.Trial:
  memory estimate: 150.66 KiB
  allocs estimate: 58
  --------------
  minimum time: 410.548 µs (0.00% GC)
  median time: 487.992 µs (0.00% GC)
  mean time: 530.543 µs (5.63% GC)
  maximum time: 49.224 ms (98.75% GC)
  --------------
  samples: 9373
  evals/sample: 1

julia> @benchmark splitstring2($s)
```

```
BenchmarkTools.Trial:
  memory estimate: 25.02 MiB
  allocs estimate: 20001
  --------------
  minimum time: 5.910 ms (16.50% GC)
  median time: 6.320 ms (15.96% GC)
  mean time: 7.289 ms (20.53% GC)
  maximum time: 67.388 ms (86.08% GC)
  --------------
  samples: 685
  evals/sample: 1
```

In the preceding code, we can observe that using string concatenation is very inefficient.

See also

In the *Working with UTF-8 strings* recipe in `Chapter 2`, *Data Structures and Algorithms*, we explain in more detail about how you can work with strings.

In the *Understanding broadcasting in Julia* recipe in `Chapter 4`, *Numerical Computing with Julia*, we give more background on how broadcasting in Julia works.

In the *Julia development workflow with Revise.jl* recipe in `Chapter 8`, *Julia Workflow*, we present another example of how `IOBuffer` can be used in practice when fetching data from the internet.

Fetching data from the internet

In this recipe, we will show how to use Julia to obtain data from the internet, and how to extract information from web pages. We will write some sample code that extracts the number of stars from GitHub projects.

Getting ready

For this recipe, you need the following packages: `HTTP.jl`, `Gumbo.jl`, and `Cascadia.jl`. These packages can simply be installed with the Julia package manager. In the Julia command line (REPL), simply press *]* key and run the following commands:

```
(v1.0) pkg> add HTTP
(v1.0) pkg> add Gumbo
(v1.0) pkg> add Cascadia
```

This will install the aforementioned packages and all their dependencies.

 In the GitHub repository for this recipe, you will find the `commands.txt` file, which contains the presented sequence of Julia commands.

How to do it...

In this example, we will read the number of GitHub stars from a set of GitHub repositories present under the umbrella of the JuliaWeb organization:

1. Start by loading the required modules as follows:

```
using HTTP, Gumbo, Cascadia
```

2. Next, we obtain the contents of the JuliaWeb site:

```
r=HTTP.get("https://github.com/JuliaWeb");
page_body = String(r.body);
```

3. Parse the website content, as follows:

```
h = Gumbo.parsehtml(page_body);
```

4. Now, we find all of the projects linked on this website from the HTML content:

```
qs = HTMLElement[]
Cascadia.matchAllInto(sel".d-inline-block.mb-1", h.root,qs);
names_links = Tuple{String,String}[]
for q in qs
    name = strip(nodeText(children(q)[1][1]))
    link = children(q)[1][1].attributes["href"]
    push!(names_links, (name, link))
end
```

5. Check whether the code worked correctly (since Julia is developing rapidly, you will see more packages when running this example):

```
julia> names_links
25-element Array{Tuple{String,String},1}:
  ("WebSockets.jl", "/JuliaWeb/WebSockets.jl")
  ("MbedTLS.jl", "/JuliaWeb/MbedTLS.jl")
  .
  .
  .
```

```
("GnuTLS.jl", "/JuliaWeb/GnuTLS.jl")
("Roadmap", "/JuliaWeb/Roadmap")
```

6. Visit each GitHub repository site from the list, and collect the number of stars for each project:

```julia
julia> stats = Dict{String,String}();
julia> @sync for (name,link) in names_links
    @async begin
        r2=HTTP.get("https://github.com"*link);
        h2 = parsehtml(String(r2.body));
        qs2 = HTMLElement[]
        Cascadia.matchAllInto(sel".social-count.js-social-count",
        h2.root,qs2);
        stats[name] = strip(nodeText(qs2[1]))
    end
end
```

7. Check the contents of `stats`:

```julia
julia> stats
Dict{String,String} with 25 entries:
  "HTTPClient.jl"   => "15"
  "JuliaWebAPI.jl"  => "81"
  "HTTP.jl"         => "125"
  ...               => ...
```

8. Convert the dictionary values into `Int64`:

```julia
julia> stats2 = Dict(key => parse(Int64, stats[key]) for key in
keys(stats))

Dict{String,Int64} with 24 entries:
  "HTTPClient.jl"   => 15
  "JuliaWebAPI.jl"  => 81
  "HTTP.jl"         => 125
  ... => ...
```

9. Finally, see which projects have the highest number of stars:

```julia
julia> m=maximum(values(stats2))
139

julia> filter(x -> x[2] == m, stats2)
Dict{String,Int64} with 1 entry:
  "HttpServer.jl" => 139
```

How it works...

The most popular protocol for communicating data over the internet is the **Hypertext Transfer Protocol (HTTP)**. Julia enables efficient networking via the HTTP.jl package. The HTTP.get function opens an HTTP connection to the server and gets the content. The operation returns an object of the HTTP.Messages.Response type, containing fields corresponding to the HTTP GET request:

- status: The status of the HTTP GET response; 200 stands for OK.

- headers: HTTP response headers that describe the response content type (including character encoding), the encoding method for the data, and other response specific fields.

- request: The content of the request that was sent by HTTP.jl to the server.

- body: The raw bytes of the server response. In the preceding example, we have assumed that the response is UTF-8 encoded, and thus we directly converted it to a string with the String(r.body) command. For other encoding types, you need to use the StringEncodings.jl package.

Once we obtained the output, we used Gumbo to parse the HTML and get the tree representation. The Gumbo-parsed data can be searched using a Cascadia selector. Cascadia enables writing selectors that perform a search over the HTML document structure. The library documentation, containing more information on this, is available at https://github.com/Algocircle/Cascadia.jl.

There's more...

Another way to access the data on web pages is via XPath. One option to handle this is to use the scrapy module from Python. We start by importing PyCall.jl and assume that PyCall has been already installed; for more information on working with PyCall in Julia, please see the recipe *Calling Python from Julia*:

```
using PyCall
```

The Python `scrapy` module can be used from an external Python installation (see the *Calling Python from Julia* recipe), or can be configured via the `Conda.jl` package (if `Conda.jl` is not installed, please go to the package manager by pressing the *]* key and installing it with the `add Conda` command):

```
using Conda
Conda.add("scrapy")
```

Now, we can import the Python `scrapy` module into Julia:

```
@pyimport scrapy.selector as ssel
```

Now, let's prepare the `Selector` object that will be used for searching (we assume that `page_body` from the main recipe in this chapter is still available in the REPL):

```
julia> s = ssel.Selector(text=page_body)
PyObject <Selector xpath=None data='<html lang="en">\n  <head>\n    <meta char'>
```

We use the XPath query to find the elements as follows:

```
julia> elems = s[:xpath]("//a[@itemprop='name codeRepository']")
25-element Array{PyObject,1}:
 PyObject <Selector xpath="//a[@itemprop='name codeRepository']" data='<a href="/JuliaWeb/WebSockets.jl" itempr'>
 .
 .
 .
 PyObject <Selector xpath="//a[@itemprop='name codeRepository']" data='<a href="/JuliaWeb/Roadmap" itemprop="na'>
```

The project names may be extracted as follows:

```
julia> strip(elems[1][:xpath]("text()")[1][:extract]())
"WebSockets.jl"

julia> strip(elems[2][:xpath]("text()")[1][:extract]())
"MbedTLS.jl"
```

Lastly, links can be extracted in the following way:

```
julia> a = elems[1][:xpath]("@href")[1][:extract]()
"/JuliaWeb/WebSockets.jl"

julia> a = elems[2][:xpath]("@href")[1][:extract]()
"/JuliaWeb/MbedTLS.jl"
```

See also

For more information on the HTTP protocol, have a look at `https://developer.mozilla.org/en-US/docs/Web/HTTP`. The Cascadia documentation is available at `https://github.com/Algocircle/Cascadia.jl`. For more documentation on `scrapy`, have a look at `https://scrapy.org/`. Finally, for information on how to use Python libraries from Julia, see the recipe on *Calling Python from Julia*.

Writing a simple RESTful service

HTTP, as described in the previous recipe, can be used to provide communication between different computers. The architectural style where HTTP is used to exchange tasks and information between machines is called **REpresentational State Transfer (REST)**. The applications that can be accessed via HTTP are called **web services**. As using HTTP for communication is straightforward on the client side as well as the server side, this is a very common method for providing cross-system communication.

Getting ready

In this recipe, we will present two approaches. The first one is a raw implementation of a web service using only the built-in Julia functions, including the standard package, `Sockets.jl`. In the second approach, we will use the `JuliaWebAPI.jl` package. This package should be installed along with `ZMQ.jl`, which will be used for handling the incoming requests. For testing purposes, we will use `HTTP.jl`.

The packages can be installed simply with the Julia package manager. In the Julia command line (REPL), press the *]* key and run the following commands:

```
(v1.0) pkg> add JuliaWebAPI
(v1.0) pkg> add ZMQ
(v1.0) pkg> add HTTP
```

This will install the `JuliaWebAPI.jl` package and its dependencies, along with the `HTTP.jl` package that we will use for testing the service.

Currently, `JuliaWebAPI.jl` also depends on the presence of the `Compat.jl` package, so you should install this as well (by executing `add Compat` in the package manager). The `Compat.jl` package provides code compatibility between older and newer versions of Julia.

In the GitHub repository for this recipe, you will find the `commands.txt` file, which contains the presented sequence of shell and Julia commands.

How to do it...

In this recipe, we consider two options:

- Building a web service from scratch that will illustrate Julia's socket network communication mechanism
- Using the `JuliaWebAPI.jl` package to publish a Julia function as a web service

Building a web service from scratch

In this example, we consider a scenario where the built-in `Sockets` package in Julia is used to write a web service:

1. The first step is to import the package as follows:

```
julia> using Sockets
```

2. Open the `server` for listening on port `8080`:

```
julia> server = Sockets.listen(8080)
Sockets.TCPServer(RawFD(0x00000014) active)
```

Opening a port for reading from the server is accomplished via the `Sockets.accept` function.

3. The following code creates a web service that can execute any Julia command:

```
julia> while true
    sock = Sockets.accept(server)
    data = readline(sock)
    print("Got request:\n", data, "\n")
    cmd = split(data, " ")[2][2:end]
    println(sock, "\nHTTP/1.1 200 OK\nContent-Type: text/html\n")
    println(sock, string("<html><body>", cmd, "=",
eval(Meta.parse(cmd)), "</body></html>"))
    close(sock)
end          #note that this will block the Julia console
```

Please be aware that the preceding code will run forever (unless there is an error in evaluating the cmd command or *Ctrl + C* is pressed in the console). Hence, in order to test our server, we will need a separate console.

4. Linux and macOS users can test the server in a bash console (on Windows, go to step 6):

```
$ curl http://127.0.0.1:8080/5+9
HTTP/1.1 200 OK
Content-Type: text/html

<html><body>5+9=14</body></html>
```

5. Once you execute the preceding command, switch back to the Julia console where the server is running. In the Julia console, you should see the following output:

```
Got request:
GET /5+9 HTTP/1.1
```

6. Another way to test the server is by pasting the URL, http://127.0.0.1:8080/5+9, into a web browser. You should see the output in the web browser, along the lines of 5+9=14.

Note that a graphical (desktop) web browser will send an additional request for an icon file (GET /favicon.ico), which will fail and stop the server. You will need to start it again for the next point.

7. It is possible to test the preceding server straight from Julia code, instead of using the web browser. Start a new Julia console (being careful not to shut down the console used to create the server) and open the connection:

```
julia> using Sockets
julia> client = Sockets.connect("127.0.0.1",8080)
TCPSocket(RawFD(0x00000013) open, 0 bytes waiting)
```

8. Please note that our server is expecting to receive some data. For example, you can try the following:

```
julia> write(client,"GET /3*8\n")
9
```

The `write` command sent the string containing the GET request content, followed by a new line character, to the `client` stream, representing a network connection to our web server. The server has logged its request. The number 9, seen in the console, represents the number of bytes written to the stream returned by the `write` function.

9. Read the data from the server:

```
julia> readlines(client)
5-element Array{String,1}:
 " "
 "HTTP/1.1 200 OK"
 "Content-Type: text/html"
 " "
 "<html><body>3*8=24</body></html>"
```

Remember that in order to stop the server, you need to press *Ctrl* + *C* in the server console.

Building a high-performance web service integrating ZeroMQ and JuliaWebAPI.jl

This time, we will use the `JuliaWebAPI.jl` package, along with the `ZMQ.jl` package, to publish a Julia function as a web service:

1. We start by loading the appropriate modules:

```
using JuliaWebAPI
using ZMQ
```

2. Define a function that will be published as a web service. Note that the `testfn` function uses two mandatory and two optional arguments:

```
function testfn(arg1, arg2; optarg1="10", optarg2="20")
    println("T: ", arg1, " ", arg2, " ", optarg1, " ", optarg2)
    return parse(Int,arg1) + parse(Int,arg2) + parse(Int,optarg1)
+ parse(Int,optarg2)
end
```

3. Define the parameters for the ZeroMQ server:

```
tr = JuliaWebAPI.ZMQTransport("tcp://127.0.0.1:9999", ZMQ.REP,
true);
apir = JuliaWebAPI.APIResponder(tr, JuliaWebAPI.JSONMsgFormat());
```

4. Register the function on the ZeroMQ server:

```
julia> register(apir, testfn; resp_json=true,
    resp_headers=Dict("Content-Type" => "application/json;
charset=utf-8"))
JuliaWebAPI.APIResponder with endpoints:
"testfn"
```

5. Run the ZeroMQ server:

```
julia> process(apir)  # note that this will block the Julia console
```

The REPL console is now blocked (it's running the ZeroMQ server) and you need another new instance of the Julia REPL (optionally, you could use the @async macro in front of the preceding command, and continue with the old console; however, it makes debugging more difficult). Finally, since our ZeroMQ server is running, we can attach an HTTP endpoint.

6. Start a new Julia console and execute the following commands:

```
julia> using JuliaWebAPI
julia> const apiclnt =
JuliaWebAPI.APIInvoker("tcp://127.0.0.1:9999");
```

7. At this point, we can run the server. Please note that the following code will run forever; the only way to terminate it is to press *Ctrl + C*:

```
julia> JuliaWebAPI.run_http(apiclnt, 8888)  #note that this will
block the Julia console
[ Info: Listening on: Sockets.InetAddr{Sockets.IPv4}(ip"0.0.0.0",
0x22b8)
```

In order to test our servers, we need a separate (third) console.

8. Linux and macOS users can test the server in a Bash console:

```
$ curl "http://127.0.0.1:8888/testfn/5/9?optarg1=100&optarg2=1000"
{"data":1114,"code":0}
```

You can see that the input is returned as JSON; the data field represents the result of the function, while the code equal to 0 means that it was successfully executed. Another way to test the server is by pasting the following URL, http://127.0.0.1:8888/testfn/5/9?optarg1=100&optarg2=1000, into a web browser. If your browser supports displaying JSON data (we recommend Chrome), you should see an output along the lines of {"data":1114,"code":0}.

9. Taking another look at the ZeroMQ console, you should see that after executing the `testfn` function, the output has changed; it now looks similar to the following:

```
julia> process(apir)
┌ Info: received
└    command = "testfn"
T: 5 9 100 1000
```

On the other hand, the output of the web server console will look like this:

```
julia> JuliaWebAPI.run_http(apiclnt, 8888)
[ Info: Listening on: Sockets.InetAddr{Sockets.IPv4}(ip"0.0.0.0",
0x22b8)
[ Info: Accept:        0↑      0↓    0s 0.0.0.0:8888:8888 ≣16
┌ Info: processing
└    target = "/testfn/5/9?optarg1=100&optarg2=1000"
[ Info: waiting for a handler
[ Info: Closed:        1↑      1↓    5s 0.0.0.0:8888:8888 ≣16
```

You can also test the preceding server directly with Julia code, instead of using the web browser.

10. Start a new (third) Julia console (being careful not to shut down the console used to create the ZeroMQ and web service server processes) and open the connection as follows:

```
julia> using HTTP
julia> res =
HTTP.get("http://127.0.0.1:8888/testfn/5/9?optarg1=100&optarg2=1000
")
HTTP.Messages.Response:
"""
HTTP/1.1 200 OK
Content-Type: application/json; charset=utf-8
Transfer-Encoding: chunked

{"data":1114,"code":0}"""
```

How it works...

You have now seen two examples of running a web service in Julia:

- Low-level (`Sockets`)
- High-level (`JuliaWebAPI`).

In fact, Julia offers a convenient way to open network connections. They are handled by the same mechanism as files. Once a network connection is open, it can be read and written to like any other data stream. In the example where a web service is built from scratch, the programmer is responsible for sending messages specific to the HTTP protocol. A minimal set of information includes the response status (`200` means *OK*) and the type of content that is being sent. Similarly, when the connection is made with the low-level `Sockets` API, the programmer is responsible for sending properly formed requests and reading the output. More information on the HTTP protocol can be found at `https://developer.mozilla.org/en-US/docs/Web/HTTP`.

The `JuliaWebAPI.jl` package simplifies the process of publishing Julia functions as web services. In order to ensure high scalability and parallelization, the functions are executed via the ZeroMQ engine. Please note that the service address given at `APIResponder` (here, `tcp://127.0.0.1:9999`) must match the service address provided to `APIInvoker`. In the provided example, we only publish one particular function, though any number of Julia functions can be published as a web service. Note how the HTTP URL, used to invoke a Julia function, is constructed. After the protocol, server address, and port (`http://127.0.0.1:8888/`), we provide the endpoint name, which must match the actual function name. The mandatory parameters are provided in the `/parameter_name/parameter_value` format, while the optional parameters are provided after the question mark, `?`, with the `parameter_name=parameter_value` format. If more than one optional parameter exists, they can be separated with the `&` symbol. Finally, please note that the ZeroMQ server and the HTTP endpoint **must** use different ports (in our example, `9999` and `8888`)—it is impossible to assign the same port to different services running at the same time.

There's more...

One thing to be aware of is that our low-level server implementation expects at least one line (along with the new line character, \n) to be written to the opened connection before the data is available. In our implementation, if you forget the new line character (for example, by executing `write(client, "GET /")`), then the `data = readline(sock)` line in the server implementation will wait for data (a complete line) to become available. If you now try to execute `readlines(client)`, this command will be waiting for data that is unavailable, and your code will be blocked. To make things worse, after this command is executed, the `while true` loop is blocked and no other connections to our simple web server are possible! A workaround to this situation would be using the `@async` macro around the code that handles data processing in our simple web server. The `@async` macro spawns the code as a new thread, and hence the Julia columns remain active. Whenever you write code where several processes communicate, you need to think about what to do when the data in the stream is not yet available for reading.

The preceding problems can be mitigated by using ready-made packages such as `JuliaWebAPI.jl`. This package provides a framework that can be used for publishing Julia functions and processing HTTP requests on any scale.

See also

More information on the ZeroMQ server is available at `http://zeromq.org/`.

Another framework for publishing Julia functions as services is `Genie.jl`, available at `https://github.com/essenciary/Genie.jl`.

Working with JSON data

JSON (short for **JavaScript Object Notation**) is a format for representing and exchanging data between computer systems in a human-readable way. The JSON format has a tree-like structure and supports list and the nesting of elements. Within many applications, JSON has replaced the XML format, being lighter and requiring less disk space. JSON has become a *de facto* standard for exchange of web data, including REST web services. Many logging systems also use the JSON format to represent events. Finally, JSON is the standard data representation format in NoSQL document-oriented database systems, such as MongoDB or Amazon DynamoDB.

Getting ready

The JSON.jl package can easily be installed with the Julia package manager. In the Julia command line (REPL), press the *J* key and run the following command:

```
(v1.0) pkg> add JSON
```

This will install the JSON.jl package and all its dependencies.

 In the GitHub repository for this recipe, you will find the commands.txt file, which contains the presented sequence of Julia commands.

How to do it...

In this example, we show how to handle processing of JSON data:

1. We start by loading the JSON module:

   ```
   using JSON
   ```

   A JSON document is a hierarchical data structure that contains key-value pairs. The values can be numbers, string, lists of other values, or key-value pairs.

2. Consider the following Julia String:

   ```
   json_txt = """{
           "key":"value",
           "number":7,
           "array":[1,2,5],
           "dict":{"k1":"val1","k2":2}
   }""";
   ```

3. Print this String variable to see its contents:

   ```
   julia> print(json_txt)
   {
           "key":"value",
           "number":7,
           "array":[1,2,5],
           "dict":{"k1":"val1","k2":2}
   }
   ```

4. We can `parse` the preceding text:

```
julia> JSON.parse(json_txt)
Dict{String,Any} with 4 entries:
  "key"    => "value"
  "dict"   => Dict{String,Any}("k1"=>"val1","k2"=>2)
  "number" => 7
  "array"  => Any[1, 2, 5]
```

Julia data structures can also be converted into JSON. Consider the following example:

```
data = Dict{Int64,Union{Int64,String}}(1=>"text", 2=>999);
```

5. In order to convert it to JSON format, use the `JSON.json` function:

```
julia> print(JSON.json(data))
{"2":999,"1":"text"}
```

Notice how the type information has been lost. In the JSON format, the keys can only be of the `String` type.

6. In order to print JSON data to a file, the `JSON.print` function can be used:

```
f = open("file.json", "w");
JSON.print(f, data);
close(f);
```

7. Reading a file can be accomplished in the same manner:

```
f = open("file.json", "r");
data2 = JSON.parse(f);
close(f);
```

For reading JSON files, Julia provides another convenient method: `JSON.parsefile`.

8. The preceding example could be executed in a more concise form, as follows:

```
julia> data_copy = JSON.parsefile("file.json")
Dict{String,Any} with 2 entries:
  "1" => "text"
  "2" => 999
```

How it works...

The JSON.jl package provides methods for interacting with JSON data, as well as JSON streams and files. Note that processing a JSON document requires reading the entire structure between the opening brace { and closing brace }. It means that the data being read needs to fit into the system memory. A common approach to this problem, which can be found, for instance, in logging systems, is to store one JSON document for each individual logged event.

 The JSON.jl package provides three functions for interacting with data streams and files: JSON.print, JSON.parse, and JSON.parsefile. In order to write JSON format data to a file, all we need to do is open a file and then write a Julia object. Note that the first argument of the JSON.print and JSON.parse functions is any kind of I/O object, and so a network connection could be used, instead of an opened file.

There's more...

JSON conversion support is not just limited to Julia AbstractDict objects; other data types can also be represented in JSON format.

For example, an Array can be converted to JSON:

```
julia> a = reshape(collect(1:8), 2, 4)
2×4 Array{Int64,2}:
 1  3  5  7
 2  4  6  8

julia> b = JSON.json(a)
"[[1,2],[3,4],[5,6],[7,8]]"
```

However, when converting back to a Julia object, the type information will be lost:

```
julia> JSON.parse(b)
4-element Array{Any,1}:
 Any[1, 2]
 Any[3, 4]
 Any[5, 6]
 Any[7, 8]
```

It is worth noting that Julia's `struct` type will be converted to a dictionary upon conversion to JSON:

```julia
julia> struct S; x1::Int64; x2::Float64; x3::String; end
julia> s = S(1, 4.5, "test");
julia> println(JSON.json(s))
{"x1":1,"x2":4.5,"x3":"test"}
julia> JSON.parse(JSON.json(s))
Dict{String,Any} with 3 entries:
  "x1" => 1
  "x2" => 4.5
  "x3" => "test"
```

If you need to store more complex data structures along with object type information, have a look at the *Using object serialization in Julia* recipe.

See also

For more information on the JSON file format, see `https://www.json.org/`. The JSON format is defined in *The JavaScript Object Notation (JSON) Data Interchange Format* document, available online at `https://tools.ietf.org/html/rfc7159`. The `JSON.jl` package is available at `https://github.com/JuliaIO/JSON.jl`.

Working with date and time

Julia offers full date and time support and arithmetic via the `Dates` base module.

In Julia, similar to other languages, handling of dates is done via two types:

- `Date`: Represents the date without the time (just the year, month, and day)
- `DateTime`: Represents the date, along with the millisecond precision time

Getting ready

No installation is required for this recipe. Simply start the Julia command line.

In the GitHub repository for this recipe, you will find the `commands.txt` file, which contains the presented sequence of Julia commands.

How to do it...

To see how dates are processed in Julia, please follow the steps as shown:

1. Support for date and time handling is available via the `Dates` standard module, which needs to be imported:

   ```
   julia> using Dates
   ```

2. In order to get the current time, use the `now` function:

   ```
   julia> ts = Dates.now()
   2018-08-15T07:54:18.044

   julia> typeof(ts)
   DateTime
   ```

   This function returns an object of `DateTime` type.

3. In order to create an arbitrary date, simply pass the year, month, and day to the `Date` constructor. Note that the month and day parameters are optional; if you skip them, then the first day of the month will be given (however, it is not possible to skip the month field, and just provide year and day):

   ```
   julia> Date(2018, 08, 15)
   2018-08-15

   julia> Date(2018, 8)
   2018-08-01

   julia> Date(2018)
   2018-01-01
   ```

4. Similarly, a `DateTime` object can be constructed by giving the year, month, day, hour of the day, minute, second, and millisecond parameters. Again, all parameters except the year are optional (see the `Date` examples):

   ```
   julia> DateTime(2018, 8, 15, 18, 22, 55, 123)
   2018-08-15T18:22:55.123
   ```

5. The `Date` and `DateTime` objects can also be created from `String`:

```
julia> dt1 = Date("2018-08-15T18:22:55.123", DateFormat("y-m-
dTH:M:S.s"))
2018-08-15
julia> dtm1 = DateTime("2018-08-15T18:22:55.123", DateFormat("y-m-
dTH:M:S.s"))
2018-08-15T18:22:55.123
```

6. Note that we can also use a `"dateformat"` string macro:

```
julia> dtm2 = DateTime("2018-08-16T19:32:55.223", dateformat"y-m-
dTH:M:S.s")
2018-08-16T19:32:55.223
```

7. We can use date arithmetic to calculate differences between multiple instances of `DateTime` (this also works for multiple `Date` objects):

```
julia> delta = dtm2 - dtm1
90600100 milliseconds
julia> typeof(delta)
Millisecond

julia> Date("2018-03-01") - Date("2018-02-01")
28 days
```

It is not possible to add one `DateTime` or `Date` object to another.

8. However, there are `Year`, `Month`, `Day`, `Hour`, `Minute`, `Second`, and `Millisecond` types that can be used in date arithmetic:

```
julia> dtm1 + Year(1) + Month(4) + Day(4) + Hour(3)
2019-12-19T21:22:55.123

julia> dtm1 + Millisecond(24*3600*1000)
2018-08-16T18:22:55.123
```

9. For the `Year`, `Month`, `Day`, `Hour`, `Minute`, `Second`, and `Millisecond` types, multiplication and division operators are defined (the arguments for the / and * operators must be integers):

```
julia> Year(1)*3 + Month(4)/2 + Day(4)*3 + Hour(3)
3 years, 2 months, 12 days, 3 hours
```

10. However, the user must ensure that the result of an operation can still be represented as an `Int`:

```
julia> Day(4)/2
2 days

julia> Day(4)/8
ERROR: InexactError: Int64(Int64, 0.5)

julia> Day(4)*0.5
ERROR: InexactError: Int64(Int64, 0.5)
```

How it works...

The internal representation of dates in the `Date` object is the number of days from the start of the current epoch:

```
julia> d1 = Date("2018-08-15")
julia> dump(d1)
Date
  instant: Dates.UTInstant{Day}
    periods: Day
      value: Int64 736921
```

The day that corresponds to the integer 1 is January 1st, 1 A.D.:

```
julia> d1 = Date("2018-08-15")
2018-08-15

julia> d1 - Day(d1.instant.periods.value)+Day(1)
0001-01-01
```

The internal representation of time in the `DateTime` objects is `Millisecond`-based:

```
julia> dt = DateTime("2018-08-15T18:22:55.123")
julia> dump(dt)
DateTime
  instant: Dates.UTInstant{Millisecond}
    periods: Millisecond
      value: Int64 63670040575123
```

Similarly, the milliseconds are counted from the start of the current epoch:

```
julia> dt = DateTime("2018-08-15T18:22:55.123");
julia> dt - Millisecond(dt.instant.periods.value) + Day(1)
0001-01-01T00:00:00
```

Note that the mathematical operations on `Dates` are content-aware. The results of `Month` arithmetic are not immediately obvious. Have a look at the following example:

```julia
julia> Date(2008,1,31) + Month(1)
2008-02-29

julia> Date(2008,1,31) + Month(1) - Month(1)
2008-01-29

julia> Date(2008,1,31) + (Month(1) - Month(1))
2008-01-31
```

In the preceding example, you can see that in `Date` arithmetic, the order of operations might be important.

There's more...

One thing to remember is that the default Julia package does not support timezones. In order to use this functionality, press *J* to start the Julia package manager, then type the following:

```julia
(v1.0) pkg> add TimeZones
```

Once the package is installed, it should be loaded as follows:

```julia
julia> using TimeZones
```

Now, we can parse a standard date that contains timezone information:

```julia
julia> dtz = parse(ZonedDateTime, "2017-11-14 11:03:53 +0100",
                   dateformat"yyyy-mm-dd HH:MM:SS zzzzz")
2017-11-14T11:03:53+01:00
```

The same applies to dates in a format often present in Apache web server logs:

```julia
julia> dtz = parse(ZonedDateTime, "22/Aug/2018:09:22:07 -0100",
                   DateFormat("dd/uuu/yyyy:H:M:S zzzzz"))
2018-08-22T09:22:07-01:00
```

Let's take a look at how the `dtz` object is represented in Julia:

```julia
julia> dump(dtz)
ZonedDateTime
  utc_datetime: DateTime
   instant: Dates.UTInstant{Millisecond}
   periods: Millisecond
```

```
value: Int64 63670616527000
timezone: FixedTimeZone
name: Symbol UTC-01:00
offset: TimeZones.UTCOffset
std: Second
value: Int64 -3600
dst: Second
value: Int64 0
zone: FixedTimeZone
name: Symbol UTC-01:00
offset: TimeZones.UTCOffset
std: Second
value: Int64 -3600
dst: Second
value: Int64 0
```

The `TimeZones.jl` package supports date arithmetic in the same way that the `Dates.jl` package does:

```
julia> using Dates
julia> dtz2 = dtz + Dates.Year(2) - Dates.Month(1) + Dates.Day(20)
2020-08-11T09:22:07-01:00
```

See also

More examples can be found in Julia's `Date` module documentation at `https://docs.julialang.org/en/v1.0.0/stdlib/Dates/`.

Using object serialization in Julia

Julia, similar to other programming languages, supports object serialization. This is a mechanism where a byte representation of any object can be acquired and stored directly to disk or sent across a network. Normally, the serialization mechanism is used for short-term data storage. It is not guaranteed to work across even minor environment upgrades or on other system architectures; different platforms might have different binary representations of data. However, if storage is needed only during runtime (for example, caching), then serialization is the recommended approach.

When data serialization is required for longer periods, along with better cross-platform compatibility, then use of the JDL2.jl or BSON.jl packages is recommended. Please note that at the time of writing, both libraries are under intensive development, so you should test which package best suits your needs. However, for long-term data storage, we recommend the BSON format, because it is compatible with other programming languages.

Getting ready

The required packages can be installed with the Julia package manager. In the Julia command line (REPL), press the *]* key and run the following commands:

```
(v1.0) pkg> add JLD2
(v1.0) pkg> add FileIO
(v1.0) pkg> add BSON
```

This will install the JLD2.jl, FileIO.jl, and BSON.jl packages and all their dependencies.

 In the GitHub repository for this recipe, you will find the commands.txt file, which contains the presented sequence of Julia commands.

How to do it...

This recipe is divided into three parts: firstly, short-term serialization with the Julia Serialization module; secondly, long-term serialization with the JLD2 module; and lastly, long-term serialization with the BSON module.

Serializing Julia objects with Julia Base.Serialization

Please follow the steps as shown:

1. The first step is to load the module with the following command:

```
using Serialization
```

2. Any Julia object can be directly written to a stream. Consider the following examples:

```
x = 1:5;
open(f -> serialize(f,x), "x.jls", "w");
```

The filename extension *.jls is recommended for data saved by the serializer.

3. Deserialization is achieved in exactly the same way:

```
y = open(deserialize, "x.jls");
```

4. Now, let's take a look at the object's contents:

```
julia> dump(y)
UnitRange{Int64}
  start: Int64 1
  stop: Int64 5
```

Note that several objects can be written to a stream, and the exact type information of every object in the stream is preserved. The following example illustrates this:

```
open("data.jls", "w") do f
    serialize(f, Array{Int8}([1, 2, 4]));
    serialize(f, Dict{Int64,String}(1=>"a", 2=>"b"));
end
```

5. Now, look at the resulting console log:

```
julia> f = open("data.jls", "r");

julia> deserialize(f)
3-element Array{Int8,1}:
 1
 2
 4

julia> deserialize(f)
Dict{Int64,String} with 2 entries:
  2 => "b"
  1 => "a"
julia> close(f)
```

Serializing Julia objects with JLD2.jl

The process of serializing Julia objects with JLD2 is similar to the Serialization API:

1. We start by loading the JLD2.jl package as follows:

```
using JLD2
using FileIO
```

2. Any Julia object can be directly written to a stream using the JLD2 module. Consider the following examples:

```
x1 = 1:5;
x2 = rand(3);
file = File(format"JLD2", "myfile.jld2")
save(file, "x1", x1, "x2", x2)
```

   In this case, the recommended extension for data saved is *.jld2.

3. Deserialization can be achieved as follows:

```
julia> data = load(file)
Dict{String,Any} with 2 entries:
  "x1" => 1:5
  "x2" => [0.486263, 0.764547, 0.715775]
```

4. Check the contents of the deserialized object:

```
julia> dump(data["x1"])
UnitRange{Int64}
  start: Int64 1
  stop: Int64 5
```

You can actually write to several objects within a single save command. The saved objects are loaded as a single object of the Dict type.

Serializing Julia objects with BSON.jl

Yet another format for data storage supported by Julia is BSON (binary JSON):

1. The first step is to load the module using the following command:

```
using BSON
```

2. Next, create some objects to serialize:

```
x = 1:5
d = Dict{Int64,String}(1=>"a", 2=>"b")
e = 5+3im
```

3. Now open the stream and serialize the objects (note that the default extension for BSON files is `*.bson`):

```
f = open("data.bson", "w")
bson(f, Dict("x" => x, "d" => d))
bson(f, Dict("e" => e))
close(f)
```

4. The last step is to read the objects back from the file:

```
julia> f = open("data.bson", "r");

julia> BSON.load(f)
Dict{String,Any} with 2 entries:
  "x" => 1:5
  "d" => Dict(2=>"b",1=>"a")

julia> BSON.load(f)
Dict{String,Complex{Int64}} with 1 entry:
  "e" => 5+3im

julia> close(f)
```

How it works...

In this recipe, you have seen three methods for permanently storing Julia objects:

- The built-in object serialization is the most time- and disk space-efficient method of storing data. Hence, this method is the recommended mechanism for handling information exchange between processes and subsequent computation runs. However, it might not be appropriate for data exchange between various environment configurations, or systems running on different hardware architectures. Moreover, the Serialization module is not intended for long-term data archiving. Subsequent Julia versions, or even different Julia package versions, could use different data structures or different binary object representations.

- The JLD2 format is based on the HDF5 format for data storage. This format is appropriate for long-term storage and exchange of data across various platforms. Additionally, the JLD2 format has a built-in data compression mechanism that can be used to save disk space (as opposed to the Julia `Serialization` module; see the following *There's more...* section for more information) and limit the number of I/O operations.
- The `BSON.jl` package uses the binary JSON format, known from MongoDB, and can be used for long-term data archival.

There's more...

For many distributed high-performance computing scenarios, data compression might be much more cost- and time-efficient than disk/network I/O. In such scenarios, it is worth thinking about compressing the data before it is serialized into a stream. The `JLD2` module provides data compression out of the box. Using the `Serialization` module requires a stream decorator. For the compression to operate, you need to install the `CodecZlib.jl` package. Just press *]* to go to the Julia package manager and execute the command:

```
(v1.0) pkg> add CodecZlib
```

For a sample serialization of a Julia object, consider the following example:

```
using CodecZlib
using Serialization
d=Dict([("txt", collect(1:1000000))]);
open("big2.bin", "w") do f
    comp = DeflateCompressorStream(f);
    serialize(comp, d);
    close(comp);
end
```

The serialized object file is 80% smaller in the compressed form than without compression. You should be aware that the `DeflateCompressorStream` needs to be closed before the actual file is closed, otherwise the compressor will fail to provide the closing flags on the data stream.

In this example, the decompressor code is as follows:

```
f=open("big2.bin", "r");
decomp = DeflateDecompressorStream(f);
d2=deserialize(decomp);
close(f);
```

In fact, the compression-decompression pattern presented here can also be applied to other types of stream. In particular, it can also be used to compress the BSON streams discussed in this recipe.

See also

The full documentation for serialization can be found in the Julia manual at `https://docs.julialang.org/en/v1.0/stdlib/Serialization/`.

The documentation for `JLD2.jl` can be found at `https://github.com/JuliaIO/JLD2.jl`.

More samples for the `BJSON.jl` package can be found at `https://github.com/MikeInnes/BSON.jl`.

Running Julia as a background process

In this recipe, you will learn how to run Julia as a background process, and pass commands to it using pipes.

We would like to thank Charles Duffy for ideas that helped to improve this recipe, as discussed at `https://stackoverflow.com/questions/48510815/named-pipe-does-not-wait-until-completion-in-bash`.

Getting ready

For this example to work, you need to run it under bash.

This would be the default under Linux. If you are on Windows, you can use the bash that is shipped with a Git installation.

 In the GitHub repository for this recipe, you will find the `commands.txt` file, which contains the presented sequence of shell and Julia commands.

Now, open your favorite terminal to execute the commands and switch to an empty folder.

How to do it...

In this recipe, you will start a Julia process in the background and then pass commands to it via a named pipe:

1. First, create a named pipe using the `mkfifo` command. We will call it `pipe`:

   ```
   $ mkfifo pipe
   ```

2. Check that a file named `pipe` was indeed created:

   ```
   $ ls
   pipe
   ```

3. Now, start Julia as a background process. Direct its standard input from `pipe`, and send standard output to `log.txt` and standard error to `err.txt`:

   ```
   $ julia <pipe >log.txt 2>err.txt &
   ```

4. Before sending jobs to Julia, redirect the 3 descriptor to the named `pipe`:

   ```
   $ exec 3>pipe
   ```

5. Now, you are ready to start sending commands to Julia. For this, you can use the `echo` command:

   ```
   $ echo "1+2" >&3
   ```

6. Now, try sending a malformed expression:

   ```
   $ echo "X" >&3
   ```

7. Finally, send `exit()` to Julia, which terminates it:

   ```
   $ echo "exit()" >&3
   ```

8. Now, you should check the contents of the `log.txt` and `err.txt` files, as follows:

   ```
   $ cat log.txt
   3
   ```

   ```
   $ cat err.txt
   ERROR: UndefVarError: X not defined
   ```

9. Finally, remember to clean up all the files you created:

```
$ rm pipe log.txt err.txt
```

How it works...

A Julia command line executable normally communicates with the environment via I/O connections, including standard input, standard output, and standard error. In this recipe, we show how you can take control of these three streams to be able to programmatically execute Julia code on a Julia executable running in the background.

The first step is creating the standard input stream, which is quite complicated. To do so, we create a named `pipe` using the `mkfifo` command. More details can be found at `https://linux.die.net/man/1/mkfifo`.

We set the newly created `pipe` as standard input for the Julia process, using the `<pipe` construct. Similarly, `>log.txt` redirects standard output to a given file and `2>err.txt` does the same for standard error. Finally, the `&` at the end makes the process start in the background.

Now, we could directly send some command to Julia via `pipe`, as follows:

```
echo "1+2" >pipe
```

However, this would close the `pipe` and make Julia terminate immediately. Therefore, we redirect the 3 file descriptor to our `pipe` using the `exec` command. Now, when we send commands to this file descriptor, `pipe` is not closed, and thus Julia is kept alive, as shown here:

```
echo "1+2" >&3
```

Finally, we terminate Julia by sending the `exit()` command to it. Alternatively, you could close the stream using `exec`:

```
exec 3<&-
```

There's more...

In this recipe, you learned how to communicate with Julia via pipes from an external process. However, in more advanced applications, you may wish to consider embedding Julia code directly in them.

How this can be achieved is described in the Julia documentation, available at `https://docs.julialang.org/en/latest/manual/embedding/`.

See also

Another popular option for ensuring you can set up a Julia server that can receive and send messages is to use the `ZMQ.jl` package, available at `https://github.com/JuliaInterop/ZMQ.jl`. This is a wrapper around the `ZeroMQ` asynchronous messaging library and has been presented in the *Writing a simple RESTful service recipe* in this chapter.

Integration of Julia with R and Python is discussed in the *Calling R from Julia* and *Calling Python from Julia* recipes in `Chapter 8`, *Julia Workflow*.

Reading and writing Microsoft Excel files

Microsoft Excel is a popular spreadsheet application. In this recipe, you will discover how to create files within Julia using the `openpyxl` Python library, as well as how to read Excel files. Specifically, we will look at how to handle Excel files in two different ways: firstly, by using Python's `openpyxl` library via `PyCall.jl`, and secondly, by using the `XLSX.jl` package.

Getting ready

For this recipe, you need the following packages: `PyCall.jl`, `Conda.jl`, `DataFrames.jl`, and `XLSX.jl`. Install them with the Julia package manager by going to the Julia command line (REPL), pressing the *J* key, and running the following commands:

```
(v1.0) pkg> add PyCall
(v1.0) pkg> add Conda
(v1.0) pkg> add DataFrames
(v1.0) pkg> add XLSX
```

This will install the required packages and their dependencies.

The `openpyxl` Python library can be installed with the following commands:

```
julia> using Conda
julia> Conda.add("openpyxl")
```

 In the GitHub repository for this recipe, you will find the `commands.txt` file, which contains the presented sequence of shell and Julia commands.

How to do it...

Since different packages provide different levels of Microsoft Excel support, this recipe is divided into two parts:

- Manipulating Excel files with `PyCall` and `openpyxl`
- Manipulating Excel files with the `XLSX.jl` package

Manipulating Excel files with PyCall.jl and openpyxl

In this recipe, you are going to create an Excel spreadsheet and find out how to read the data from it:

1. Start by loading the required modules:

   ```
   using PyCall
   using Dates
   using Random
   @pyimport openpyxl as xl
   ```

2. Now create a workbook, then select a worksheet within that workbook:

   ```
   julia> wb = xl.Workbook();

   julia> ws = wb[:active]
   PyObject <Worksheet "Sheet">
   ```

3. Create cells A1 and A2 within the worksheet:

   ```
   julia> ws[:cell](1, 1, "Data generated on:")
   PyObject <Cell 'Sheet'.A1>

   julia> ws[:cell](2, 1, Dates.now())
   PyObject <Cell 'Sheet'.A2>
   ```

This is how data is copied from a Julia `Array` to Excel:

```
Random.seed!(0)
dat = rand(3, 5)
for i in 1:size(dat)[1]
    ws[:append]((dat[i, :]..., ))
end
```

4. Now, it is time to write the workbook to the disk:

```
wb[:save]("sample1.xlsx")
```

You can check the generated file with Microsoft Excel (note that we have manually adjusted the width of the first column):

A1	▼	:	✕	✓	*fx*	Data generated on:	

◢	A	B	C	D	E	F
1	Data generated on:					
2	2018-10-26 15:43:15					
3	0.823647508	0.177329	0.042302	0.973216	0.260036	
4	0.910356538	0.27888	0.068269	0.585812	0.910047	
5	0.164565798	0.203477	0.361828	0.539289	0.167036	
6						

Before going on to the next step, make sure that the file does not remain open in Microsoft Excel.

5. Now, read in the Excel file and select the worksheet:

```
wb = xl.load_workbook(filename = "sample1.xlsx")
ws = wb[:active]
```

6. Once you have the workbook, it is time to read the cell contents:

```
julia> println(ws[:cell](1, 1)[:value], "\n", ws[:cell](2,
1)[:value])
Data generated on:
2018-10-26T15:43:15.265
```

7. Cells containing dates will automatically be converted to the Julia `Date` type:

```
julia> typeof(ws[:cell](2, 1)[:value])
DateTime
```

8. If you ask for a non-existent cell, then `nothing` will be returned:

```
julia> ws[:cell](20, 221)[:value] == nothing
true
```

9. You can iterate over rows and columns within the Excel file:

```
julia> using Printf
julia> for row in ws[:rows]
    for cell in row
        print("|")
        if typeof(cell[:value]) <: Number
            @printf("%.3f", cell[:value])
        else
            show(cell[:value])
        end
    end
    println("|")
end
|"Data generated on:"|nothing|nothing|nothing|nothing|
|2018-10-26T13:46:15.265|nothing|nothing|nothing|nothing|
|0.824|0.177|0.042|0.973|0.260|
|0.910|0.279|0.068|0.586|0.910|
|0.165|0.203|0.362|0.539|0.167|
```

10. Once completed, you can close the workbook:

```
wb[:close]()
```

Manipulating Excel files with XLSX.jl

The `XLSX.jl` package provides a Julia-native package for manipulating Microsoft Excel files:

1. Start by loading the module:

```
using XLSX
```

Once the module has been loaded, you can create a Microsoft Excel file (as in the previous `openpyxl` example). Note the use of the `do` syntax, which ensures that the Excel file is closed at the end of the code block:

```
XLSX.openxlsx("sample2.xlsx", mode="w") do xf
    sheet = xf[1]
    XLSX.rename!(sheet, "SheetName")
    sheet["A1"] = "Data generated on:"
```

```
sheet["A2"] = Dates.now()
dat = rand(3, 5)
for row in 1:3
    for col in 1:5
        XLSX.setdata!(sheet, XLSX.CellRef(2+row, col), rand())
    end
end
end
```

2. Load in the workbook:

```
julia> wb = XLSX.readxlsx("sample2.xlsx")

sheetname = XLSX.sheetnames(wb)[1]XLSXFile("sample2.xlsx")
containing 1 Worksheets
        sheetname size        range
-------------------------------------------------
        SheetName 5x5         A1:E5
```

3. Now, obtain the sheet name and get an object representing a worksheet:

```
julia> sheetname = XLSX.sheetnames(wb)[1]
"SheetName"

julia> ws = wb[sheetname]
5×5 XLSX.Worksheet: ["SheetName"](A1:E5)
```

4. Finally, obtain the information about the available cells and get the data from the worksheet:

```
julia> dim = ws.dimension
A1:E5

julia> ws[dim]
5×5 Array{Any,2}:
 "Data generated on:"  missing   missing    missing   missing
 2018-10-26T14:44:01   missing   missing    missing   missing
 0.838118              0.914712  0.300075   0.72285   0.119653
 0.76707               0.801924  0.0353445  0.484661  0.899199
 0.951691              0.801119  0.124323   0.114269  0.0795545
```

5. Now, you can close the workbook:

```
XLSX.close(wb)
```

One thing you might find useful to know is that the XLSX.jl package provides a convenient mechanism for manipulating our DataFrame objects.

6. You can check this functionality out by creating two `DataFrame` objects:

```
using DataFrames
df1 = DataFrame(a=[1, 2, 3], b=[4, 5, 6]);
df2 = DataFrame(x1=[1, 2, 3], x2=["A", "B", "C"]);
```

7. Now, use the following code to save them to disk:

```
XLSX.writetable("sample3.xlsx",
  SheetName1=( DataFrames.columns(df1), DataFrames.names(df1) ),
  SheetName2=( DataFrames.columns(df2), DataFrames.names(df2) ));
```

You have now managed to create an Excel file, with a `DataFrame` in each separate worksheet:

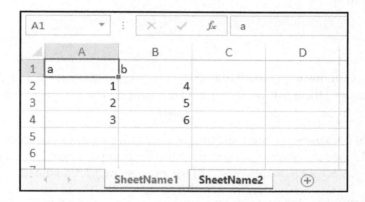

How it works...

An Excel spreadsheet is a hierarchical data structure. The spreadsheet is represented as a workbook object. A workbook contains a collection of sheets, with each sheet containing a number of rows, where each row is a collection of cells. This layout structure determines how Excel spreadsheets should be manipulated.

The `openpyxl` library provides a mature option for manipulating Excel files, while `XLSX.jl` is a new Julia-native package developed by the Julia community. In particular, at the time of writing, you can expect broader compatibility from `openpyxl` for various Excel file formats. For example, `openpyxl` can read files created by `XLSX.jl`, but on the other hand, `XLSX.jl` can only read `openpyxl` files once they have been opened and re-saved in Microsoft Excel.

There's more...

It should be noted that for handling some sophisticated spreadsheets, the most powerful library is Apache POI, which is written for Java. The Apache POI library can be called from Julia using the `JavaCall.jl` package (Java users can find Apache POI documentation on the project website at `https://poi.apache.org/`). There is a Julia wrapper package for POI, named `Taro.jl`, which is currently under development. Unfortunately, it has not yet been updated for the Julia 1.0 specification, although this situation might soon change. The full documentation of the Taro package is available at `http://aviks.github.io/Taro.jl/`.

Please also note that there are no Excel data retrieval packages that would guarantee 100% MS Excel compatibility (unless it is Microsoft Office itself), so caution is advised every time you process Excel files.

See also

The `openpyxl` documentation is available at `https://openpyxl.readthedocs.io/en/stable/`. The documentation for `XLSX.jl` can be found on the project's website, available at `https://felipenoris.github.io/XLSX.jl/latest/`.

There are yet more packages for the handling of Excel files in the Julia ecosystem. Another package is named `ExcelReaders.jl` and uses the Python package `xlrd` (available at `https://github.com/python-excel/xlrd`) for processing spreadsheet data.

More information on `DataFrame`'s can be found in `Chapter 7`, *Handling Analytical Data*.

Handling Feather data

Feather is a file format that provides binary columnar serialization of data. Feather files use the Apache Arrow data format for data frame storage. This format is supported for data exchange across many platforms, including Python and GNU R.

Getting ready

In this recipe, you will learn how to use Feather.jl to store and retrieve a DataFrame object. The Feather.jl and DataFrames.jl packages can be installed with the Julia package manager. Additionally, the packages RCall.jl and PyCall .jl will be used to illustrate our examples in R and Python (see the *Calling R from Julia* and *Calling Python from Julia* recipes for more details on how those packages work). In the Julia command line, press *]* and run the following commands:

```
(v1.0)  pkg>  add  DataFrames
(v1.0)  pkg>  add  Feather
(v1.0)  pkg>  add  RCall
(v1.0)  pkg>  add  PyCall
(v1.0)  pkg>  add  Conda
```

This will install the required packages and all their dependencies.

 In the GitHub repository for this recipe, you will find the commands.txt file, which contains the presented sequence of Julia commands.

How to do it...

Please follow the steps as shown:

1. The first step is to load the modules:

    ```
    using Feather
    using DataFrames
    ```

    As we will be using random numbers in this recipe, set the seed value so that you can reproduce the results:

    ```
    using Random
    Random.seed!(0);
    ```

2. Now, create a `DataFrame` object:

```julia
julia> df = DataFrame(x1=[1:3..., missing],
                      x2=rand(4),
                      x3=rand(1:10, 4))
```

| Row | x1 | x2 | x3 |
	Int64	Float64	Int64
1	1	0.823648	1
2	2	0.910357	1
3	3	0.164566	4
4	missing	0.177329	9

3. Save the data using the `Feather.jl` package:

```julia
julia> Feather.write("df.dat", df);
```

The data can now be read into Julia:

```julia
julia> df2 = Feather.read("df.dat");
```

4. Now, try comparing both `DataFrame` objects and check their data types:

```julia
julia> isequal(df, df2)
true
```

```julia
julia> describe(df)[[1:3..., 5, 7, 8]]
```
3×6 DataFrame

| Row | variable | mean | min | max | nmissing | eltype |
	Symbol	Float64	Real	Real	Union...	DataType
1	x1	2.0	1	3	1	Int64
2	x2	0.518975	0.164566	0.910357		Float64
3	x3	3.75	1	9		Int64

```julia
julia> describe(df2)[[1:3..., 5, 7, 8]]
```
3×6 DataFrame

| Row | variable | mean | min | max | nmissing | eltype |
	Symbol	Float64	Real	Real	Union...	DataType
1	x1	2.0	1	3	1	Int64
2	x2	0.518975	0.164566	0.910357		Float64
3	x3	3.75	1	9		Int64

Now, we will read the data in R. This time, we will show an R console, which can be done either as a separate process or by using `RCall.jl`. Although `RCall.jl` allows for `DataFrame` objects to be transferred directly between Julia and R, here it will merely be used for illustrative purposes.

5. Start by loading the module (please make sure that you have installed `RCall`; if not, see the *Calling R from Julia* recipe):

```
using RCall
```

6. Now, start the R session in Julia's REPL by pressing the $ key (we assume that the R library `feather` has already been installed; if it hasn't, run the command `install.packages("feather")` in a separate R console):

```
R> library(feather)
R> dfR <- read_feather("df.dat")
┌ Warning: RCall.jl: Warning: Coercing int64 to double
│ Warning: Coercing int64 to double
└ @ RCall ~/.julia/packages/RCall/Q4n8R/src/io.jl:110
```

7. Take a peek at the R `DataFrame`:

```
R> dfR
# A tibble: 4 x 3
     x1    x2    x3
  <dbl> <dbl> <dbl>
1     1 0.824     1
2     2 0.910     1
3     3 0.165     4
4    NA 0.177     9
```

8. Then, retrieve the variable from the R session (press *backspace* to exit the `RCall` REPL console):

```
julia> dfR = @rget dfR
4×3 DataFrame
| Row | x1      | x2       | x3      |
|     | Float64 | Float64  | Float64 |
|-----|---------|----------|---------|
| 1   | 1.0     | 0.823648 | 1.0     |
| 2   | 2.0     | 0.910357 | 1.0     |
| 3   | 3.0     | 0.164566 | 4.0     |
| 4   | missing | 0.177329 | 9.0     |
```

Since R supports only 32-bit integer columns, the `Int` columns in our `DataFrame` have been converted to `Float64`:

```
julia> describe(dfR)[[1:3..., 5, 7, 8]]
3×6 DataFrame
| Row | variable | mean     | min      | max      | nmissing | eltype   |
|     | Symbol   | Float64  | Float64  | Float64  | Union... | DataType |
|-----|----------|----------|----------|----------|----------|----------|
| 1   | x1       | 2.0      | 1        | 3        | 1        | Float64  |
| 2   | x2       | 0.518975 | 0.164566 | 0.910357 |          | Float64  |
| 3   | x3       | 3.75     | 1        | 9        |          | Float64  |
```

The Feather format is also supported in Python. We will show here how it can be used via a `PyCall` session. Make sure that you have the `Conda.jl` package installed (if not, press `]` to go to the package manager and type `add Conda`).

9. We start by installing Feather support for the Julia Python installation:

```
using Conda
Conda.runconda(`install feather-format -c conda-forge -y`)
```

Now, the Python `feather` library can be verified via the `PyCall` module:

```
using PyCall
@pyimport feather
```

10. The imported module can then be used to read the Feather file as a Python object (`PyObject`):

```
julia> dat = feather.read_dataframe("df.dat")
PyObject     x1        x2     x3
0            1.0  0.823648   1
1            2.0  0.910357   1
2            3.0  0.164566   4
3            NaN  0.177329   9
```

How it works...

The Feather format was originally developed to facilitate data exchange between Python and R.

`Feather.jl` itself supports only a limited set of column types, which must correspond to formats that are described by the Feather standard. The list of supported types (according to the `Feather.jl` documentation) is the following: `Integer` types, `Float32`, `Float64`, `String`, `Date`, `DateTime`, and `Time`, along with `CategoricalArray{T}`, where `T` is a supported type.

There's more...

Note that for most scenarios, the `PyCall` and `RCall` modules can be used to ensure interoperability between Julia, Python, and R. Yet another format that can be considered for data exchange is HDF5, which is available via the `HDF5.jl` package.

See also

`Feather.jl` documentation is available at `http://juliadata.github.io/Feather.jl/stable/`. Documentation for the Feather data format can be found at `https://github.com/wesm/feather`, while documentation for Apache Arrow can be found at `https://arrow.apache.org/`.

There is also a must-read blog post on Feather written by the authors of the Feather data format (Wes McKinney and Hadley Wickham), available at `https://blog.cloudera.com/blog/2016/03/feather-a-fast-on-disk-format-for-data-frames-for-r-and-python-powered-by-apache-arrow/`.

More information on the `DataFrame`'s can be found in `Chapter 7`, *Handling Analytical Data*.

Reading CSV and FWF files

Reading **comma-separated value (CSV)** and **fixed-width files (FWF)** are commonly needed operations in data processing. In this recipe, we look at how Julia supports these operations.

Getting ready

Start the Julia command line and create two `IOBuffer` objects from which we'll read data:

```
julia> csv = """a,b,c
                11,2,3
                4,555,6
                7,8,9999"""
"a,b,c\n11,2,3\n4,555,6\n7,8,9999"

julia> iocsv = IOBuffer(csv)
IOBuffer(data=UInt8[...], readable=true, writable=false, seekable=true,
append=false, size=29, maxsize=Inf, ptr=1, mark=-1)

julia> fwf = """a  b      c
                11 2      3
                4  555    66
                7  8      9999"""
"a b    c\n11 2    3\n4 555    66\n7 8 9999"

julia> iofwf = IOBuffer(fwf)
IOBuffer(data=UInt8[...], readable=true, writable=false, seekable=true,
append=false, size=47, maxsize=Inf, ptr=1, mark=-1)
```

 In the GitHub repository for this recipe, you will find the `commands.txt` file, which contains the presented sequence of Julia commands.

Now, open your favorite terminal to execute the commands.

How to do it...

The first step is to read the CSV file, which can be done by using the `DelimitedFiles.jl` package that is bundled with Julia:

1. Start by loading it into the namespace:

   ```
   julia> using DelimitedFiles
   ```

2. Now, read the file as follows:

   ```
   julia> datacsv, headercsv = readdlm(iocsv, ',', header=true)
   ([11.0 2.0 3.0; 4.0 555.0 6.0; 7.0 8.0 9999.0], AbstractString["a"
   "b" "c"])
   ```

```julia
julia> headercsv
1×3 Array{AbstractString,2}:
 "a"  "b"  "c"

julia> datacsv
3×3 Array{Float64,2}:
 11.0    2.0     3.0
  4.0  555.0     6.0
  7.0    8.0  9999.0
```

3. For FWF, there is no built-in functionality allowing them to be read. Therefore, it is necessary to create a helper function to extract the data from a string:

```julia
julia> function getsubstring(s::AbstractString,
                             charfrom::Int,
                             charto::Int)
           SubString(s, nextind.(s, 0, (charfrom, charto))...)
       end
getsubstring (generic function with 1 method)
```

4. This helper function can then be used to define a simple parser of FWF files:

```julia
julia> function readfwf(io, ranges::AbstractVector{<:Pair})
           datafwf = []
           starts = first.(ranges)
           ends = last.(ranges)
           while !eof(io)
               line = readline(io)
               push!(datafwf, getsubstring.(line, starts, ends))
           end
           [datafwf[i][j] for i in 1:length(datafwf), j in
       1:length(ranges)]
       end
readfwf (generic function with 1 method)
```

Now, you are able to read in data from the file:

```julia
julia> datafwf = readfwf(iofwf, [1=>2, 4=>6, 8=>11])
4×3 Array{SubString{String},2}:
 "a "  "b "   "  c"
 "11"  "2 "   "  3"
 "4 "  "555"  " 66"
 "7 "  "8 "   "9999"
```

Finally, you can extract the data from the previous step into a more suitable format:

```
julia> parse.(Int, datafwf[2:end, :])
3×3 Array{Int64,2}:
  11   2    3
   4 555   66
   7   8 9999
```

How it works...

First, we create in-memory streams using `IOBuffer`, as explained in the *Using IOBuffer to efficiently work with in-memory streams* recipe. This is a convenient technique for writing test code for I/O functions.

Reading CSV files is simple. We invoke the `readdlm` function from the `DelimitedFiles.jl` package with two options included: our delimiter (`','` in this case), and a flag telling us if the file contains a header. As its output, in this case, `readdlm` produced a tuple containing the data read in and the header line.

In order to read in an FWF file, a custom parser is needed. Here, we implemented a minimal example of how you can do it. Some noteworthy points of this code are as follows:

1. The `nextind.(s, 0, (charfrom, charto))...` construct broadcasts the `nextind` function over the `(charfrom, charto)` tuple, and then splats the result as positional arguments to `SubString` using `...`.
2. The signature of the `readfwf` function for the `pairs` argument is `AbstractVector{<:Pairs}` in order to allow any concrete type implementing `Pairs` to be an element of `AbstractVector`; the reason for this is that types in Julia are invariant, as explained in the *Understanding subtyping in Julia* recipe in `Chapter 5`, *Variables, Types and Functions*.
3. If you read all data from the `IOBuffer` object then it becomes empty; for example, running `readdlm(iocsv, ',', header=true)` in the recipe will fail if you try to run it for the second time, because `iocsv` got emptied after the first call to `readdlm`;
4. Finally, the last line shows how you can easily transform a vector of vectors into a matrix, where each vector constitutes its row by using comprehensions.

There's more...

You can look up the help of the `readdlm` function in the Julia command line to find out what other options it provides for more fine-tuned reading of data.

See also

In the *Reading CSV data from the internet* recipe in `Chapter 7`, *Handling Analytical Data*, we describe more advanced methods to read and write data from `DataFrame`.

Numerical Computing with Julia

4

In this chapter, we discuss the following recipes:

- Traversing matrices efficiently
- Executing loops efficiently with conditional statements
- Generating full factorial designs
- Approximating π using partial series sums
- Running Monte Carlo simulations
- Analyzing a queuing system
- Working with complex numbers
- Writing a simple optimization routine
- Estimating linear regression
- Understanding broadcasting in Julia
- Improving code performance using `@inbounds`
- Creating a matrix from a set of vectors as rows
- Using array views to avoid memory allocation

Introduction

In this chapter, we provide recipes showing how computing tasks can be performed in the Julia language. Each recipe implements a relatively simple and standard algorithm to show a specific feature of the language. Therefore, the reader can concentrate on the implementation issues. However, we provide a reference to source materials for each problem for any readers interested in deeper understanding of the algorithmic part.

Traversing matrices efficiently

Matrices are a basic building block of any numerical computing workflow. In this introductory recipe, we show how to work with them using loops.

The important point to consider here is that in order to traverse a matrix efficiently in Julia you should traverse it column-wise, as this is the memory layout used internally. Other languages that use column-major order are Fortran, MATLAB, and R.

Getting ready

Make sure that you have the `BenchmarkTools.jl` package installed. If it is missing then run the following command: `using Pkg; Pkg.add("BenchmarkTools")`.

> In the GitHub repository for this recipe, you will find the `commands.txt` file that contains the presented sequence of shell and Julia commands and the `sums.jl` file that contains definitions of functions used in this recipe.

Now open your favorite terminal to execute the commands.

How to do it...

First, we define two ways we could implement a function that takes the sum of all elements of an array. After this, we will compare their performance:

1. Execute the contents of the `sums.jl` file by running `include("sums.jl")` in the Julia command line to define the following two functions:

```
function sum_by_col(x)
    s = zero(eltype(x))
    for j in 1:size(x, 2)
        for i in 1:size(x, 1)
            s += x[i, j]
        end
    end
    s
end

function sum_by_row(x)
    s = zero(eltype(x))
    for i in 1:size(x, 1)
```

```
        for j in 1:size(x, 2)
            s += x[i, j]
        end
    end
    s
end
```

2. Test the code by entering the following commands in the Julia console:

```
julia> using BenchmarkTools

julia> x = rand(10^4, 10^4);

julia> @btime sum_by_row(x)
  1.072 s (1 allocation: 16 bytes)
5.000042698338314e7

julia> @btime sum_by_col(x)
  113.323 ms (1 allocation: 16 bytes)
5.000042698340571e7

julia> @btime sum(x)
  55.591 ms (1 allocation: 16 bytes)
5.0000426983395495e7
```

Observe that the code traversing the matrix by columns is much faster than the one using row traversal. Additionally, due to a finite precision of floating point arithmetic, the results of all three functions are not exactly identical, because they perform the summation in different orders.

How it works...

When you design your computations, you must be aware that Julia stores the data in columns (so-called **column-major order**). This means that due to caching on modern processors, it is often much faster to process matrices column-wise than row-wise. In our case, there is a difference of almost *10x* in the time taken.

First, note that the sum function built into Julia is even faster than our sum_by_col function. The difference is caused by the fact that it uses SIMD processor instructions (see https://www.intel.com/content/www/us/en/support/articles/000005779/processors.html for a discussion of SIMD extensions available on Intel processors).

Also, observe that when adding numbers, the order of summation actually matters: the `sum_by_row`, `sum_by_col`, and `sum` functions all return a slightly different result.

Importantly, you should be aware that Python stores data in row-major order, so often the most efficient way to implement an algorithm in Julia and in Python will differ.

Additionally, observe that in the recipe, we initialize `s` to be zero of the `eltype(x)` type. In this way, we make sure that the produced code is type stable.

See also

See the *Executing loops efficiently with conditional statements* recipe for the `@simd` macro description.

See the *Ensuring type stability of your code* recipe in `Chapter 6`, *Metaprogramming and Advanced Typing,* for a discussion of type stability.

Executing loops efficiently with conditional statements

In this recipe, we want to calculate a sum of the positive entries of a large vector in an efficient way.

Getting ready

Open the Julia console. Make sure that you have the `BenchmarkTools.jl` package installed. If it is missing you can add it by running the following commands: `using Pkg; Pkg.add("BenchmarkTools")`.

Before we begin, load the required packages and generate the vector over which we will perform a sum:

```
julia> using Random, BenchmarkTools

julia> Random.seed!(1);

julia> x = randn(10^6);
```

Notice that we use `;` at the end of the expressions to suppress the output of the results.

 In the GitHub repository for this recipe, you will find the `commands.txt` file that contains the presented sequence of shell and Julia commands.

Now open your favorite terminal to execute the commands.

How to do it...

In the following steps, we investigate different methods for how the sum of positive values in a vector can be calculated, and then compare the performance:

1. A simple way to calculate this sum would be the following:

```julia
julia> @btime sum(v for v in x if v > 0)
  5.446 ms (3 allocations: 48 bytes)
398244.60749279766
```

This implementation is simple and easy to read, so we would probably use it in non-performance-critical code.

2. Now consider a roughly equivalent, more verbose implementation, using explicit loops:

```julia
julia> function possum1(x)
           s = zero(eltype(x))
           for v in x
               if v > 0
                   s += v
               end
           end
           s
       end
possum1 (generic function with 1 method)

julia> @btime possum1(x)
  2.198 ms (1 allocation: 16 bytes)
398244.60749279766
```

It is already faster. However, having a conditional statement inside a loop often hinders execution performance. Therefore, we will consider the third implementation.

3. Consider the following function, calculating the sum using `ifelse`:

```
julia> function possum2a(x)
           s = zero(eltype(x))
           for v in x
               s += ifelse(v > 0, v, zero(s))
           end
           s
       end
possum2a (generic function with 1 method)

julia> @btime possum2a(x)
  1.487 ms (1 allocation: 16 bytes)
398244.60749279766
```

This can be refined even further since it is clear that we are repeatedly performing the same operation, although this refinement may very slightly alter the result of the computation.

4. Now add the `@simd` macro annotation to the loop:

```
julia> function possum2b(x)
           s = zero(eltype(x))
           @simd for v in x
               s += ifelse(v > 0, v, zero(s))
           end
           s
       end
possum2b (generic function with 1 method)

julia> @btime possum2b(x)
  459.094 µs (1 allocation: 16 bytes)
398244.6074928036
```

How it works...

A typically poor implementation of a function performing the summation is as follows:

```
julia> function possum2c(x)
           s = 0
           for v in x
               s += ifelse(v > 0, v, 0)
           end
           s
       end
possum2c (generic function with 1 method)
```

```
julia> @btime possum2c(x)
 14.670 ms (1000001 allocations: 15.26 MiB)
398244.60749279766
```

The difference between this and our preceding code is that we initiate the s variable using an Int value, and then ifelse(v > 0, v, 0) returns either a variable of the typeof(v) type or Int (which is of the 0 type). The problem is that in this case the Julia compiler is not able to determine the type of s uniquely (so, we say that s is not type stable). We can see that this significantly degrades code performance. In the *Ensuring type stability of your code* recipe in Chapter 6, *Metaprogramming and Advanced Typing*, we explain in detail how to detect such problems in your code.

In order to overcome this problem, we use zero(eltype(x)) and zero(s) to make sure that we use zero of a proper type.

The other two key features in this code are the following:

- Using the ifelse function makes Julia avoid branching in compiled assembly code; the cost is that both values (one for the true value, and one for the false value of the condition) have to be computed; if performing both computations is cheap (as in our example), then avoiding branching can significantly speed up the loop.
- The second feature is the use of the @simd macro, which tells Julia to use the SIMD processor instructions (see http://www.tech-faq.com/simd.html or https://en.wikipedia.org/wiki/SIMD) that can further speed up computations. Not every loop will be faster when @simd is used; the conditions for its efficiency are explained in detail at https://docs.julialang.org/en/latest/manual/performance-tips/.

There's more...

In our example, we could also use the type in the signature of a method:

```
julia> function possum2d(x::AbstractArray{T}) where T
           s = zero(T)
           @simd for v in x
               s += ifelse(v > 0, v, zero(T))
           end
           s
       end
possum2d (generic function with 1 method)

julia> @btime possum2d(x)
```

```
   465.990 µs (1 allocation: 16 bytes)
398244.6074928036
```

As you can see, we can now refer directly to the T type in the code of the function to ensure type stability. The `where T` clause is shorthand for `where T<:Any`, and in our example is only used to extract the type that parametrizes the x array.

Another useful function, similar to `ifelse`, is `clamp`. It takes three arguments, x, lo, and hi, and makes sure that the returned value is x, clamped to the `[lo, hi]` interval. It also avoids branching of code.

See also

More details of code benchmarking are provided in the *Benchmarking code* recipe in Chapter 8, *Julia Workflow*.

Generating full factorial designs

Often in scientific computing, we are interested in generating a full factorial design of a computational experiment (see, for example, http://www.socialresearchmethods.net/kb/expfact.php or https://en.wikipedia.org/wiki/Factorial_experiment). A typical application of this design is performing a grid search in hyperparameter tuning of machine learning models (see https://cloud.google.com/ml-engine/docs/tensorflow/hyperparameter-tuning-overview or https://en.wikipedia.org/wiki/Hyperparameter_optimization#Grid_search).

Assume that we are given a list of vectors and we want to generate all possible combinations of values taken from those vectors. For instance, if we have the x=[1,2] and y=['a', 'b'] vectors, we have four possible combinations of values taken from them, namely, (1,'a'), (2, 'a'), (1,'b'), and (2,'b'). In general, if we have k vectors, and vector i has n_i elements, then there are $\prod_{i=1}^{k} n_i$ such combinations. In this recipe, we will show how to use the matrix manipulation functions built into Julia to generate a full factorial design from a given list of input vectors.

Our function is similar to the `expand.grid` function in the GNU R programming language.

 In the GitHub repository for this recipe, you will find the `commands.txt` file that contains the presented sequence of shell and Julia commands and the `expand.jl` file that contains the definition of a function used in this recipe.

Now open your favorite terminal to execute the commands.

How to do it...

In this recipe, we first define a function that generates a full factorial design, and then we test it on sample data. Here is a list of steps to be followed:

1. Execute the `expand.jl` file by running `include("expand.jl")` in the Julia command line to define the following function:

```
function expandgrid(levels...)
    lengths = length.(levels)
    inner = 1
    outer = prod(lengths)
    grid = []
    for i in 1:length(levels)
        outer = div(outer, lengths[i])
        push!(grid, repeat(levels[i], inner=inner, outer=outer))
        inner *= lengths[i]
    end
    Tuple(grid)
end
```

The function takes vectors as a list of its arguments and returns a tuple representing a full factorial design.

2. Run the following examples in the Julia console to test this function:

```
julia> expandgrid(1:2, 'a':'b')
([1, 2, 1, 2], ['a', 'a', 'b', 'b'])

julia> hcat(expandgrid(1:3, [true, false], 'a':'b')...)
12x3 Array{Any,2}:
 1   true   'a'
 2   true   'a'
 3   true   'a'
 1   false  'a'
 2   false  'a'
```

```
3   false   'a'
1    true   'b'
2    true   'b'
3    true   'b'
1   false   'b'
2   false   'b'
3   false   'b'
```

The last operation could be also written as `reduce(hcat, expandgrid(1:3, [true, false], 'a':'b'))`.

How it works...

The `expandgrid` function takes the `levels...` argument. The `...` inside the definition means that we can pass any number of positional arguments to this function, and they will become accessible inside the function as a tuple. This is a convenient way of defining functions that take a variable number of arguments.

Next, by running `length.(levels)`, we apply the `length` function to each element of the `levels` tuple. This is achieved by adding `.` after the function name. If ww wrote `length(levels)`, we would get the length of the tuple.

The crucial element in the design of our procedure is the built-in `repeat` function. It takes a vector, `v`, and two arguments, `inner` and `outer`. First, each element of the vector is repeated `inner` times, then the entire resulting vector is repeated `outer` times. For instance, consider the following code:

```julia
julia> repeat([1,2], inner=2, outer=3)
12-element Array{Int64,1}:
 1
 1
 2
 2
 1
 1
 2
 2
 1
 1
 2
 2
```

Using this function, it is relatively simple to generate a full factorial design. What we need to do is to generate each vector so as to have the `prod(lengths)` length. We ensure that for the ith vector, we set the `inner` keyword argument to be the product of the lengths of vectors from 1 to i-1, and the `outer` keyword argument is the product of the lengths of vectors from i+1 to `length(levels)`.

We collect those results into the `grid` vector, which we later convert into a tuple.

Finally, we use ... in `hcat(expandgrid(1:3, [true, false], 'a':'b')...)` to extract elements of a tuple as positional arguments to the `hcat` function.

See also

More examples on how you can work with `hcat` and similar array combination functions are given in the recipe *Creating a matrix from a set of vectors as rows*.

Often, you may wish to put the results of a full factorial design in `DataFrame`. In Chapter 7, *Handling Analytical Data*, we explain how you can work with the `DataFrame` type.

Approximating π using partial series sums

One of the powers of Julia is its flexibility in applying its numeric type system. In this recipe, we explain how to write flexible code that can adjust to the required type, using the example of approximating π.

Getting ready

Approximation of π is a long-standing problem in mathematics. You can find many formulas for its calculation at `http://mathworld.wolfram.com/PiFormulas.html`.

One of the more interesting methods is the use of an infinite sum of terms $n!/(2n+1)!!$ for n, ranging from zero to infinity. The denominator in each summed fraction is a double factorial (see `http://mathworld.wolfram.com/DoubleFactorial.html` or `https://en.wikipedia.org/wiki/Double_factorial`). Formally, we have the following relationship:

$$\pi = 2 \sum_{n=0}^{+\infty} \frac{n!}{(2n+1)!!}$$

In this recipe, we will use this formula with different numeric types as a basis for the calculations.

 In the GitHub repository for this recipe, you will find the `commands.txt` file that contains the presented sequence of shell and Julia commands.

Now open your favorite terminal to execute the commands.

How to do it...

Firstly, we implement the function that approximates π, and then we will test it with different numeric types, as follows:

1. In the Julia console, define a function as follows:

```julia
julia> function our_pi(n, T)
           s = one(T)
           f = one(T)
           for i::T in 1:n
               f *= i / (2i+1)
               s += f
           end
           2s
       end
our_pi (generic function with 1 method)
```

2. Now we will test `our_pi` for different numeric types by running the following code in the Julia console:

```julia
julia> for T in [Float16, Float64, BigFloat]
           display([our_pi(2^n, T) for n in 1:10] .- big(π))
       end
10-element Array{BigFloat,1}:
-2.07998903589793238462643383279502884197169399375105820974944592307
81e-01
-4.39364035897932384626433832795028841971693993751058209749445923078
16e-02
-2.92077858979323846264338327950288419716939937510582097494459230781
64e-03
-9.67653589793238462643383279502884197169399375105820974944592307816
40e-04
-9.67653589793238462643383279502884197169399375105820974944592307816
40e-04
```

```
-9.676535897932384626433832795028841971693993751058209749445923078164
0e-04
-9.676535897932384626433832795028841971693993751058209749445923078164
0e-04
-9.676535897932384626433832795028841971693993751058209749445923078164
0e-04
-9.676535897932384626433832795028841971693993751058209749445923078164
0e-04
-9.676535897932384626433832795028841971693993751058209749445923078164
0e-04
10-element Array{BigFloat,1}:
-2.082593202564601123709413133087237632750807763282308209749445923078164e-01
-4.317995517709517539637050332880069379799477500105820974944592307816e-02
-2.12297294364262068719613863999445800774679195323082097494459230781e-03
-6.25755273299145195738503156651620858297359385582097494459230781640e-06
-7.00472017127499913089578307151137353126058209749445923078164062861980e-11
-1.01064309961486055006151192770015635582097494459230781640628619802e-15
-1.01064309961486055006151192770015635582097494459230781640628619802e-15
-1.01064309961486055006151192770015635582097494459230781640628619802e-15
-1.01064309961486055006151192770015635582097494459230781640628619802e-15
-1.01064309961486055006151192770015635582097494459230781640628619802e-15
10-element Array{BigFloat,1}:
-2.082593202564599051293100499461695508638360660417724876416112589744e-01
-4.317995517709482576423068486680447149875670096240740827653189389511e-02
-2.122972943642004076114879103939885104758542258366351294298441073429e-03
-6.257552731792070508295743788487240468397453131043771934107556099005e-06
-7.004652017792807785231708478601873166539334803007259111293615461272e-11
-1.17624725174958900219955191596676373409332105600785622950813691937441e-20
-4.555467456395812571863354028257417095625126183776878405020450217779e-40
1.036340226611333355046362223536047948533920043723537662028444164202e-76
```

```
1.036340226611333355046362223536047948533920043732353776620284441642
023e-76
1.036340226611333355046362223536047948533920043732353776620284441642
023e-76
```

3. For the `BigFloat` type, we can improve the precision of computations using the `setprecision` function:

```
julia> our_pi(1000, BigFloat) - pi
1.036340226611333355046362223536047948533920043732353776620284441642
0231e-76
```

```
julia> setprecision(1000) do
           our_pi(1000, BigFloat)-pi
       end
3.733054474012875515960358178895268678468365785486832098486857359 18
386764390310253781776130839152440943837995972129697049686195008 5416
129579366083268815723024937642664553300601095980303943607326044 4019
631850604524729620500591837351632207130845016604152427935154177 0592
4477879256914643836888070651641771 19e-301
```

4. Finally, we run the same calculations using rational numbers:

```
julia> [our_pi(n, Rational) for n in 1:10]
10-element Array{Rational{Int64},1}:
        8//3
       44//15
       64//21
      976//315
    10816//3465
   141088//45045
    47104//15015
  2404096//765765
 45693952//14549535
 45701632//14549535
```

5. If we try running the same code for n=23, we get the following result:

```
julia> our_pi(23, Rational)
ERROR: OverflowError: 462382939977023488 * 47 overflowed for type
Int64
Stacktrace:
 [1] throw_overflowerr_binaryop(::Symbol, ::Int64, ::Int64) at
.\checked.jl:158
 [2] checked_mul at .\checked.jl:292 [inlined]
 [3] +(::Rational{Int64}, ::Rational{Int64}) at .\rational.jl:249
 [4] our_pi(::Int64, ::Type) at .\REPL[1]:6
 [5] top-level scope at none:0
```

6. This now gives an overflow error, but by switching to the `Rational{BigInt}`
   type, we can obtain a proper result:

   ```
   julia> our_pi(23, Rational{BigInt})
   67386041794822144//21449643578668305
   ```

How it works...

In this recipe, we discuss several important features of Julia. The first is how we constrain
the types of parameters of `our_pi`. The second argument of this method is a type using the
calculations that should be performed.

In order to make sure that we perform calculations on the desired T type, we bind the value
of this type to the s and t variables. Additionally, by writing `i::T`, we ensure that any
value that would be bound to the i variable will be converted to the T type. One crucial
consequence of this is that `i/(2i+1)` will be evaluated as the T type, because we know that
T is either `Rational` or `AbstractFloat`, and for any subtype of one of these types,
multiplication by integer, addition of integer, and division also produce a result of
the T type (exceptions to this rule will be explained as we proceed further). Also, observe
that we use the one function to get a value of 1, represented as a T type.

Another important feature discussed in this recipe is a way to improve the precision of
calculations on `BigFloat` using the `setprecision` function. Here, it is crucial that our
evaluation of π was also performed with high precision (within the do block of
`setprecision`). Otherwise, we would have got the following output:

```
julia> setprecision(() -> our_pi(1000, BigFloat), 1000) - pi
1.096917440979352076742130626395698021050758236508687951179005716992142688
513354e-77
```

This would happen because π would be evaluated using the default 256-bit precision.

Finally, we learned how to use `Rational` type and that it performs overflow checking.
Remember, however, that standard operations on integer types, such as `Int`, are not
overflow safe.

There's more...

We could restrict the list of accepted arguments of our function in the following way:

```
function our_pi(n::Integer, T::Type{<:Union{AbstractFloat, Rational}})
```

This is specified using the `Type{...}` type. An important condition here is that we want to allow only `AbstractFloat` or `Rational` as accepted types, so we need to use `Union` in order to take both. Finally, because the Julia type system is invariant (for an explanation of invariance, see https://docs.microsoft.com/en-us/dotnet/standard/generics/covariance-and-contravariance

or https://en.wikipedia.org/wiki/Covariance_and_contravariance_(computer_scienc e) and the *Understanding subtyping in Julia* recipe in Chapter 5, *Variables, Types, and Functions*), we have to use the `<:` subtyping symbol to express the fact that we accept any type that is a subtype of `AbstractFloat` or `Rational`.

Using the preceding signature, you could pass an abstract type as T to `our_pi`. As you will see in the *Understanding the structure of Julia numeric types with introspection* recipe in Chapter 6, *Metaprogramming and Advanced Typing*, the allowed abstract types in our case are `AbstractFloat` and `Rational`, and the concrete types using an abstract type as a parameter are `Rational{Integer}`, `Rational{Signed}`, and `Rational{Unsigned}`. This means that in the first two cases (abstract types), the `t` and `s` variables must get some other type. It is straightforward to check this (we use the `∘` operator, which denotes function composition; you can input it by typing `\circ` and pressing *Tab*):

```
julia> (typeof∘one).([AbstractFloat, Rational])
2-element Array{DataType,1}:
 Float64
 Rational{Int64}
```

On the other hand, it is not clear how the concrete subtypes of `Rational` that are based on abstract types would behave under mathematical operations. Once again, it is easy enough to check, as follows:

```
julia> typeof(2*one(Rational{Integer}))
Rational{Int64}

julia> typeof(2*one(Rational{Signed}))
Rational{Int64}

julia> typeof(2*one(Rational{Unsigned}))
Rational{UInt64}
```

See also

In the *Understanding the structure of Julia numeric types with introspection* recipe in `Chapter 6`, *Metaprogramming and Advanced Typing*, we investigate the full tree of Julia numeric types in detail and discuss the difference between concrete and abstract types in Julia.

Running Monte Carlo simulations

The Monte Carlo simulation (see the example, `http://news.mit.edu/2010/exp-monte-carlo-0517` or `https://en.wikipedia.org/wiki/Monte_Carlo_method`) is one of the elementary computational techniques. In this recipe, we will explain how it can be implemented efficiently in Julia.

Getting ready

Consider the following problem. Assume that on each day, a random volume of water leaks from a pipe to a container. The amount of water that leaks out is greater than zero, but less than one. How many days do we need to wait till a container having a volume equal to one is filled, if on each day the amount of water that leaks is a uniformly random value between zero and one?

Formally, we repeatedly draw independent random numbers from a uniform distribution on the $[0, 1[$ interval. How many draws, on average, are required until the sum of drawn numbers is greater than or equal to 1? Let $X_i \sim U([0, 1[)$ be a sequence of independent random variables. We want to find the following:

$$E\left(\min\left\{k: \sum_{i=1}^{k} X_i \geq 1\right\}\right)$$

We will approximate this value by calculating the average of many simulations of the preceding process.

Make sure that you have the `OnlineStats.jl` package installed. If it is missing you should add it using the following commands in the Julia command line: `using Pkg; Pkg.add("OnlineStats")`.

In the GitHub repository for this recipe, you will find
the `commands.txt` file that contains the presented sequence of shell and
Julia commands and the `simwalk.jl` file that contains definitions of
functions used in this recipe.

Now open your favorite terminal to execute the commands.

How to do it...

In this recipe, the first step is to define our simulation function. Next, we compare several
alternatives for running it. Finally, we make sure that it produces the result that is
predicted by the analytical solution:

1. Using `include("simwalk.jl")` run the following code, that is contained in the
   `simwalk.jl` file in the Julia command line by:

   ```
   using OnlineStats, Random

   function simwalk()
       jumps = 0
       distance = 0.0
       while true
           jumps += 1
           distance += rand()
           distance ≥ 1.0 && return jumps
       end
   end

   function incremental(n)
       s = Mean()
       for i in 1:n
           fit!(s, simwalk())
       end
       value(s)
   end
   ```

2. Test `simwalk` by running a Monte Carlo simulation in four different ways, as
   follows, in the Julia console:

   ```
   julia> n = 10^6;

   julia> Random.seed!(1);

   julia> res1 = mean([simwalk() for i in 1:n])
   2.718453
   ```

```
julia> res2 = mean(map(x -> simwalk(), 1:n))
2.717532

julia> res3 = mean(simwalk() for i in 1:n)
2.718537

julia> res4 = incremental(n)
2.717549999999901
```

3. Compare the performance of the four considered methods by increasing n to 10^8:

```
julia> n = 10^8;

julia> @time mean([simwalk() for i in 1:n]);
  3.391541 seconds (53.10 k allocations: 765.577 MiB, 0.67% gc
time)

julia> @time mean(map(x -> simwalk(), 1:n));
  3.607314 seconds (62.64 k allocations: 766.063 MiB, 5.02% gc time)

julia> @time mean(simwalk() for i in 1:n);
  2.811260 seconds (276.21 k allocations: 13.419 MiB)

julia> @time incremental(n);
  2.867631 seconds (5 allocations: 176 bytes)
```

4. We can get closer to the true value of Napier's constant by increasing the number of samples taken:

```
julia> MathConstants.e - incremental(10^9)
-6.026543315051924e-6
```

We see that the result of running `incremental(10^9)` is quite close to the value of e provided in the `Base.MathConstants` module. In the *Analyzing a queuing system* recipe, we will discuss how to assess the accuracy of such an approximation.

How it works...

A discussion of the mathematical proof for our assertion that the process converges to the constant e can be found at http://mathworld.wolfram.com/UniformSumDistribution.html.

From a programming perspective, we have discussed four ways to run the simulation:

- The first method calculated a mean of the data captured in a comprehension as [simwalk() for i in 1:n]). This is the simplest method for running the simulation many times. Its benefit is that it retains all the results of the simulation, which can then be used for future analysis. The downside is that, as we have seen, it is relatively slow if we are interested only in the mean.
- The second method using map(x -> simwalk(), 1:n) is very similar, as it also stores all the results of the simulations. This time, we used a functional programming approach.
- A significant difference to the first two methods is provided by the third approach, which uses a mean(simwalk() for i in 1:n) approach. This time we are creating a generator that is passed to the mean function. In this case, no intermediate results were stored. An alternative way to perform computations using this approach would be with mean(x -> simwalk(), 1:n).
- Finally, the incremental function refers to the OnlineStats.jl package, which is designed to efficiently calculate statistics in an incremental way.

Also, note that we have used the @time macro to measure the performance of our code. This is the most basic method for performance analysis of code in Julia. Here, an important factor was that we used the @time macro the second time each approach was called, so we were sure that all the methods used had been precompiled by Julia. More details about compilation time and performance measurement are given in the *Benchmarking Code* recipe in Chapter 8, *Julia Workflow*.

There's more...

As usual in Julia, if you are willing to complicate your code a bit, there is room for performance improvement. Here is an implementation in which repetitions of a Monte Carlo simulation are fused within the simwalk function itself:

```julia
julia> function simwalk(n)
           jumps = 0
           for i in 1:n
               distance = 0.0
```

```
            while true
                jumps += 1
                distance += rand()
                distance ≥ 1.0 && break
            end
        end
        jumps / n
    end
simwalk (generic function with 1 method)
```

Now, running this code, we get the following:

```
julia> simwalk(10^6)
2.717539

julia> @time simwalk(10^8)
  1.953019 seconds (6 allocations: 192 bytes)
2.71824124
```

And we can see a significant performance improvement. One particular advantage of Julia is that using `for` or `while` loops do not lead to performance degradation when compared to MATLAB, R, or Python.

Another remark regarding the preceding code is that it only works correctly on 64-bit machines. The reason is that the `jumps` variable will have the `Int64` type, and we can guarantee that we won't overflow it by consecutive additions. On 32-bit architectures, `jumps` have the `Int32` type, and the maximum value of this type is `2147483647` (you can check it by running the `typemax(Int32)` command), which would result in an overflow if you ran `simwalk(10^9)`. On 64-bit machines, you can check it yourself by manually changing the type of the `jumps` variable, as shown:

```
julia> function simwalk(n)
           jumps = Int32(0)
           for i in 1:n
               distance = 0.0
               while true
                   jumps += Int32(1)
                   distance += rand()
                   distance ≥ 1.0 && break
               end
           end
           jumps / n
       end
simwalk (generic function with 1 method)
```

The lesson from this example is that you should be careful to check whether an integer overflow problem will not happen in your code. Fortunately, by running `typemax(Int64)`, we see that it is equal to 9223372036854775807, so in most situations we will be safe. If the possibility of an overflow is a concern, there are two solutions. Either use the `BigInt` type, or apply checked versions of standard mathematical operations on integers. Julia offers the following list: `checked_neg`, `checked_abs`, `checked_add`, `checked_sub`, `checked_mul`, `checked_div`, `checked_rem`, `checked_fld`, `checked_mod`, and `checked_cld`. They are not exported from the `Base` module, so their usage has to be qualified with the `Base.` prefix; for example, `Base.checked_add(1, 2)`, or else they have to be explicitly imported. You should also be aware that checked operations are slower than standard arithmetic, and they throw an `OverflowError` exception on overflow.

See also

You can read about the functionalities of the `OnlineStats` package on its GitHub page, available at `https://github.com/joshday/OnlineStats.jl`.

We will discuss more advanced benchmarking methods in the *Benchmarking Code* recipe in `Chapter 8`, *Julia Workflow*.

Analyzing a queuing system

In the *Running Monte Carlo simulations* recipe, we presented basic methods for running a Monte Carlo simulation. Now, we will show you how you can calculate the confidence interval of a simulation output using bootstrapping.

Getting ready

First, you need to understand how an M/M/1 queue works. A basic introduction to this topic can be found at `https://www.britannica.com/science/queuing-theory` or `https://en.wikipedia.org/wiki/M/M/1_queue`. For our purposes, it is sufficient to know that in this model the time between two consecutive arrivals of a customer to the system has an exponential distribution (see `http://mathworld.wolfram.com/ExponentialDistribution.html` or `https://en.wikipedia.org/wiki/Exponential_distribution`). Customers are then served by a single server in a first-in/first-out schedule. The time taken by the service is also exponentially distributed.

Here is a simple visualization of a single server queue:

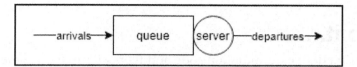

We are interested in the average time, over the long term, that a random customer stays in the system (that is, from entering it, to finishing the service). As a reference, it is known that, under the preceding assumptions, if the expected customer mean interarrival time is a and the expected customer service time is s, then this theoretical value is equal to $1/(1/s - 1/a)$.

We will run a simulation of an M/M/1 queue many times. Then we will calculate a confidence interval of the simulated mean time spent using bootstrapping (see `http://mathworld.wolfram.com/BootstrapMethods.html` or `https://en.wikipedia.org/wiki/Bootstrapping_(statistics)`). In particular, we will use the percentile bootstrapping method (see `https://www.sciencedirect.com/science/article/pii/0167715289901211` or `https://en.wikipedia.org/wiki/Bootstrapping_(statistics)#Deriving_confidence_intervals_from_the_bootstrap_distribution`). The idea behind this is relatively simple. Given an X vector of data that has a length of 1 and a statistic we want to use (we assume mean in this recipe), we choose the number of runs of a simulation as r. Then, for r times, we repeat the same action: we draw 1 sample from X with replacement and calculate the mean. By the end of this procedure, we will have r means. If we want to calculate a confidence interval of confidence C, we simply take $(1-C)/2$ and $(1+C)/2$ percentiles of the distribution as the bounds. For instance, for 95% confidence intervals, these would be the 2.5% and 97.5% percentiles.

For this recipe, you will need to have the `Distributions.jl` and `OnlineStats.jl` packages installed. If they are missing then you can add them using the following commands:

```julia
julia> using Pkg

julia> Pkg.add("Distributions")

julia> Pkg.add("OnlineStats")
```

In the GitHub repository for this recipe, you will find the `commands.txt` file that contains the presented sequence of shell and Julia commands and the `mm1.jl` file that contains definitions of functions used in this recipe.

Now open your favorite terminal to execute the commands.

How to do it...

In this recipe, we first define a simulation code and then we run it on some sample data as follows:

1. Check out the code contained in the `mm1.jl` file:

```julia
using Distributions, OnlineStats

function queue1(until::Real, burnin::Real,
                ad::Distribution, sd::Distribution)
    now, nextArrival, nextDeparture = 0.0, rand(ad), Inf
    queue, waits = Float64[], Mean()
    while now < until
        if nextArrival < nextDeparture
            now = nextArrival
            if isempty(queue)
                nextDeparture = nextArrival + rand(sd)
            end
            push!(queue, nextArrival)
            nextArrival += rand(ad)
        else
            now = nextDeparture
            insystem = nextDeparture - popfirst!(queue)
            burnin < now < until && fit!(waits, insystem)
            nextDeparture += isempty(queue) ? Inf : rand(sd)
        end
    end
    value(waits)
end

mm1_exact(ad::Exponential, sd::Exponential) =
1/(1/mean(sd)-1/mean(ad))

function bootCI(data, stat::Function, CI::Float64, reps::Integer)
    boot = [stat(rand(data, length(data))) for i in 1:reps]
    low, high = quantile(boot, [(1-CI)/2, (1+CI)/2])
    (value=stat(data), low=low, high=high)
end
```

2. Start Julia in interactive mode while loading the mm1.jl file:

```
$ julia -i mm1.jl
```

3. Now run the simulation and measure the performance:

```
julia> ad = Exponential(1.3)
Exponential{Float64}(θ=1.3)

julia> sd = Exponential(0.95)
Exponential{Float64}(θ=0.95)

julia> @time res = [queue1(2^14, 2^12, ad, sd) for i in 1:2^12];
  3.318662 seconds (148.73 k allocations: 11.630 MiB)

julia> exact = mm1_exact(ad, sd)
3.5285714285714285

julia> @time println(bootCI(res .- exact, mean, 0.99, 2^14))
(value = -0.003943780433664523, low = -0.013200074798619505, high =
0.005321844047221419)
  1.146994 seconds (32.84 k allocations: 513.533 MiB, 12.15% gc
time)
```

How it works...

The queue1 function is a queue simulator, and takes four arguments:

- until tells it how long the simulation should run
- burnin specifies the time after which we want to start collecting performance data
- ad is a distribution of interarrival times
- sd is a distribution of service times

Note that ad and sd do not have to be exponentially distributed (although, later in the code, we use exponential distributions for testing purposes). This is one of the advantages of the simulator over an analytical solution. We use the Distributions.jl package to supply us with the library of distributions.

The simulator follows the logic of processing events we described earlier. It has four key variables:

- `now` keeps track of the current time in the simulation; the simulation starts at time 0.
- `nextArrival` holds the time when the next arrival of the customer will occur.
- `nextDeparture` stores the time when the next service of the customer will finish. Here, we have a special situation whereby a system may be empty; in such cases, there is no scheduled next departure, so we say that it is "infinity" and set this variable to `Inf`.
- `queue` holds information about the arrival times of customers that are currently in the system (either being served, or waiting in a queue to start their service); initially, it is empty.

The main `while` loop of the simulator moves the `now` time forward to the next event. If it is an arrival (that is when `nextArrival < nextDeparture`), we do the following:

- Check if this is the only customer in the system, in which case we start the service immediately and schedule `nextDeparture` time
- Add the customer to a queue
- Schedule the arrival of the next customer

On the other hand, if the next event is the departure of the customer, we do the following instead:

- Remove one customer from the queue
- Register the customer sojourn time, but only if the current time is after the `burnin` time but before the `until` time
- Start serving the next customer in the queue, or note that there is no service taking place by setting `nextDeparture` to `Inf`

We keep track of the average time in the system using the `OnlineStats.jl` package, outlined in the *Running Monte Carlo simulations* recipe. Observe that implementing a simple single server queue was very simple in Julia—we achieved this with just 20 lines of code.

Next, note that the `mm1_exact` function has the `Exponential` requirement for the arguments in its signature, as opposed to `queue1`, which allowed any `Distribution`. This is an illustration of how in Julia you can control which arguments are applicable in which case. The `queue1` function is fully general, but `mm1_exact` only works for an M/M/1 queuing system.

In the `bootCI` function, the `rand(data, length(data))` expression performs sampling with replacement. The `quantile` function calculates the required ends of a confidence interval using the percentile bootstrap method. We return the result of the procedure as `NamedTuple`.

When running the code, observe that we measure the execution time of lengthy operations using the `@time` macro (note that timings also include the compilation time). Also, in order to clearly see if our confidence interval coincides with the theoretical value, we analyze the difference of collected data from the analytical result. In the data, we use a 99% confidence interval, which means that in 99 out of 100 simulation runs, we expect the interval to have zero inside.

In fact, we could make the `bootCI` function even more efficient, by avoiding excess memory allocation. An improved implementation is presented as follows:

```
function bootCI(data, stat::Function, CI::Float64, reps::Integer)
    tmp = similar(data)
    boot = [stat(rand!(tmp, data)) for i in 1:reps]
    low, high = quantile(boot, [(1-CI)/2, (1+CI)/2])
    (value=stat(data), low=low, high=high)
end
```

Avoiding reallocation using the `rand!` function reduces execution time by roughly 10%.

There's more...

In Julia, it is also simple to implement not only standard frequentist bootstrapping but also the Bayesian bootstrap (https://projecteuclid.org/euclid.aos/1176345338). Here is a sample implementation for the mean:

```
using StatsBase, Distributions

function bayesbootCI(data, stat, CI::Float64, reps::Integer)
    d = Dirichlet(length(data), 1)
    boot = [stat(data, weights(rand(d))) for i in 1:reps]
    low, high = quantile(boot, [(1-CI)/2, (1+CI)/2])
    (value=stat(data), low=low, high=high)
end
```

In this case, the `stat` function must accept two arguments—the data vector and the weight vector. Such a method for `mean` is defined in the `SatsBase.jl` package (if you wanted to run this example and the `StatsBase.jl` is missing then you can install it using the commands: `using Pkg; Pkg.add("StatsBase")`).

The `run` function for the same simulation results as used earlier produces very similar results:

```
(mean = 0.0013208713432, low = -0.007849598425, high = 0.010608716624)
```

The interpretation of the resulting interval is obviously different (Bayesian vs frequentist).

See also

Usage of the `OnlineStats.jl` package is discussed in the *Running Monte Carlo simulations* recipe.

Working with complex numbers

Julia has first-class support for complex number arithmetic. Coupling this with powerful comprehension functionality allows you to easily perform complex computations. In this recipe, we will show how to plot a Julia set.

Getting ready

Make sure you have the `PyPlot.jl` package installed. If it is missing run the `using Pkg; Pkg.add("PyPlot")` commands in the Julia command line.

We would like to count how many iterations are required for repeated application of a mapping $f(x) = x^2 - 0.4 + 0.6i$ to reach a value whose norm is greater than two. The number of iterations depends on the point from which we start the iterations. We will plot a heat map showing this relationship. You can find more details about the Julia set at http://mathworld.wolfram.com/JuliaSet.html or https://en.wikipedia.org/wiki/Julia_set.

 In the GitHub repository for this recipe, you will find the `commands.txt` file that contains the presented sequence of shell and Julia commands.

Now open your favorite terminal to execute the commands.

How to do it...

In this recipe, we will write some code that generates the plot of the Julia set as follows:

1. First, define the following `juliapoint` function:

```
julia> function juliapoint(z, c)
           for n in 1:255
               z = z^2 + c
               abs2(z) > 4 && return n
           end
           return 256
       end
juliapoint (generic function with 1 method)
```

2. Next, test the `juliapoint` function on sample input data:

```
julia> using PyPlot

julia> xs = -1.4:0.002:1.4;

julia> ys = -1.05:0.002:1.05;

julia> c = -0.4+0.6im;

julia> res = [juliapoint(complex(x, y), c) for y in ys, x in xs];

julia> imshow(res, extent=[extrema(xs)..., extrema(ys)...],
cmap="gray_r")
PyObject <matplotlib.image.AxesImage object at 0x00000000014448D0>
```

After you run the cell, you should get the following diagram as a product:

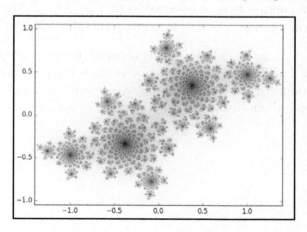

How it works...

We use several important features of Julia in this example.

Firstly, observe that the `juliapoint` function is fast. Loops in Julia incur no penalty, contrary to a typical scripting language. The second thing to notice is that there is nothing special in how you write your code to handle complex numbers—it just works. All operations (addition, among many others) have specialized methods supporting complex numbers.

Notice that we use the `abs2` function—it is faster than the `abs` function because it avoids taking a square root.

An expression such as `-1.4:0.002:1.4` is a handy way to define a range of values with a given step (`0.002` in this case).

The `res` vector is created using a comprehension with a general form of `[expression for i in collection]`. We supplied two variables over which the loop is run, `ys` and `xs`, so in the end result, we got a matrix that can be checked by using the `size` function. In the next Jupyter Notebook cell, write:

```
julia> size(res)
```

This should give us the following output:

```
(1051, 1401)
```

We have used the `imshow` function from the `PyPlot.jl` package to plot a heat map of the `res` matrix. The resulting plot is correctly displayed in Jupyter Notebook.

You can see that we can naturally pass parameters that are required by `imshow` in `matplotlib`. This shows you how easy it is to integrate Julia with Python.

The `[extrema(xs)..., extrema(ys)...]` command deserves attention, as it performs two actions in a single line. The `extrema` function extracts the minimum and maximum element from a collection. Additionally, since `imshow` requires a single array of ranges for the x and y axes, we split them (using `...` operator) into a vector construction literal.

We can confirm that this is actually how it behaves by running the following code:

```julia
julia> [extrema(xs)..., extrema(ys)...]
4-element Array{Float64,1}:
 -1.4
  1.4
 -1.05
  1.05
```

There's more...

You can find more details on how Julia handles complex numbers at `https://docs.julialang.org/en/latest/manual/complex-and-rational-numbers/`.

See also

Please refer to the `PyPlot.jl` package documentation for details about its usage. This can be found at `https://github.com/JuliaPy/PyPlot.jl`.

Writing a simple optimization routine

Performing optimization is a common data science task. In this recipe, we implement a simple optimization routine using the Marquardt algorithm. For more information on this, see `http://mathworld.wolfram.com/Levenberg-MarquardtMethod.html` or `https://en.wikipedia.org/wiki/Levenberg%E2%80%93Marquardt_algorithm`. In the process of optimizing, we will also discover how Julia handles linear algebra and numerical differentiation.

The basic idea of the procedure is the following. Given a twice differentiable function, $f: R^n \to R$, and some point, $x \in R^n$, we want to find another point, $x' \in R^n$, such that $f(x') < f(x)$. By repeating this process, we want to reach the local the minimum of the f function.

The rule for finding x' is as follows:

$$x' = x - \left(\nabla^2 f(x) + \lambda I\right)^{-1} \nabla f(x)$$

The idea is that we mix two standard algorithms: the Newton algorithm, where the step is $\left(\nabla^2 f(x)\right)^{-1} \nabla f(x)$, and the gradient descent algorithm, where the step is $\lambda^{-1} \nabla f(x)$, where λ is a parameter. We accept x' if it leads to a decrease in the value of f.

The additional rule is that if we have found the direction in which our function decreases, then in the next step we divide λ by α. Consequently, gradient descent gets less weight (the Newton algorithm can be expected to be faster). On the other hand, if the direction did not lead to a decrease, then we multiply λ by α (the search direction was not accurate, so we give more weight to gradient descent).

Getting ready

Make sure you have the `ForwardDiff.jl` package installed. If this package is missing then you can add it by running the following `using Pkg;`
`Pkg.add("ForwardDiff")` commands in the Julia command line.

> In the GitHub repository for this recipe, you will find the `commands.txt` file that contains the presented sequence of shell and Julia commands and the `marquardt.jl` file that contains definition of a function used in this recipe.

Now open your favorite terminal to execute the commands.

How to do it...

In this recipe, we first define the custom optimization routine. Then we define the function we wish to optimize, and, finally, we test it to see if our function works as follows:

1. Run the `marquardt.jl` file using the `include("marquardt.jl")` command in the Julia command line to execute the following code:

```julia
using ForwardDiff
using LinearAlgebra

function marquardt(f, x₀; ε=1e-6, maxiter=1000, λ=10.0^4, α=2)
    x = x₀
    fx = f(x)
    for i in 1:maxiter
        g = ForwardDiff.gradient(f, x)
        norm(g) ≤ ε && return (x=x, converged=true, iters=i)
        x' = x .- (ForwardDiff.hessian(f, x) + λ*I) \ g
        fx' = f(x')
```

```
            if fx' < fx
                λ *= 0.5
                fx = fx'
                x = x'
            else
                λ *= 2.0
            end
        end
        (x=x, converged=false, iters=maxiter)
    end
```

2. Define the function to be optimized in the Julia command line:

```
julia> rosenbrock(x) =
        sum([(1-x[i])^2 + 100(x[i+1]-x[i]^2)^2 for i in
1:length(x)-1])
rosenbrock (generic function with 1 method)
```

3. Finally, test the code:

```
julia> marquardt(rosenbrock, rand(20))
(x = [1.0, 1.0, 1.0, 1.0, 1.0, 1.0, 1.0, 1.0, 1.0, 1.0, 1.0, 1.0,
1.0, 1.0, 1.0, 1.0, 1.0, 1.0, 1.0, 1.0], converged = true, iters =
38)
```

How it works...

`ForwardDiff` is a powerful package, enabling accurate and rapid calculation of derivatives. In this case, we use it for computation of the gradient and Hessian of the optimized function.

Note that ε is a parameter that governs the stopping of our procedure. If the norm of the gradient of the optimized function is below this value, we determine that the algorithm has converged.

In general, we cannot be sure that the Marquardt procedure will always converge. Therefore, we run it for a maximum of `maxiter` steps.

The key line in the code is `x' = x .- (ForwardDiff.hessian(f, x) + λ*I) \ g`, which is an equivalent of the $x' = x - \left(\nabla^2 f(x) + \lambda I \right)^{-1} \nabla f(x)$ formula. In particular, the `A\B` formula yields a solution to the `A*X=B` equation.

There is one additional detail about the preceding code that is worth noting. We use x' and fx' identifiers, which are perfectly valid in Julia; they make the connection between mathematical formulae and code easier to grasp. In order to input a ' type in the Julia console, use \prime and press *Tab*. Similarly, in order to the x_0 input in the function signature, you type x_0 and then press *Tab*.

There's more...

In this recipe, we used the following signature for our method:

```
function marquardt(f, x₀; ε=1e-6, maxiter=1000, λ=10.0^4, α=2)
```

In practice, this is fine. However, if we were preparing a package, it would probably be a good idea to explicitly restrict the allowed types of function arguments. Consider the following example:

```
function marquardt(f::Function, x₀::AbstractVector{<:Real};
                   ε::Real=1e-6, maxiter::Real=1000, λ::Real=10.0^4,
                   α::Real=2)
```

In particular, observe that x_0::AbstractVector{<:Real} means that our function will accept Vector{Int} or Vector{Float64} for the x_0 argument. Note that if we had written x_0::AbstractVector{Real}, then such vectors would not be acceptable, because the Julia type system is invariant. See the *Understanding subtyping in Julia* recipe in Chapter 5, *Variables, Types, and Functions*, for an explanation.

See also

Optimization packages and recipes are given in Chapter 9, *Data Science*.

A full explanation of type stability of the code is given in *Ensuring type stability of your code* recipe in Chapter 6, *Metaprogramming and Advanced Typing*.

Estimating a linear regression

Linear regression is one of the basic models for predictive modeling. In this recipe, we show you how to implement a fully functional method that allows the estimation of such models. This recipe mainly concentrates on array manipulation, but also shows a typical example of more complex Julia code, combining several standard functionalities.

Getting ready

Make sure you have the `DataFrames.jl` and `CSV.jl` packages installed. If they are missing, add them using the following commands:

```julia
julia> using Pkg

julia> Pkg.add("DataFrames")

julia> Pkg.add("CSV")
```

Linear regression is a model following the $y = \alpha_0 + \sum_{i=1}^{k} \alpha_i x_i + \varepsilon$ formula. It is known that if you define vector Y as the observations of the explained variables and a matrix $X = [1, X_1, X_2, \ldots, X_k]$ of explanatory variables, then the least squares estimator of α is $(X^T X)^{-1} X^T Y$.

We can see that, in this formula, both explained and explanatory variables must be numeric. In practice, a typical challenge is that raw explanatory variables are often nominal. In such cases, these variables are encoded using a one-hot approach (see https://scikit-learn.org/stable/modules/generated/sklearn.preprocessing.OneHotEncoder.html or https://en.wikipedia.org/wiki/One-hot) with a selected reference class. This is the approach we will use in our procedure.

In the GitHub repository for this recipe, you will find the `commands.txt` file that contains the presented sequence of shell and Julia commands and the `lm.jl` file that contains the definition of a function used in this recipe. Also the `wages.csv` file, containing the data which we will use for estimation, is located in the repository.

Now open your favorite terminal to execute the commands.

How to do it...

In the first step of the recipe, we define a function estimating linear regression, then in the second step, we test it out on a simple example:

1. Run the `include("lm.jl")` command in the Julia command line to execute the following code that is contained in the `lm.jl` file:

```
using DataFrames

function df2mm(df::DataFrame)
    n = size(df, 1)
    mm_raw = [fill(1.0, n, 1)]
    mm_name = ["const"]
    for (name, value) in eachcol(df)
        if eltype(value) <: Real
            push!(mm_raw, hcat(Float64.(value)))
            push!(mm_name, string(name))
        else
            uvalue = unique(value)
            length(uvalue) == 1 && continue
            dvalue = Dict(v=>i for (i, v) in enumerate(uvalue))
            mvalue = zeros(n, length(uvalue))
            for i in 1:n
                mvalue[i, dvalue[value[i]]] = 1.0
            end
            push!(mm_raw, mvalue[:, 2:end])
            append!(mm_name, string.(name, "_", uvalue[2:end]))
        end
    end
    (data=hcat(mm_raw...), names=mm_name)
end

function lm(df, y, xs)
    yv = Float64.(df[y])
    xv, xn = df2mm(df[[xs;]])
    params = (transpose(xv)*xv)\(transpose(xv)*yv)
    DataFrame(name = xn, estimate=params)
end
```

2. Now test it on an example data set:

```
julia> using CSV

julia> wages = CSV.read("wages.csv",
                        allowmissing=:none,
                        categorical=true);
```

```
julia> lm(wages, :LWage, setdiff(names(wages), [:LWage]))
12×2 DataFrame
 | Row | name        | estimate   |
 |     | String      | Float64    |
 |-----|-------------|------------|
 |  1  | const       | 5.45403    |
 |  2  | Exp         | 0.0103709  |
 |  3  | Wks         | 0.00494447 |
 |  4  | BlueCol_yes | -0.148634  |
 |  5  | Ind         | 0.0530578  |
 |  6  | South_no    | 0.0532101  |
 |  7  | SMSA_yes    | 0.145304   |
 |  8  | Married_no  | -0.0660799 |
 |  9  | Sex_female  | -0.353302  |
 | 10  | Union_yes   | 0.102076   |
 | 11  | Ed          | 0.0571539  |
 | 12  | Black_yes   | -0.167123  |
```

How it works...

We have two methods defined in the preceding code, df2mm and lm. The first one transforms DataFrame of explanatory variables into a matrix, using one-hot encoding if needed. The second performs model estimation.

The df2mm method, which prepares a model matrix, is more complex. It iteratively scans all columns of df. If a column contains real values, then it is simply added to the model matrix; if not, a one-hot encoding is applied and an mvalue submatrix is created. We use a dvalue dictionary to map levels to their numbers. Note that we drop the first column of this matrix to avoid linear dependence of columns in the resulting matrix.

In parallel, the function generates the column names of the matrix created.

The lm function is simpler. It takes a DataFrame df, the name of the y explained column, and the names of the xs explanatory columns. One idiom that is worth commenting on in its body is [xs;]. If xs is a vector, then the result is also a vector. However, if xs is a single value, it gets wrapped in a vector. In this way, we can pass a single column as an xs argument to lm without having to wrap it in a vector. The reason for doing this is that passing a single symbol to getindex of the DataFrame object would yield a vector, not a DataFrame.

In this recipe, we read in the data from the wages.csv file into a DataFrame using the CSV.jl package. More details about working with data frames are presented in Chapter 7, *Handling Analytical Data*.

There's more...

Implementing ordinary least squares is a good exercise, allowing you to learn how to implement it in Julia, but in practice you would not use this code directly (unless you have a very simple problem and do not want to introduce dependencies in your code). There are advanced packages allowing estimation of regression in the Julia ecosystem. The most popular one is `https://github.com/JuliaStats/GLM.jl`. It has a more advanced functionality, along with statistical inference.

Also, note that the `df2mm` function has two important special cases.

The first one is that it is possible that an array can contain only numbers, but can have some more general type. For instance, `Any[1, 2, 3]` would be considered by this function as a categorical variable and would get one-hot encoded. As this behavior can be sometimes desirable, it can be left unchanged. The only thing to remember is to pass numeric values in a vector of numeric type.

The other case is the handling of `missing` values since linear regression does not accept them. Fortunately, it is easy to filter out rows with `missing` data in `DataFrame`. Here is a modified `lm` function that does precisely that:

```
function lm(df, y, xs)
    df = disallowmissing!(dropmissing!(df[[y; xs]]))
    yv = Float64.(df[y])
    xv, xn = df2mm(df[[xs;]])
    params = (transpose(xv)*xv)\(transpose(xv)*yv)
    DataFrame(name = xn, estimate=params)
end
```

We remove the rows with missing values in two steps:

1. The `dropmissing!` function removes rows with missing data in explained or explanatory variables.
2. The `disallowmissing!` function makes sure that the type of the resulting vector does not allow `missing` (which is important, as, in `df2mm`, we only treat columns of the `AbstractVector{<:Real}` type as numeric).

See also

Additional information about working with the `DataFrame` type and about working with `missing` values is given in `Chapter 7`, *Handling Analytical Data*.

Understanding broadcasting in Julia

Julia has a very powerful piece of built-in functionality for vectorizing operations. It is very simple, as you only need to add a dot, `.`, after the name of a function, or annotate an expression with `@.` to vectorize it. In this recipe, we will explain in detail how this mechanism works.

A common operation in data science is getting a subset of the original dataset. In this recipe, we will generate a vector and then will randomly select 50% of its odd rows.

Getting ready

Now open your favorite terminal to execute the commands.

 In the GitHub repository for this recipe, you will find the `commands.txt` file that contains the presented sequence of shell and Julia commands.

How to do it...

We will compare different options for applying to broadcast to a vector of data:

1. First, generate the vector we want to work within the Julia console:

```
julia> x = [1:10;]
10-element Array{Int64,1}:
  1
  2
  3
  4
  5
  6
  7
  8
  9
 10
```

We have a `10` element column vector. We want to randomly select 50% of its odd rows. For this, we want to create a Boolean row selector.

2. Here are two equivalent ways to generate the vector (run this code in the Julia console):

```julia
julia> s = isodd.(x) .& (rand(length(x)) .< 0.5)
10-element BitArray{1}:
 true
 false
 false
 false
 false
 false
 false
 false
 true
 false
julia> s = @. isodd(x) & ($rand($length(x)) < 0.5)
10-element BitArray{1}:
 true
 false
 false
 false
 false
 false
 false
 false
 true
 false
```

Observe that in the first case we have applied . to all the functions we wanted to broadcast, and when using the @. macro, we have protected the functions we did not want to broadcast with $. Using $ protects the function from being broadcasted over.

Another minor issue to note is operator precedence. We had to take rand(length(x)) .< 0.5 in parentheses, as, otherwise, the .& operation would be performed first. This is an important case because the && and || control flow operators have lower precedence than comparison operators such as <, whereas & and | have the same precedence as multiplication.

How it works...

In order to understand how the dot operator (.) works, it is best to study the possible results from different ways of applying to broadcast to `rand(length(x))` in our preceding example:

- **Case 1**: Not broadcasting `rand(length(x))`—in this case, the result is a 10-element `Vector{Float64}`.

- **Case 2**: Broadcasting the `rand.(length(x))` outer function—in this case, the result is also a 10-element `Vector{Float64}`. The reason for this is that `rand.(length(x))` is rewritten by Julia to something similar to `broadcast(v -> rand(v), length(x))`, and because we are effectively broadcasting over one element where `length(x)` is 10, and nothing changes.

- **Case 3**: Broadcasting the `rand(length.(x))` inner function—in this case, the result is 1. This is puzzling. The reason is that `rand(length.(x))` is rewritten by Julia as something similar to `rand(broadcast(v -> length(v), x))`. But elements of `x` are scalars so `broadcast(v -> length(v), x)` produces a 10-element vector containing only value 1. When `rand` gets a vector as an input, it draws a single element from it. Since the vector contains the same value 10 times over—it is returned.

- **Case 4**: Broadcasting both `rand.(length.(x))` functions—in this case, the result is a 10-element array of arrays containing one random value. This looks like the following (note that you might have different numbers because we used a random number generator):

  ```
  10-element Array{Array{Float64,1},1}:
   [0.391009]
   [0.0199535]
   [0.606183]
   [0.3963]
   [0.239723]
   [0.320903]
   [0.699059]
   [0.026546]
   [0.3563]
   [0.86077]
  ```

Why did we get such a result? We already know that `rand.(length.(x))` is rewritten by Julia as something similar to `broadcast(v -> rand(length(v)), x)`, and we are effectively applying a composition of the `rand` and `length` functions to consecutive elements of `x`. Because they are scalars, the `length` function always returns 1, and as a consequence we call `rand(1)`, which produces one element random vector.

As a rule of thumb, we recommend using `@.` only if there is a lot of broadcasting in your expression, and you are absolutely sure that you have remembered to escape all functions that must not be broadcasted over, with `$` in the expression. As you can imagine, this is easy to forget, so in practice it is safer to be explicit about which functions you want to broadcast over. You can easily make a mistake when you use functions that specifically expect vectors as their arguments (like `rand` or `length`, in our example).

There's more...

As we have seen, a chain of broadcasted functions is rewritten by Julia to perform only a single pass over the arguments. Consider the following example:

```
exp.(sin.(cos.(log.(1:100))))
```

The preceding code is fused into an operation similar to the following:

```
broadcast(v -> exp(sin(cos(log(v)))), 1:100)
```

The consequence is that there is only one allocation of memory to produce the final result of the operation. In standard scripting languages, each step of the computation would typically use up new memory. This is both computationally inefficient and memory expensive. Such seemingly minor details make Julia shine in numerical computing applications.

See also

You can read more about broadcasting in the Julia manual in the following sections:

- https://docs.julialang.org/en/latest/manual/mathematical-operations/#man-dot-operators-1
- https://docs.julialang.org/en/latest/manual/functions/#man-vectorized-1

- https://docs.julialang.org/en/latest/manual/arrays/#Broadcasting-1
- https://docs.julialang.org/en/latest/base/arrays/#Broadcast-and-vectorization-1

Improving code performance using @inbounds

Often, especially in performance-critical code, we want to squeeze the maximum speed out of Julia. If you are working with arrays, the @inbounds macro can be used to significantly reduce access time to the elements. The drawback is that you have to be sure that you are not trying to access an out-of-bounds location.

Getting ready

Inspect the inbounds.jl file that contains the following contents:

```
using BenchmarkTools
mode = ["normal", "@inbounds"]
i = 0
for inbounds in ["", "@inbounds"]
    global i += 1
    eval(Meta.parse("""function f$i(x::AbstractArray{<:Real})
                    y = 0
                    $inbounds for i in eachindex(x)
                        y += x[i] > 0.5
                    end
                    y
                end"""))
end

x = rand(10^7)
for (idx, f) in enumerate([f1, f2])
    println("\n", mode[idx])
    @btime $f($x)
end
```

In the GitHub repository for this recipe, you will find the commands.txt file that contains the presented sequence of shell and Julia commands and the inbounds.jl file that contains definitions used in this recipe.

Now open your favorite terminal to execute the commands.

How to do it...

Run the following three commands from the OS shell:

```
$ julia inbounds.jl
normal
 11.705 ms (0 allocations: 0 bytes)
@inbounds
 5.488 ms (0 allocations: 0 bytes)

$ julia --check-bounds=yes inbounds.jl
normal
 11.778 ms (0 allocations: 0 bytes)
@inbounds
 11.772 ms (0 allocations: 0 bytes)

$ julia --check-bounds=no inbounds.jl
normal
 5.519 ms (0 allocations: 0 bytes)
@inbounds
 5.485 ms (0 allocations: 0 bytes)
```

How it works...

Normally, when you try to access any element of an array in Julia, it checks whether the index is valid. See the following code snippet as an example:

```
julia> x = [1,2,3]
3-element Array{Int64,1}:
 1
 2
 3
julia> x[4]
ERROR: BoundsError: attempt to access 3-element Array{Int64,1} at index [4]
```

You can disable bounds checking, using the @inbounds macro. In our example, it halved the execution time. You can see the difference in the assembly code emitted by Julia, depending on the bounds checking flag, by analyzing the following example (the @code_native macro prints native assembly instructions generated for a method call):

```julia
julia> f(x) = @inbounds x[1]
f (generic function with 1 method)

julia> g(x) = x[1]
g (generic function with 1 method)

julia> @code_native f([1])
 .text
; Function f {
; Location: REPL[3]:1
        pushq %rbp
        movq %rsp, %rbp
; Function getindex; {
; Location: array.jl:731
        movq (%rcx), %rax
        movq (%rax), %rax
;}
        popq %rbp
        retq
        nopl (%rax)
;}

julia> @code_native g([1])
 .text
; Function g {
; Location: console[2]:1
; Function getindex; {
; Location: console[2]:1
 cmpq $0, 8(%rcx)
 je L14
 movq (%rcx), %rax
 movq (%rax), %rax
;}
 retq
L14:
 pushq %rbp
 movq %rsp, %rbp
; Function getindex; {
; Location: array.jl:661
 movl $16, %eax
 movabsq $1897086832, %r11 # imm = 0x71133F70
 callq *%r11
```

```
    subq %rax, %rsp
    movq %rsp, %rdx
    movq $1, (%rdx)
    subq $32, %rsp
    movabsq $jl_bounds_error_ints, %rax
    movl $1, %r8d
    callq *%rax
    addq $32, %rsp
    ud2
    nopl (%rax)
;}}
```

We can also see that the `--check-bounds` switch makes Julia disregard the `@inbounds` macro, and either enables or disables bounds checking throughout the entire program.

In this code, we also see three important elements of Julia in their simplest form:

- Using the `eachindex` function to traverse all the indices of an array; this approach is fully general, as different specialized arrays might define non-standard indexing.
- Dynamic generation of code using the `Meta.parse` and `eval` functions: we have created two almost identical functions; they differed by whether they had the `@inbounds` macro invocation. We had a string containing Julia code, into which `$inbounds` interpolated an appropriate value of the `inbounds` variable string; then this string was interpreted as Julia code.
- Benchmarking code performance, using the `@btime` macro from the `BenchmarkTools.jl` package.

There's more...

If you are developing a function in which you want to allow its user to disable bounds checking, you can use the `@boundscheck` macro. Here is an example function definition from `base/bitarray.jl`:

```
@inline function getindex(B::BitArray, i::Int)
    @boundscheck checkbounds(B, i)
    unsafe_bitgetindex(B.chunks, i)
end
```

This annotation will only have an effect if the function, `getindex` in this case, is inlined into a caller. Therefore, the `@inline` macro is used at the beginning of its definition.

Additional tips about performance annotations can be found at https://docs.julialang.org/en/latest/manual/performance-tips/#man-performance-annotations-1.

See also

Information about benchmarking Julia code is given in the *Benchmarking Code* recipe in Chapter 8, *Julia Workflow*.

Code parsing and evaluation from a string are easy to understand, but it is error-prone and there are more powerful tools for automatic code manipulation in Julia. More advanced examples of Julia metaprogramming facilities are discussed in Chapter 6, *Metaprogramming and Advanced Typing*.

Creating a matrix from a set of vectors as rows

Julia has a powerful set of matrix manipulation features. However, since vectors are one-dimensional and matrices are two-dimensional, people often need to switch from one to the other. In this recipe, we show an example of how to create a matrix from a set of vectors as rows.

Getting ready

Let's assume that you have the following input dataset:

```
julia> input = [[10i+1:10i+5;] for i in 1:3]
3-element Array{Array{Int64,1},1}:
 [11, 12, 13, 14, 15]
 [21, 22, 23, 24, 25]
 [31, 32, 33, 34, 35]
```

From that dataset, you wish to create the following matrix:

```
julia> output = [10i+j for i in 1:3, j in 1:5]
3×5 Array{Int64,2}:
 11 12 13 14 15
 21 22 23 24 25
 31 32 33 34 35
```

Make sure that the `input` and `output` variables are defined as before in your Julia console before trying out the recipe so that you can test whether proper results are obtained.

 In the GitHub repository for this recipe, you will find the `commands.txt` file that contains the presented sequence of shell and Julia commands.

Now open your favorite terminal to execute the commands.

How to do it...

We will go through several possible attempts to achieve the desired result, and compare the effects:

1. As a first step, it is natural to begin by applying the `hcat` or `vcat` functions to `input`:

```
julia> hcat(input...)
5×3 Array{Int64,2}:
 11  21  31
 12  22  32
 13  23  33
 14  24  34
 15  25  35

julia> vcat(x...)
15-element Array{Int64,1}:
 11
 12
 13
 14
 15
 21
 22
 23
 24
 25
 31
 32
 33
 34
 35
```

Unfortunately, they both produce a result different than `output`. The reason is that the entries of `input` are treated as column vectors.

2. This suggests to us a hint: using `vcat` transposed vectors (this time, we used the `reduce` function on the `vcat` function, instead of splitting):

```julia
julia> reduce(vcat, transpose.(input))
3x5 Array{Int64,2}:
 11 12 13 14 15
 21 22 23 24 25
 31 32 33 34 35
```

This solution worked.

3. For completeness, check that running the `hcat` function on the transposed vectors gives the following result:

```julia
julia> hcat(transpose.(input)...)
1x15 LinearAlgebra.Transpose{Int64,Array{Int64,1}}:
 11 12 13 14 15 21 22 23 24 25 31 32 33 34 35
```

Of course, this should be expected.

4. Another approach is to transpose the result of `hcat` of the original vectors:

```julia
julia> transpose(hcat(input...))
3x5 LinearAlgebra.Transpose{Int64,Array{Int64,2}}:
 11 12 13 14 15
 21 22 23 24 25
 31 32 33 34 35
```

5. An alternative to the `transpose` function is to use the `reshape` function:

```julia
julia> vcat(reshape.(input, 1, :)...)
3x5 Array{Int64,2}:
 11 12 13 14 15
 21 22 23 24 25
 31 32 33 34 35
```

And once again, we get the desired result.

How it works...

Observe the following:

```julia
julia> hcat(input[1])
5×1 Array{Int64,2}:
 11
 12
 13
 14
 15
```

This allows you to transform a one-dimensional column vector to a two-dimensional column matrix.

It is worth remembering that `transpose` creates a thin wrapper around the original array. This means that if we modify the transposed matrix, the original will also be modified. See the following code as an example:

```julia
julia> x = [1 2; 3 4]
2×2 Array{Int64,2}:
 1 2
 3 4

julia> y = transpose(x)
2×2 LinearAlgebra.Transpose{Int64,Array{Int64,2}}:
 1 3
 2 4

julia> y[1] = 100
100

julia> x
2×2 Array{Int64,2}:
 100 2
   3 4
```

There's more...

Additionally, `transpose` is a recursive function, since it is designed to be used in linear algebra applications. If you do not want the recursive operation, use the `permutedims` function:

```julia
julia> hcat(permutedims.(input)...)
1×15 Array{Int64,2}:
```

```
11 12 13 14 15 21 22 23 24 25 31 32 33 34 35

julia> vcat(permutedims.(input)...)
3×5 Array{Int64,2}:
 11 12 13 14 15
 21 22 23 24 25
 31 32 33 34 35

julia> permutedims(hcat(input...))
3×5 Array{Int64,2}:
 11 12 13 14 15
 21 22 23 24 25
 31 32 33 34 35
```

Additionally, we can see that `permutedims` allocates a fresh array.

Finally, you might wonder how to perform a reverse transformation, that is, to generate `input` from `output`. This is very easy to achieve using comprehensions:

```
julia> [output[i,:] for i in 1:size(output, 1)]
3-element Array{Array{Int64,1},1}:
 [11, 12, 13, 14, 15]
 [21, 22, 23, 24, 25]
 [31, 32, 33, 34, 35]
```

We could have used a comprehension to get `output` from `input` like this:

```
julia> [input[i][j] for i in 1:length(input), j in 1:length(input[1])]
3×5 Array{Int64,2}:
 11 12 13 14 15
 21 22 23 24 25
 31 32 33 34 35
```

But, the drawback is that, here, we assume that all elements of the `input` vector have the same length without checking it and that the `input` vector has at least one element.

You can find more details about how arrays work in Julia by referencing the official documentation, available at https://docs.julialang.org/en/v1.0/.

Using array views to avoid memory allocation

Sudoku is a popular mathematical puzzle. If you have never played this game it is worth reading a description of it at https://www.kristanix.com/sudokuepic/sudoku-rules.php or https://en.wikipedia.org/wiki/Sudoku.

In this recipe, we will show how you can solve this puzzle using a backtracking approach. The general idea of this algorithm is to incrementally test candidate solutions of Sudoku, and if they fail, go back (backtrack) one step. You can read more about this method at https://www.geeksforgeeks.org/backtracking-introduction/ or https://en.wikipedia.org/wiki/Backtracking.

Solving Sudoku using backtracking is a basic computational technique. In this recipe, we will show how using array views can improve the performance of such code.

Getting ready

We want to solve 50 Sudoku problems specified in the Project Euler problem 96, see https://projecteuler.net/problem=96. The task is to find the sum of 50 three-digit numbers present in the top left corner of the solution to the puzzles given in the p096_sudoku.txt file. The initial lines of this file are the following:

```
Grid 01
003020600
900305001
001806400
008102900
700000008
006708200
002609500
800203009
005010300
Grid 02
200080300
060070084
030500209
000105408
000000000
402706000
301007040
720040060
004010003
```

In this file, each puzzle consists of nine lines of nine digits. Where digits from 1 to 9 denote the known parts of the Sudoku puzzle and digit 0 represents the unknown parts.

Next, inspect the sudoku.jl file that contains the code that we will run and modify in this recipe:

```
blockvalid(x, v) = count(isequal(v), x) ≤ 1

function backtrack!(x)
    pos = findfirst(isequal(0), x)
    isa(pos, Nothing) && return true
    iloc = 3div(pos[1]-1, 3) .+ (1:3)
    jloc = 3div(pos[2]-1, 3) .+ (1:3)
    for k in 1:9
        x[pos] = k
        blockvalid(view(x, pos[1], :), k) || continue
        blockvalid(view(x, :, pos[2]), k) || continue
        blockvalid(view(x, iloc, jloc), k) || continue
        backtrack!(x) && return true
    end
    x[pos] = 0
    return false
end

function ssolve(lines, i)
    t = [lines[10i-j][k] - '0' for j in 8:-1:0, k in 1:9]
    backtrack!(t)
    sum([100, 10, 1] .* t[1, 1:3])
end

lines = readlines("p096_sudoku.txt")
@time sum(ssolve(lines, i) for i in 1:50)
@time sum(ssolve(lines, i) for i in 1:50)
```

 In the GitHub repository for this recipe, you will find the commands.txt file that contains the presented sequence of shell and Julia commands, the sudoku.jl file that contains definitions of functions used in this recipe, and the p096_sudoku.txt file that contains the input data for the Sudoku puzzles.

Now open your favorite terminal to execute the commands.

How to do it...

We will analyze how the `view` function can improve the performance of your code, firstly by running the code using views, and then by changing it to work on creating new arrays:

1. Execute the `sudoku.jl` file from the system shell:

```
$ julia sudoku.jl
  1.033830 seconds (1.09 M allocations: 61.133 MiB, 0.72% gc time)
  0.264584 seconds (26.52 k allocations: 1.545 MiB)
```

2. Change lines 10-12 in the `sudoku.jl` file so as not to use `view`, but rather the standard `getindex` routine that copies a matrix. The altered lines should look like this:

```
blockvalid(x[pos[1], :], k) || continue
blockvalid(x[:, pos[2]], k) || continue
blockvalid(x[iloc, jloc], k) || continue
```

3. Now run the file again:

```
$ julia sudoku.jl
  1.555036 seconds (10.94 M allocations: 1.544 GiB, 2.87% gc time)
  0.844457 seconds (10.05 M allocations: 1.496 GiB, 3.86% gc time)
```

As you can see, the execution time and memory usage have increased significantly (the second result is important and bears close examination, as the first one also includes compilation time and memory usage).

How it works...

In the code we have the following three functions:

- `blockvalid`: This is a helper function that tests if a given block of data, x, contains at most one occurrence of a value, v.
- `backtrack!`: This is a core function of the recipe; it takes a matrix, x, and as a result returns `true` or `false`, depending on whether x is a valid Sudoku problem; the function modifies x in place (so if it returns `true`, then x contains the solution to the problem), and therefore we add `!` at its end (this is a standard convention in Julia).

- `ssolve`: This is a data preparation function. It preprocesses the lines read from the `p096_sudoku.txt` file to a matrix, and after calling `backtrack!`, it extracts the first three numbers in the upper-left corner of the Sudoku solution as it was described in the *Getting ready* section. After the preprocessing, we obtain a 9 x 9 matrix. It contains zeros in places where information about a number in the puzzle is missing and values from 1 to 9 in places where we have the information.

The key part of the recipe is understanding the `backtrack!` function. It works by means of the following steps:

1. First, it tries to find the first 0 in the x matrix.
2. If `pos` is `nothing` (a value of type `Nothing`), this means that 0 was not found, so the puzzle has been solved and we return `true`.
3. Otherwise, `pos` is the location of the first 0. The type of this value is `CartesianIndex`; we can access its first and second dimensions using `pos[1]` and `pos[2]`.
4. The `iloc` and `jloc` values give us the range of a 3 x 3 square in Sudoku, where `pos` is located.
5. Next, we try to put values from 1 to 9 into the `pos` location; if entering some number there creates a valid row, column, and 3 x 3 square, then we recursively call `backtrack!` again with this position filled. If instead, it returns `true`, then we are done with solving the puzzle, so we also return `true`.
6. If we moved through values from 1 to 9 and couldn't solve the puzzle for any of them, this means that we have to backtrack, since we must have made a wrong decision earlier. Therefore, we set `x[pos]` to 0 to clean up all changes made and return `false`.

The most time-consuming part of the procedure is calling the `blockvalid` function. We saw earlier that it is much more efficient to pass a view of x to this function, instead of allocating small slices of data into new structures.

There's more...

You can make the code in this recipe even faster with a few optimizations:

```
function backtrack!(x, z, idx)
    idx > length(z) && return true
    pos = z[idx]
    iloc = 3div(pos[1]-1, 3)
    jloc = 3div(pos[2]-1, 3)
    filled = 0
    @inbounds for k in 1:9
        filled |= x[pos[1], k] | x[k, pos[2]]
    end
    @inbounds for k1 in 1:3, k2 in 1:3
        filled |= x[iloc+k1, jloc+k2]
    end
    @inbounds for i in 1:9
        k = 1<<i
        if k & filled == 0
            x[pos] = k
            backtrack!(x, z, idx+1) && return true
        end
    end
    x[pos] = 1
    return false
end

function ssolve(lines, i)
    t = [1 << (lines[10i-j][k] - '0') for j in 8:-1:0, k in 1:9]
    z = findall(isequal(1), t)
    backtrack!(t, z, 1)
    sum([100, 10, 1] .* trailing_zeros.(t[1, 1:3]))
end
```

In the preceding code, we did not change the core algorithm. The optimizations we performed are as follows:

- We keep track of zeros in the Sudoku table so that we can avoid running findfirst repeatedly.
- When checking a cell in order to check which entries are possibly valid, we traverse the row, column, and 3 x 3 square only once, remembering which values appeared (now the checks are inlined into the backtrack! function).
- In order to efficiently keep track of the values encountered, we use binary encoding in the integer variable called filled; instead of processing values as ranging from 0 to 9, we process them as ranging from 2^0 to 2^9.

Here are the results from timing the preceding code if it is put in the sudoku.jl file:

```
$ julia sudoku.jl
  0.733585 seconds (867.89 k allocations: 49.576 MiB, 1.05% gc time)
  0.068187 seconds (27.02 k allocations: 1.676 MiB)
```

We can see that we managed to speed up the code by a factor of nearly four.

Further speedups are possible with a smarter search strategy. You can read about alternative algorithms at https://www.kristanix.com/sudokuepic/sudoku-solving-techniques.php or https://en.wikipedia.org/wiki/Sudoku_solving_algorithms.

See also

We could experiment with speeding up the execution of the code even more if we used static arrays, as discussed in the *Using static arrays* recipe in Chapter 6, *Metaprogramming and Advanced Typing*.

Variables, Types, and Functions

5

The chapter contains the following recipes:

- Understanding subtyping in Julia
- Using multiple dispatch to handle branching behavior
- Using functions as variables in Julia
- Functional programming in Julia
- The scope of variables in Julia
- Handling exceptions in Julia
- Working with NamedTuples

Introduction

In this chapter, we present topics related to variables and their scoping, Julia type systems and processing functions, and exceptions in Julia.

We begin by discussing the subtyping mechanism and explaining how to use Julia's multiple dispatch mechanism. We then move on to processing functions and functional programming. Next, we explain how the scoping of variables works in Julia, including differences in the scoping mechanism between global and local scopes. In the next recipe, we show how to handle exceptions and how to create custom-exception objects. Furthermore, we show how named tuples can be used for efficient data structure creation and manipulation.

Understanding subtyping in Julia

In this recipe, we explain how subtyping in Julia works and how you should design method signatures to properly handle subtyping.

Getting ready

In this recipe, we reveal how to define a type that handles Gaussian integers with additional metadata.

A **Gaussian integer** is a complex number whose real and imaginary parts are both integers.

 In the GitHub repository for this recipe you will find the `commands.txt` file that contains the presented sequence of shell and Julia commands.

Now open your favorite terminal to execute commands.

How to do it...

Start with defining the custom `Point` type, and next learn how to store it in an array as follows:

1. First, define the type that you will be working with:

```
julia> struct Point{T<:Integer, S<:AbstractString}
           pos::Complex{T}
           label::S
       end

julia> Point(x::T, y::T, label::S) where {T<:Integer,
                                          S<:AbstractString} =
           Point{T,S}(Complex(x,y), label)
Point

julia> Point(x, y, label) = Point(promote(Integer.((x,y))...)...,
                                  label)
Point
```

2. Next, create a few instances of this type:

```
julia> p1 = Point(1, 0, "1")
Point{Int64,String}(1 + 0im, "1")

julia> p2 = Point(1, 0, SubString("1", 1))
Point{Int64,SubString{String}}(1 + 0im, "1")

julia> p3 = Point(true, false, "1")
Point{Bool,String}(Complex(true,false), "1")

julia> p4 = Point(2, 0, "2")
Point{Int64,String}(2 + 0im, "2")
```

3. Now, test some array constructors:

```
julia> [p1, p2, p3, p4]
4-element Array{Point,1}:
 Point{Int64,String}(1 + 1im, "1")
 Point{Int64,SubString{String}}(1 + 1im, "1")
 Point{Bool,String}(Complex(true,false), "1")
 Point{Int64,String}(2 + 0im, "2")

julia> [p1, p2]
2-element Array{Point{Int64,S} where S<:AbstractString,1}:
 Point{Int64,String}(1 + 1im, "1")
 Point{Int64,SubString{String}}(1 + 1im, "1")

julia> [p1, p3]
2-element Array{Point{T,String} where T<:Integer,1}:
 Point{Int64,String}(1 + 1im, "1")
 Point{Bool,String}(Complex(true,false), "1")

julia> [p1, p4]
2-element Array{Point{Int64,String},1}:
 Point{Int64,String}(1 + 1im, "1")
 Point{Int64,String}(2 + 0im, "2")
```

4. Suppose that you wish to write a method that takes an array of `Point` and returns a new `Point` type that is the sum of passed `Point` instances with an empty label:

```
julia> sumpoint1(v::AbstractVector{Point}) =
           Point(sum(p.pos for p in v), "")
sumpoint1 (generic function with 1 method)
```

Trying this yields the following:

```julia
julia> sumpoint1([p1, p2])
ERROR: MethodError: no method matching
sumpoint1(::Array{Point{Int64,S} where S<:AbstractString,1})
Closest candidates are:
  sumpoint1(::AbstractArray{Point,1}) at REPL[22]:1
Stacktrace:
 [1] top-level scope at none:0
```

5. Let's try another definition:

```julia
julia> sumpoint2(v::AbstractVector{<:Point}) =
           Point(sum(p.pos for p in v), "")
sumpoint2 (generic function with 1 method)
```

The aim of this is to allow the following:

```julia
julia> sumpoint2([p1, p2])
Point{Int64,String}(2 + 2im, "")
```

6. Now we can try defining another function, which takes a single instance of Point:

```julia
julia> foo(p::Point) = "generic definition"
foo (generic function with 1 method)

julia> foo(p::Point{Int, <:AbstractString}) = "default Int passed"
foo (generic function with 2 methods)

julia> foo(p::Point{<:Integer, String}) = "default String passed"
foo (generic function with 3 methods)
```

7. And now we can test it on several point instances:

```julia
julia> foo(Point(true, true, s"12"))
"generic definition"

julia> foo(Point(1, 1, s"12"))
"default Int passed"

julia> foo(Point(true, true, "12"))
"default String passed"

julia> foo(Point(1, 1, "12"))
ERROR: MethodError: foo(::Point{Int64,String}) is ambiguous.
Candidates:
  foo(p::Point{#s1,String} where #s1<:Integer) in Main at
```

```
REPL[13]:1
  foo(p::Point{Int64,#s1} where #s1<:AbstractString) in Main at
REPL[12]:1
Possible fix, define
  foo(::Point{Int64,String})
Stacktrace:
  [1] top-level scope at none:0
```

8. We see that it's necessary to define a specific method for the intersection of types:

```
julia> foo(p::Point{Int, String}) = "most specific method"
foo (generic function with 4 methods)

julia> foo(Point(1, 1, "12"))
"most specific method"
```

How it works...

In this recipe, we define a type, `Point`, which has two parameters, `T` and `S`. Such a definition in itself defines only one type of constructor, and so we add two custom constructors. Here, it is worth highlighting that in the `Point(x, y, label)` constructor, we take its two arguments, `x` and `y`, try converting them to `Integer,` and then `promote` them to a common type so that we ensure that the other constructor accepts the passed data, if required conversions are possible.

The second important feature is storing parametric types in collections. As we could see in the recipe, standard constructors try to find the narrowest possible type that can hold the passed data. This means that if we can expect to encounter heterogeneous data types in the collection, then we should manually specify an appropriate type; for instance, the first example shown fails, while the second works:

```
julia> push!([p1], p2)
ERROR: MethodError: Cannot `convert` an object of type
Point{Int64,SubString{String}} to an object of type Point{Int64,String}
Closest candidates are:
  convert(::Type{T}, ::T) where T at essentials.jl:123
  Point{Int64,String}(::Any, ::Any) where {T<:Integer, S<:AbstractString}
at REPL[1]:2
Stacktrace:
  [1] push!(::Array{Point{Int64,String},1},
::Point{Int64,SubString{String}}) at .\array.jl:830
  [2] top-level scope at none:0

julia> push!(Point[p1], p2)
2-element Array{Point,1}:
```

```
Point{Int64,String}(1 + 0im, "1")
Point{Int64,SubString{String}}(1 + 0im, "1")
```

The final difficult question related to parametric types is the Julia subtyping algorithm, which is important in method dispatch. In Julia, most parametric types are invariant. This means that subtyping of type parameters does not translate to subtyping of parametric types. By way of illustration, consider the following:

```
julia> Int <: Integer
true
```

```
julia> Point{Int, String} <: Point{Integer, String}
false
```

In order to allow for subtyping of types in function signatures, the < : operator is used, for example:

```
julia> Point{Int, String} <: Point{<:Integer, String}
true
```

```
julia> Point{Int, String} <: Point{T, String} where T<:Integer
true
```

The preceding two expressions are equivalent.

Next, it is important to understand that if a parametric type has more than one parameter, we can partially restrict them to a subset, so let's consider the following examples:

```
julia> Point{Int}
Point{Int64,S} where S<:AbstractString
```

```
julia> Point{<:Signed, String}
Point{#s2,String} where #s2<:Signed
```

```
julia> Point{Int}{String}
Point{Int64,String}
```

```
julia> Point{Int, String}
Point{Int64,String}
```

The last two expressions are equivalent, as they represent the application of two parameters to a type.

We can see that type invariance is important in the definition of the `sumpoint1` function, as it only accepts subtypes of `AbstractVector{Point}` and `[p1, p2]` creates `Vector{Point{Int}}`, which is not its subtype. However, the following statement works:

```
julia> sumpoint1(Point[p1, p2])
Point{Int64,String}(2 + 0im, "")
```

Note that we have explicitly set the type of the vector holding `p1` and `p2`. This is a common pitfall in Julia. Fortunately, it is simple to solve this using the `<:` operator, as shown in the `sumpoint2` function.

The last important challenge in defining methods working with parametric types is making sure that we do not leave method dispatch ambiguities. This is shown in the example of the `foo` method. We see that `Point{Int, String}` is a subtype of both `Point{Int, <:AbstractString}` and `Point{<:Integer, String}`. Yet, at the same time, `Point{Int, <:AbstractString}` and `Point{<:Integer, String}` are not subtypes of each other. In this instance, Julia complained that the function call with the `Point{Int, String}` parameter was ambiguous, and we had to define a more specific method removing the ambiguity.

There's more...

You can easily check what methods you have defined for your function using the `methods` function. Let's test it on our `foo` example:

```
julia> methods(foo)
# 4 methods for generic function "foo":
[1] foo(p::Point{Int64,String}) in Main at REPL[24]:1
[2] foo(p::Point{Int64,#s1} where #s1<:AbstractString) in Main at
REPL[12]:1
[3] foo(p::Point{#s1,String} where #s1<:Integer) in Main at REPL[13]:1
[4] foo(p::Point) in Main at REPL[11]:1
```

It is also important to remember that the preceding type invariance rules are not applicable to tuples that are covariant. In short, this means that tuple subtyping behaves as if the `<:` operator were added to every variable in the tuple definition. For instance, consider this example (it has been made complex on purpose to show that subtyping of every entry of `Tuple` type is subtyped):

```
julia> Tuple{Point{Int, String}, Point{Bool, SubString{String}}} <:
Tuple{Point{Int}, Point}
true
```

The consequence is that with tuples, we do not specify < : to get the subtyping behavior we discussed earlier:

```julia
julia> sumpoint_tuple(v::Tuple{Vararg{Point}}) =
           Point(sum(p.pos for p in v), "")
sumpoint_tuple (generic function with 2 methods)

julia> sumpoint_tuple((p1, p2, p3))
Point{Int64,String}(3 + 0im, "")
```

See also

The discussion of parametric types is available at `https://docs.julialang.org/en/v1.0/manual/types/#Parametric-Types-1` in the Julia manual.

Using multiple dispatch to handle branching behavior

Let's assume you have and object of the `DataFrame` type with heterogeneous contents. In this recipe, we will discuss how you can efficiently work with such data using multiple dispatch.

Getting ready

The `DataFrame` type is designed to hold different types of columns. Therefore, you often have a challenge to dynamically decide which operation to perform on a column, depending on its type. In this recipe, we want to create a simplified version of the `describe` function, which will behave differently depending on which type of column passed in.

In order to follow this recipe you need to have the `DataFrames.jl` package installed. If it is missing then you can add it by executing the following commands `using Pkg; Pkg.add("DataFrames")` in the Julia command line.

In the GitHub repository for this recipe you will find the `commands.txt` file that contains the presented sequence of shell and Julia commands.

Now open your favorite terminal to execute commands.

How to do it...

Start with creating a data frame, and next define a function providing its custom description and test how it works.

First, create a sample `DataFrame` object:

```julia
julia> using DataFrames

julia> df = DataFrame(s = categorical(["a", "b", "c"]),
                      n = 1.0:3.0,
                      f = [sin, cos, missing])
3×3 DataFrame
| Row | s            | n       | f        |
|     | Categorical... | Float64 | Function |
|-----|--------------|---------|----------|
| 1   | a            | 1.0     | sin      |
| 2   | b            | 2.0     | cos      |
| 3   | c            | 3.0     | missing  |
```

Here is how we want to display different types of data:

```julia
julia> simpledescribe(v) = "unknown type"
simpledescribe (generic function with 1 method)

julia> simpledescribe(v::Vector{<:Number}) = "numeric"
simpledescribe (generic function with 2 methods)

julia> simpledescribe(v::CategoricalArray) = "categorical"
simpledescribe (generic function with 3 methods)
```

Now, we create a function that walks through a data frame:

```julia
julia> simpledisplay(df) =
           foreach(x -> println(x[1], ": ",
                                 simpledescribe(x[2])),
                   eachcol(df))
simpledisplay (generic function with 1 method)
```

Finally, we can test our `simpledisplay` function:

```
julia> simpledisplay(df)
s: categorical
n: numeric
f: unknown type
```

How it works...

This recipe presents the fundamentals of multiple dispatch in Julia. When the `simpledisplay` function calls the `simpledescribe` function, an appropriate method of this function is called depending on the type of the passed argument.

 In the Julia language we use the following definitions. A **function** is an object that maps a tuple of arguments to some return value. A function can have multiple definitions of possible behavior depending on the types of arguments passed to it. Each such specific behavior defined for a function is called a **method**. When particular arguments are passed to a function, the most specific method applicable to those arguments is applied.

We can inspect which methods are defined for the `simpledescribe` function, using the `methods` function:

```
julia> methods(simpledescribe)
# 3 methods for generic function "simpledescribe":
[1] simpledescribe(v::Array{#s1,1} where #s1<:Number) in Main at REPL[16]:1
[2] simpledescribe(v::CategoricalArray) in Main at REPL[19]:1
[3] simpledescribe(v) in Main at REPL[15]:1
```

There's more...

Such an approach to dispatching is not only convenient but can also speed up computations. In particular, the `DataFrame` type does not convey information about column type to the compiler, so this technique is especially useful. It is called a **barrier function**. Here is an example (you need to install the `BenchmarkTools.jl` package for this example to work; if it is missing then you can add it by executing the following commands `using Pkg; Pkg.add("BenchmarkTools")` in the Julia command line):

```
julia> df = DataFrame(x=1:10^6);

julia> function helper(x)
```

```
                s = zero(eltype(x))
                for v in x
                    s += v
                end
                s
            end
helper (generic function with 1 method)

julia> function fun1(df)
                s = zero(eltype(df[1]))
                for v in df[1]
                    s += v
                end
                s
            end
fun1 (generic function with 1 method)

julia> fun2(df) = helper(df[1])
fun2 (generic function with 1 method)

julia> using BenchmarkTools

julia> @btime fun1(df)
  97.066 ms (3998948 allocations: 76.28 MiB)
500000500000

julia> @btime fun2(df)
  493.591 μs (1 allocation: 16 bytes)
500000500000
```

The reason for the difference is that fun1 is not specialized by the Julia compiler to the type of df[1], while in fun2, the work is passed to a helper function that knows the type of x during compilation time, and Julia is able to generate efficient code computing the desired value.

See also

You can find more details about multiple dispatch in Julia at https://docs.julialang.org/en/v1.0/manual/methods/.

If you want to learn in detail how the DataFrames.jl package works, check out Chapter 7, *Handling Analytical Data*.

Using functions as variables in Julia

In Julia, programming language functions are first-class objects that can be processed and passed as parameters to other functions. This allows for great flexibility in the language syntax.

In this recipe, we will show how to use Julia to manipulate a collection of `struct` objects to carry out a simplified multi-agent simulation model.

Getting ready

For this recipe, no package installation is required. Firstly, start the Julia command line.

In this recipe, we use random numbers—if you want to get exactly the same results such as the ones shown in this recipe, set the random seed value to 0:

```
using Random
Random.seed!(0);
```

 In the GitHub repository for this recipe you will find the `commands.txt` file that contains the presented sequence of Julia commands.

How to do it...

In this example, we will consider a simplified agent-based simulation model, where a group of agents moves randomly over a two-dimensional surface. Additionally, we assume that, at each step of the simulation, the closer the agent to the starting point, the lower the probability of movement—the probability of a change in an agent's location is equal to $1/k$, where k is the rank of an agent (the agent that managed to travel the longest distance from its origin has the highest rank). In order to run the simulation, follow the steps as shown:

1. We start by defining an agent:

```
mutable struct Agent
    id::Int
    x::Float64
    y::Float64
    times_moved::Int
end
```

2. We define the function by describing the movement of agents:

```
function move!(agent::Agent)
    angle = rand()*2π
    agent.x += cos(angle)
    agent.y += sin(angle)
    agent.times_moved += 1
end
```

3. Next, we create a population of 30 agents. Note the use of the broadcasting operator .:

```
pop = Agent.(1:30, 0, 0, 0)
```

4. Now we define what happens at each simulation step:

```
function step!(pop::Array{Agent,1})
    sort!(pop, by = a -> √(a.x*a.x + a.y*a.y), rev=true)
    foreach(i -> (rand() < (1/i)) && move!(pop[i]), 1:length(pop))
end
```

5. Now we can run the simulation:

```
foreach(s -> step!(pop), 1:1000)
```

6. Finally, let's filter out the agents that are at least 25 units away from the origin:

```
julia> filter(a -> √(a.x*a.x + a.y*a.y) >= 25, pop)
2-element Array{Agent,1}:
 Agent(12, -21.782926370813627, 24.238199368699437, 436)
 Agent(4, -22.711361031074716, 17.81154946976432, 322)
```

If you set the random seed to 0 at the beginning of the simulation, you should see exactly the same results.

How it works...

In Julia, a function is a first-class object. We start by defining struct that we will operate on. We also define a move! function that mutates an agent's state.

The map function takes two parameters: a function and a collection. The function given as the parameter is executed over each element of the collection, and the result is returned as Array.

In the `step!` function, when sorting with `sort!`, we provide the `by=` parameter. The value of this parameter is an anonymous function that calculates a weight for each `Array`'s element. The `foreach` function allows us to execute the `move!` function for each agent. Once again, we provide an anonymous function as a parameter to the `move!` function.

Finally, we again use the `foreach` function to actually run the simulation. The `filter` function can be used to filter out those `Array` elements having a desired set of values.

There's more...

Please note that we cannot use the `fill` function to generate the agent population because, in this case, all array elements will reference the same object instance. Please see the example shown:

```
julia> pop = fill(Agent(1, 0.0, 0.0, 0), 3)
3-element Array{Agent,1}:
 Agent(1, 0.0, 0.0, 0)
 Agent(1, 0.0, 0.0, 0)
 Agent(1, 0.0, 0.0, 0)

julia> pop[2].id = 2
2

julia> pop
3-element Array{Agent,1}:
 Agent(2, 0.0, 0.0, 0)
 Agent(2, 0.0, 0.0, 0)
 Agent(2, 0.0, 0.0, 0)
```

In such cases, another alternative to using the dot operator in the `Agent.()` form is to use a comprehension mechanism. For example:

```
julia> pop = [Agent(i, 0.0, 0.0 ,0) for i in 1:3]
3-element Array{Agent,1}:
 Agent(1, 0.0, 0.0, 0)
 Agent(2, 0.0, 0.0, 0)
 Agent(3, 0.0, 0.0, 0)
```

See also

The behavior of Julia functions is described in great detail in the Julia manual at https://docs.julialang.org/en/v1/manual/functions/index.html.

Functional programming in Julia

In this recipe, we will demonstrate how to use Julia to achieve functional style programming. We will create a function that takes another function as a parameter and returns a function again. Such an approach could be useful in writing computational code.

Getting ready

For the main part of this recipe, no installation is required. However, we will also show a plot of the processed function using the UnicodePlots.jl package. In order to install the package, press] key in the package manager type:

```
(v1.0) pkg> add UnicodePlots
```

This will install the UnicodePlots.jl package and all its requirements.

> In the GitHub repository for this recipe you will find the commands.txt file that contains the presented sequence of Julia commands.

How to do it...

To see how functional programming works in Julia, observe the following steps:

1. In this recipe, we start by creating a function that generates as its result a new function that is a derivative of the original:

```
function deriv(f::Function)::Function
    h = √eps()
    f1(x) = (f(x+h)-f(x))/h
    return f1
end
```

2. Let's test the deriv function. We will use the UnicodePlots.jl package to plot a 2x*x+ 5x-4 function and its derivative. Let's us now test the deriv function. We will use the UnicodePlots.jl package to plot a 2x*x+ 5x-4 function and its derivative:

```
using UnicodePlots
f(x) = 2x*x + 5x - 4;
x = -5:3;
```

3. Now we perform the plotting in the Julia command line:

```
plot = lineplot(x, f.(x), width=45, height=15, canvas=DotCanvas,
name="f(x)");
plot = lineplot!(plot, x, deriv(f).(x), name="f'(x)")
```

As a result, you will see the following output:

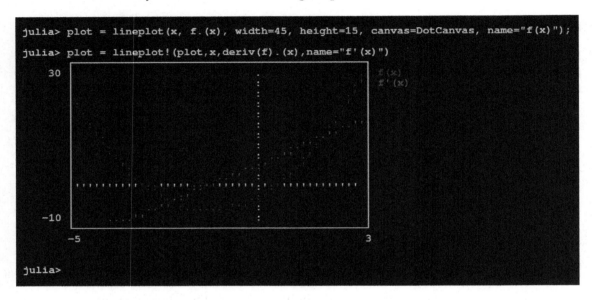

4. Next, we can construct a function that solves any quadratic equation in the form $ax^2 + bx + c = 0$, given as a Julia function:

```
function q_solve(f)
    c = f(0)
    f1 = deriv(f)
    b = f1(0)
    a = f(1)-b-c
    d = √(b*b-4*a*c)
    return ((-b-d)/(2*a),(-b+d)/(2*a))
end
```

5. We now test the solver:

```
julia> q_solve(x -> (x-1)*(x+7))
(-7.0, 1.0)

julia> q_solve(x -> x*x + 1)
ERROR: DomainError with -3.9999999403953552:
```

6. Since we did not restrict the types in the function definition, it can also work with complex numbers:

```
julia> q_solve(x -> x*x + 1 + 0im)
(-7.450580707946132e-9 - 1.0000000074505806im,
 -7.450580707946132e-9 + 1.0000000074505806im)
```

How it works...

We have constructed a Julia `deriv` function that takes another function as a parameter and returns a function. Such a function can be used to numerically calculate the derivative of any other argument function.

Next, we created a quadratic solver function that takes any quadratic function as its argument. Such functions can be presented as `f(x)=a*x*x+b*x+c`, and we calculate `f(0)` to get the `c` value. Next, we calculate `deriv(f)(0)`, which is `(2*a*x+b)(0)`, and hence obtain a numerical approximation of the value of `b`. Finally, we calculate `a`, and now we can calculate root values of the `f` function.

Since we did not specify types, our function works not only for real numbers but also for complex numbers. This can be observed when comparing the calls `q_solve(x -> x*x + 1)` and `q_solve(x -> x*x + 1 + 0im)`. The first one fails because `x*x+1` does not have a solution in the real domain. On the other hand - the second one - using complex numbers, works.

There's more...

We also advise you to try other values for the `canvas` parameter in the `lineplot` function: `BrailleCanvas` (best looking, using ASCII codes), `AsciiCanvas` (uses only ASCII characters for plotting—this plot is good for terminals that do not support all Unicode fonts), `BlockCanvas` (using square blocks), and `DensityCanvas` (using square blocks of different color saturation).

See also

The examples presented in this recipe were selected to show how to program simple functions in Julia. For actual production code, try the specific Julia packages available for differentiation (https://github.com/JuliaDiff/).

Scope of variables in Julia

In this chapter, we will illustrate some variable scoping issues that might not be obvious to all Julia users. A variable can be defined in one of two scopes—either local or global.

Getting ready

For this recipe, you do not need to install any packages.

 In the GitHub repository for this recipe you will find the `commands.txt` file that contains the presented sequence of Julia commands.

How to do it...

To test how variable scoping works in Julia, follow the steps:

1. Firstly, to illustrate variable scoping in Julia, run the following code:

```
julia> a, b = 1, 2;

julia> let a=30, b=40
           let b=500
               println("inner scope $a $b")
           end
           println("outer scope $a $b")
       end
inner scope 30 500
outer scope 30 40

julia> println("global scope $a $b")
global scope 1 2
```

We can see that with each scoping level (created by a `let...end` block), the meaning of variables changes. The `let` statement creates a new scope for variables.

2. Observe the following code:

```
julia> x=5;

julia> let
           println(x+1)
       end
6

julia> let
           x = x+1
       end
ERROR: UndefVarError: x not defined

julia> let
           global x = x+1
       end
6
```

The situation here is caused by the mechanism governing how Julia decides whether a variable is in a local scope—namely, variables that are written to (set to a new binding) are always treated as local—unless the global keyword is used (though be aware that assigning an element to an array does not result in variable rebinding).

3. Let's repeat a similar scenario with a loop. This will consist of code that creates a set of two-grams (two character substrings) from a given string. Try this code:

```
#this function will fail when run
function twogram(s::AbstractString)
    twograms = String[]
    for (i, c) in enumerate(s)
        if i == 1
            prev = c
        else
            push!(twograms, string(prev, c))
            prev = c
        end
    end
    twograms
end
```

4. Attempting to run the preceding function results in the following error:

```
julia> twogram("ABCD")
ERROR: UndefVarError: prev not defined
```

The `prev` variable has been declared in a loop scope, and hence its value is lost in each pass of the loop. This can be corrected (we have added `local prev` before the loop in order to declare `prev` in an outer local scope):

```
function twogram2(s::AbstractString)
    twograms = String[]
    local prev
    for (i, c) in enumerate(s)
        if i == 1
            prev = c
        else
            push!(twograms, string(prev, c))
            prev = c
        end
    end
    twograms
end
```

Now the code runs as expected:

```
julia> twogram2("ABCD")
3-element Array{String,1}:
 "AB"
 "BC"
 "CD"
```

Please note that the code of `twograms2` will not run as expected, if copied directly to the Julia command line:

```
julia> s="ABCD";

julia> twograms = String[];

julia> local prev

julia> for (i, c) in enumerate(s)
           if i == 1
               prev = c
           else
               push!(twograms, string(prev, c))
               prev = c
           end
       end
ERROR: UndefVarError: prev not defined
```

5. In order to run the preceding code, we need to create a local scope, for example using the `let` command:

```julia
julia> s="ABCD";

julia> twograms = String[];

julia> let
           local prev
           for (i, c) in enumerate(s)
               if i == 1
                   prev = c
               else
                   push!(twograms, string(prev, c))
                   prev = c
               end
           end
           twograms
       end
3-element Array{String,1}:
 "AB"
 "BC"
 "CD"
```

6. Yet another option is to prepend each assignment to `prev` with the `global` keyword:

```julia
julia> s="ABCD";

julia> twograms = String[];

julia> for (i, c) in enumerate(s)
           if i == 1
               global prev = c
           else
               push!(twograms, string(prev, c))
               global prev = c
           end
       end

julia> twograms
3-element Array{String,1}:
 "AB"
 "BC"
 "CD"
```

How it works...

In Julia, there are two types of scope—global scope and local scope. In the Julia command line, variables are created in the global scope by default, while in functions the variables are created in local scopes. This means that if you want to copy the body of a Julia function to the Julia command line (for example, for testing), you have to surround it with a `let...end` block. Otherwise, your code in the Julia command line will resolve variables differently compared with the code inside a Julia function.

It is important to note that within a local scope (such as `for` or `while`) the global variables by default are only available for reading but not for assignment (more precisely whenever you try to assign a value to a global variable within a local scope, it will be immediately treated by the compiler as a local variable). There are two ways around this:

- Put an explicit `global` in front of each assignment

- Wrap everything around a `let ... end` block (in this scenario a previously global variable will now be locally scoped)

Note that each module has its own global scope. The Julia command line works in the global scope of the `Main` module. If you define some code within a module, it will be global within this module. All the presented rules are valid. For example, consider the following module:

```
module B
    x = 1
    function getxplusone()
        return x+1
    end
    function increasex()
        return x+=1
    end
    function increasexglob()
        return global x+=1
    end
end
```

Now we test it and observe very similar behavior to the previous examples:

```
julia> B.getxplusone()
2

julia> B.increasex()
ERROR: UndefVarError: x not defined
```

```
julia> B.increasexglob()
2
```

Last but not least, a function creates a new local scope. Remember that scoping within a function (local scope) and within the Julia command line (global scope) exposes completely different behavior. Consider the following code:

```
function f()
    x = 1
    for a in 1:10
        x +=1
    end
    x
end
```

Now we run this function in the Julia command line:

```
julia> f()
11
```

Now, consider an example where you want to test code fragments of a function inside the Julia command line:

```
julia> x=1;
julia> for a in 1:10
            x +=1
        end
ERROR: UndefVarError: x not defined
```

The problem is that if variable x is defined in a local scope (as e.g. in the function body in this example) then it is available for writing to in a nested local scope. However, this rule does not apply to variables defined in the global scope.

There are two ways to run the preceding code—surround it with `let` block so that a local scope is created, or use the `global` keyword whenever x is referenced. For example:

```
julia> let
            x = 1
            for a in 1:10
                x +=1
          end
            x
        end
11

julia> x = 1
1
```

```
julia> for a in 1:10
           global x += 1
       end

julia> x
11
```

There's more...

In Julia, loops and comprehensions create a new scope, and hence we can make a similar test with a comprehension:

```
julia> z=5;
julia> [(x=z+i;x) for i in 1:2]
2-element Array{Int64,1}:
 6
 7
```

However, if we try to assign a value to z , it will not work (the comprehension creates a new local scope):

```
julia> z = 5;
julia> [(z=z+i;z) for i in 1:2]
ERROR: UndefVarError: z not defined
```

We can, though, set z to be global , and now it is reachable within the comprehension:

```
julia> z = 5;
julia> [(global z=z+i;z) for i in 1:2]
2-element Array{Int64,1}:
 6
 8
```

The let statement can also create a new environment that can hold values that are stored even when the scope of the let block is left:

```
julia> let state = 0
           global counter() = (state += 1)
       end;

julia> counter()
1

julia> counter()
2
```

Please note that the value of the `state` variable is visible only in the local scope of the `let` block—it is not available in the global scope:

```
julia> state
ERROR: UndefVarError: state not defined
```

See also

The documentation for Julia variable scoping is available at
https://docs.julialang.org/en/v1/manual/variables-and-scoping/.

Handling exceptions in Julia

In this recipe, you will discover how to make use of Julia's exception handling mechanism.

Getting ready

For this recipe, no package installation is required.

 In the GitHub repository for this recipe you will find
the `commands.txt` file that contains the presented sequence of Julia
commands.

How to do it...

Sometimes executing code results in an unexpected error. A typical example could be working with a file:

1. Start the Julia command line and define the following two logger functions that append a log to a file:

```
function loglines(filename, lines...)
    f = open(filename, "a")
    foreach(line -> (println(f, line)), lines)
    sqrt(-2)
    close(f)
end
```

2. Now, run the functions in the REPL:

```
julia> loglines("mylog.txt", "Test log:")
ERROR: DomainError with -2.0:
sqrt will only return a complex result if called with a complex
argument. Try sqrt(Complex(x)).
```

The try-catch block makes it possible to suppress the error:

```
julia> try
            loglines("mylog.txt", "Test log:")
        catch e
            dump(e)
        end
DomainError
  val: Float64 -2.0
  msg: String "sqrt will only return a complex result if called
with a complex argument. Try sqrt(Complex(x))."
```

3. Suppose that this command executes within a try-catch block somewhere in the logging system, for example:

```
for i in 1:100_000
    try
        loglines("mylog2.txt", string(i))
    catch
    end
end
```

4. Now try to examine the file contents:

```
julia> f = open("mylog2.txt")
ERROR: SystemError: opening file mylog2.txt: Too many open files
```

5. If the mylog2.txt file is opened using some external editor, output similar to the following may be seen (note the skipped and empty lines):

```
1


7478
49786
```

6. Since no more files can be opened, the REPL is now unusable, so it needs to be closed:

```
julia> exit()
```

7. Start a new Julia command line session and define a new function:

```
function loglines2(filename, lines...)
    f = open(filename, "a")
    try
        foreach(line -> println(f, line),lines)
        sqrt(-2)
    finally
        close(f)
    end
end
```

8. Testing this function reveals that it still executes with an error:

```
julia> loglines2("mylog3.txt", "Test log:")
ERROR: DomainError with -2.0:
sqrt will only return a complex result if called with a complex
argument. Try sqrt(Complex(x)).
```

9. Run the modified function `100_000` times:

```
open("mylog3.txt", "w") do f end   #makes sure the file is empty
for i in 1:100_000
    try
        loglines2("mylog3.txt", string(i))
    catch e
        if !(e isa DomainError)
            rethrow(e)
        end
    end
end
```

10. Now, read the file contents and check whether all the logs were actually written to:

```
julia> lines = open("mylog3.txt") do f
            readlines(f)
        end;

julia> all([lines[i]==string(i) for i in 1:100_000])
true
```

How it works...

In the recipe, we have shown a common programming problem; namely, that failing to release a resource leads to data corruption. We start by creating a function that generates an error. The error can be controlled within a try-catch block. However, whenever a program allocates some resource that should be released, a finally block is required. The finally block will always execute regardless of whether the code in the catch block succeeds or not. Hence, this is the recommended approach for handling allocation and release of resources in a Julia program.

Please note that when the finally block has a return statement, this will suppress the actual exception; see the following example. Though there is no catch block, DomainError will not be thrown—the function executed the return statement and continues:

```julia
julia> function ff(a)
           res = missing
           try
               res = sqrt(a)
           finally
               return res
           end
       end;

julia> ff(4)
2.0

julia> ff(-2)
missing
```

Please note that in try-catch blocks, a good practice is to provide separate error handling for various Exception types. In the recipe, we use the e isa DomainError expression to check whether Exception matches the expected type.

There's more...

You should also consider using the @warn and @error macros for nicely formatted reporting of errors. Consider the following function:

```julia
function divide(a,b)
    b == 0 && @warn "Division by zero"
    a/b
end
```

Let's try it out:

```
julia> divide(3, 5)
0.6

julia> divide(3, 0)
┌ Warning: Division by zero
└ @ Main REPL[25]:2
Inf
```

Similarly, you can use the @error macro to display an error message:

```
function divide2(a, b)
  b == zero(typeof(b)) && @error "Division by zero"
  a/b
end
```

Note that the divide2 function will get executed despite using the @error macro (the @error macro just displays a nicely formatted error message—no actual Exception is thrown):

```
julia> divide2(3, 0)
┌ Error: Division by zero
└ @ Main REPL[28]:2
Inf
```

If you want to actually disallow zero-division, you need to call the error method:

```
function divide3(a, b)
    if b == zero(typeof(b))
        @error "Division by zero"
        throw(ErrorException("Division by zero"))
    end
    a/b
end
```

And now the code will execute, throwing an error:

```
julia> divide3(3, 0)
┌ Error: Division by zero
└ @ Main REPL[43]:3
ERROR: Division by zero
Stacktrace:
 [1] macro expansion at .\logging.jl:307 [inlined]
 [2] divide3(::Int64, ::Int64) at .\REPL[43]:3
 [3] top-level scope at none:0
```

Note that instead of `throw(ErrorException("Division by zero"))`, we could also have used a shorter `error("Division by zero")` version—this will also throw `Exception` of type `ErrorException`. Finally, please bear in mind that there are several built-in exception types that you can use in your code to match your actual requirements. You can run `subtypes(Exception)` to see the full list:

```
julia> subtypes(Exception)
55-element Array{Any,1}:
 ArgumentError
 AssertionError
 Base.CodePointError
 Base.IOError
 Base.InvalidCharError
 ⋮
 Test.TestSetException
 TypeError
 UndefKeywordError
 UndefRefError
 UndefVarError
```

You can always extend the preceding list by adding your own `Exception` types. For instance:

```
julia> struct MyException <: Exception
           msg::String
       end

julia> throw(MyException("something went wrong"))
ERROR: MyException("something went wrong")
Stacktrace:
 [1] top-level scope at none:0
```

Finally, in this recipe we used the `throw` and `rethrow` functions to throw an exception. The difference is that the `rethrow` function does not change the current exception backtrace. This is useful when we want to throw a previously caught exception within the `catch` block.

See also

The documentation for working with `Exception`s in Julia can be found at https://docs.julialang.org/en/v1/manual/control-flow/#Exception-Handling-1.

For a broader discussion of Julia loggers (`@error` and `@warn`), see the *Setting up logging in your code* recipe in the Chapter 8, *Julia Workflow*.

Working with NamedTuples

The `NamedTuple` abstract type is a convenient immutable data structure that allows its elements to be accessed by name and by index. A typical way of thinking about them is that they are tuples with optional name information attached to data slots. However, there is one important distinction between these two types. While tuples are covariant, named tuples are invariant. In other words, `NamedTuple`, in terms of subtyping, behaves like any other `struct` type. This has important consequences for the method dispatch mechanism.

Getting ready

 In the GitHub repository for this recipe you will find the `commands.txt` file that contains the presented sequence of shell and Julia commands.

Now open your favorite terminal to execute commands.

How to do it...

The first step is to create two tuples and two named tuples:

```julia
julia> t1 = (1, 2)
(1, 2)

julia> t2 = (1.0, 2)
(1.0, 2)

julia> nt1 = (a=1, b=2)
(a = 1, b = 2)

julia> nt2 = (a=1.0, b=2)
(a = 1.0, b = 2)
```

Now, because tuples are covariant, both `t1` and `t2` are subtypes of `Tuple{Real, Int}`:

```julia
julia> t1 isa Tuple{Real, Int}
true

julia> t2 isa Tuple{Real, Int}
true
```

However, named tuples are invariant, so the same rule does not work for them:

```
julia> nt1 isa NamedTuple{(:a, :b), Tuple{Real,Int64}}
false

julia> nt2 isa NamedTuple{(:a, :b), Tuple{Real,Int64}}
false
```

In order to specify their common supertype, you have to use the `where` clause:

```
julia> nt1 isa NamedTuple{(:a, :b), Tuple{T,Int64}} where T<:Real
true

julia> nt2 isa NamedTuple{(:a, :b), Tuple{T,Int64}} where T<:Real
true
```

How it works...

The consequence of different subtyping of tuples and named tuples is apparent in situations where collections of heterogeneous objects of this type are created. For instance, consider:

```
julia> [t1, t2]
2-element Array{Tuple{Real,Int64},1}:
 (1, 2)
 (1.0, 2)

julia> [nt1, nt2]
2-element Array{NamedTuple{(:a, :b),T} where T<:Tuple,1}:
 (a = 1, b = 2)
 (a = 1.0, b = 2)
```

And we see that in the case of `Tuple`, Julia is able to identify a narrower common type than for `NamedTuple`. In the former case, we would add only tuples that are subtypes of `Tuple{Real,Int64}` to our collection, while in the second case any `NamedTuple` that has field names `a` and `b` would be accepted.

There's more...

Julia uses `NamedTuple` objects to pass keyword arguments to functions. This allows the compiler to specialize function code to the type of keyword arguments passed (although it is not permitted to have method implementations to be different for different keyword argument types).

To understand how Julia works around the problem of invariance of the NamedTuple objects, it is worth looking at the following example:

```
julia> foo(x; y::Integer) = (x, y)
foo (generic function with 1 method)

julia> @code_lowered foo(1, y=1)
CodeInfo(
 1 ─ %1  = Base.haskey(%%#temp#@_2, :(:y))::Any    │
 └──       goto 3 if not %1                         │
 2 ─ %3  = Base.getindex(%%#temp#@_2, :(:y))::Any   │
 │        #temp#@_6 = (Core.typeassert)(Core.SSAValue(3), Main.Integer)   │
 └──       goto 4                                    │
 3 ─ %6  = Core.UndefKeywordError(:(:y))::Any        │
 └──       #temp#@_6 = (Core.throw)(Core.SSAValue(6))  │
 4 ─  y   = Core.Compiler.Argument(6)                │
 │    %9  = (:y,)::Any                               │
 │    %10 = Core.apply_type(Core.NamedTuple, %9)::Any  │
 │    %11 = Base.structdiff(%%#temp#@_2, %10)::Any   │
 │    %12 = Base.pairs(%11)::Any                     │
 │    %13 = Base.isempty(%12)::Any                   │
 └──       goto 6 if not %13                         │
 5 ─       goto 7                                    │
 6 ─       Base.kwerr(%%#temp#@_2, %%, %%x)          │
 7   %17 = Main.:(#foo#5)(%%y, %%, %%x)::Any         │
 └──       return %17                                │
)
```

We can see that Julia does not perform matching on the type of NamedTuple passed in, since NamedTuple{(:y,),Tuple{Int64}} is not a subtype of NamedTuple{(:y,),Tuple{Integer}}, but in fact it directly checks the names of keyword arguments supplied and whether their types are correct by using the typeassert function.

See also

The definition of invariance for normal types and covariance of tuples was presented in this chapter in the recipe *Understanding subtyping in Julia* recipe.

6
Metaprogramming and Advanced Typing

This chapter contains the following recipes:

- Metaprogramming
- Macros and generated functions
- Defining your own types—linked list
- Defining primitive types
- Understanding the structure of Julia numeric types with introspection
- Using static arrays
- The efficiency of mutable versus immutable types
- Ensuring type stability of your code

Introduction

In this chapter, we present various advanced programming topics in Julia.

We start by introducing metaprogramming for manipulating the **Abstract Syntax Tree (AST)** of parsed Julia code, and we use this approach for writing macros. We show how to specify user-defined types—complex and primitive. Finally, we focus on important language features that affect code execution speed. We present static arrays—a mechanism built on the base of generating functions that can greatly increase the speed of array operations. We discuss how performance is affected by the use of mutable and immutable data types and data type stability.

Metaprogramming

By **metaprogramming**, we refer to the ability of a program to interact with its own code, where the code itself is represented in the data structures of that language. In Julia, this powerful functionality is available on many levels. In this recipe, we will introduce metaprogramming concepts by showing how Julia `struct` data types can be generated automatically on the base of input data. This example could be useful in situations where some data has a structure which is not known in advance and subsequently needs to be processed and stored in Julia data structures.

Getting ready

For this recipe, no package installation is required. Simply start the Julia command line.

 In the GitHub repository for this recipe, you will find the `commands.txt` file that contains the presented sequence of Julia commands.

How to do it...

Consider a situation where we have some comma-separated data:

```
data="""
id,val,class
1,4,A
2,39,B
3,44,C
"""
```

This data could be contained in a file but, in our example, for purposes of simplicity, they are in a string variable. We will create a function that parses such a dataset and produces `Array` of `struct` objects with fields matching the data structure (note that `NamedTuple` could be used instead of `struct` but we use `struct` as an illustrative example).

We present two variants of this recipe:

- Working with strings representing Julia using the `eval` function
- A more advanced method—working with ASTs

Working with the eval function

Here is a list of steps to be followed:

1. Consider the following Julia function:

```
function new_struct(fields::Vector{Tuple{String,DataType}})
    name =  "A" * string(hash(fields), base=16)
    code = "begin\nstruct $name\n"
    for field in fields
        code *= field[1]*"::"*string(field[2])*"\n"
    end
    eval(Meta.parse(code * "end\n$name\nend"))
end
```

This function generates a name for `struct` (the name is evaluated from the `struct`'s `fields`) and assembles Julia code that will contain the `struct` definition.

2. The next step is to test this function in the Julia command line:

```
julia> MyS = new_struct([("a", Int), ("b", String), ("c", Int)]);
julia> dump(MyS)
A5cc33285fde10b33 <: Any
  a::Int64
  b::String
  c::Int64
```

3. Now define a function that parses text data to obtain the column names and types:

```
function parse_data(data::AbstractString)
    lines = filter(x->length(x)>0, strip.(split(data, ('\n',
'\r'))))
    colnames = string.(split(lines[1], ','))
    row1=split(lines[2], ',')
    coltypes = [occursin(r"^-?\d+$", val) ? Int64 : String for val
in row1]
    (lines[2:end], new_struct(collect(zip(colnames, coltypes))))
end
```

4. Let's test it out. Incidentally, in order to simplify the code, we support only `String` and `Int64` data types (a `Float64` data type will be treated as a `String` data type):

```julia
julia> dump(parse_data("col1,col2,col3\nabc,123,123.5")[2])
A39a03927131d3fa0 <: Any
  col1::String
  col2::Int64
  col3::String
```

5. Next, define a function, `parse_text`, to parse the text data into `Vector` of `struct`'s (two types are supported, `Int` and `String`):

```julia
function parse_text(data::AbstractString)
    lines, MyStruct = parse_data(data)
    res = MyStruct[]
    for line in lines
        colvals = split(line, ',')
        f = (t, v)->t<:Int ? parse(Int, v) : string(v)
        vals = f.(MyStruct.types, colvals)
        push!(res, Base.invokelatest(MyStruct, vals...))
    end
    return res
end
```

6. This function is then used to parse the `data` object:

```julia
julia> parse_text(data)
3-element Array{A56d02402a5387976,1}:
 A56d02402a5387976(1, 4, "A")
 A56d02402a5387976(2, 39, "B")
 A56d02402a5387976(3, 44, "C")
```

Abstract Syntax Tree (AST)

It is possible to generate the code without using the `parse` function, but rather by directly generating the AST structure of the code to be executed. The type `Expr` enables dynamic construction of code blocks as Julia data structures:

1. Have a look at the following `new_struct2` function, which is the equivalent of the `new_struct` function created in the preceding recipe:

```julia
function new_struct2(fields::Vector{Tuple{String,DataType}})
    name =  "A" * string(hash(fields), base=16)
    c = Expr(:block,
```

```
                Expr(:struct,false,Symbol(name),
                     Expr(:block, [Expr(:(::), Symbol(f[1]),
                                   f[2]) for f in fields]...)),
                Symbol(name))
        eval(c)
    end
```

It is possible to use a still shorter notation, `:()`, instead of `Expr()`. In this case, `Expr(:(::),Symbol(f[1]), f[2])` could be represented as `:($(Symbol(f[1]))::$(f[2]) )`, where `$` is an interpolation operator.

2. We can test this function:

```
julia> MyS2 = new_struct2([("a", Int), ("b", String), ("c", Int)]);
julia> dump(MyS2)
A5cc33285fde10b33 <: Any
  a::Int64
  b::String
  c::Int64
```

3. The new function is actually identical to the previously created `new_struct`. You can check if the `MyS` object is still present in your REPL:

```
julia> MyS == MyS2
true
```

How it works...

In the recipe, we have shown how to programmatically construct Julia code and execute it. Since a new data type was created, we needed to supply a name for it. The name of the type is created on the basis of the hash code of the parameter vector. This construction means that the name of the generated `struct` is determined by its structure and, in particular, the same set of fields and types always results in the same `struct` name.

We create a `MyS` object that contains the newly created `struct` type. The `dump` function allows us to display the contents of any Julia object. For example, you can use this feature to see how Julia stores its version number:

```
julia> dump(VERSION)
VersionNumber
  major: UInt32 0x00000001
  minor: UInt32 0x00000000
  patch: UInt32 0x00000001
  prerelease: Tuple{} ()
  build: Tuple{} ()
```

Having a function generating arbitrary `struct`s enables us to write code based on information from the header line of a file (for field names) and the first line of data (to determine data types). In order to check whether a `String` value may be converted to `Int`, we use a regular expression: `r"^-?\d+$"`. In this expression, we have the following:

- `^` means the beginning of a string
- `?` means that the character `–` will be observed zero or one time
- `\d` means any number character
- `+` means one or more occurrences of such characters
- `$` means the end of the string

Hence, this expression will match only strings that contain one or more number characters.

The key function used in this recipe is `eval`, which evaluates the expression passed to it in the global scope of containing module (in our example this module is `Main`, as this is the module used by the Julia command line).

In the recipe, we show two ways to create an expression that is passed to the `eval` function:

- By calling `Meta.parse` function on a string that is a properly formed Julia code. This approach is taken in the `new_struct` function.
- By manually constructing the expression using `:(...)` or `Expr` calls. This approach is taken in the `new_struct2` function.

In more advanced applications it is recommended to work with expressions rather than to parse a string.

Finally, there are two more advanced issues that are important in this recipe.

Firstly, we had to generate a unique name for our newly created structures. We have used `"A" * string(hash(fields), base=16)` construct to achieve this. In this way, if we call the `new_struct` function with the same argument we will get the same name. The downside of this approach is that there is a minimal risk that this name is already taken (it is small as we base it on a hash value of the `fields` argument). Another approach, that guarantees that the created symbol does not conflict with variable names, is to use the `gensym` function. The downside of this approach is that it generates a unique symbol on every call. Thus, calling `new_struct` with the same argument twice would generate two different names for the resulting struct.

Secondly, it is important why we had to use the `Base.invokelatest` function in our recipe. The reason is that in the `parse_text` function we are calling `MyStruct`, which is defined when `parse_text` is running (or, in other words, `MyStruct` is not defined when the `parse_text` function is compiled). Here is a simpler example that shows why the call to the `Base.invokelatest` function is needed:

```julia
julia> function f1()
           eval(:(g1() = 10))
           g1()
       end

julia> function f2()
           eval(:(g2() = 10))
           Base.invokelatest(g2)
       end

julia> f1()
ERROR: MethodError: no method matching g1()
The applicable method may be too new: running in world age 25085, while
current world is 25086.

julia> f2()
10
```

There's more...

Please note that the `new_struct2` function could be changed to a macro. Such a macro could take a name, along with a set of field names and types, and then generate the appropriate code. We discuss macros in the next recipe.

See also

The Julia documentation on metaprogramming can be found at https://docs.julialang.org/en/v1/manual/metaprogramming/.

Please note that several Julia packages rely heavily on the dynamic type and method creation with the metaprogramming mechanism. A notable example is the `JLD2.jl` package. We advise more advanced Julia users to examine its source code at https://github.com/simonster/JLD2.jl.

Macros and generated functions

Julia provides a very powerful macro system that lets include generated code in the body of your program. They are executed at compile time and enable you to operate on the source code's Abstract Syntax Tree (AST).

Getting ready

Macros and generated functions are a built-in language functionality, and hence no installation is required. However, in this recipe, we will be also measuring the code performance. For this purpose, the `BenchmarkTools.jl` package will be used. In order to install it press the *]* key to start the Julia package manager and type:

```
(v1.0) pkg> add BenchmarkTools
```

 In the GitHub repository for this recipe, you will find the `commands.txt` file that contains the presented sequence of Julia commands.

How to do it...

This recipe contains two parts. In the first part, we will illustrate how to use Julia to construct a macro to cache the results of a function. In the second part, we will show you how to write a generated function that speeds up computing by loop unrolling.

Using macros to cache function results

Here is a list of steps to be followed to cache the results of the function:

1. In this example, we will write a macro capable of caching data. To illustrate this, let's start with a function which determines the nth element of the Fibonacci sequence:

```
function fib(n)
    n <= 2 ? 1 : fib(n-1) + fib(n-2)
end
```

2. Let us check how long it takes to evaluate this function for n=40 (note that we call the function before measuring the actual time to enforce its compilation):

```julia
julia> fib(4)
3
julia> @time fib(40)
  0.499755 seconds (5 allocations: 176 bytes)
102334155
```

You should be aware that calculating such recursive functions requires evaluating f(n) many times recursively, and hence, even for small values of n, the computing time is very long.

3. We will now implement a buffering mechanism to avoid recomputing f(n) for the same parameter values. Consider the following function:

```julia
function memoit(f::Function, p)
    if !isdefined(Main, :memoit_cache)
        global memoit_cache = Dict{Function,Dict{Any,Any}}()
    end
    c = haskey(memoit_cache, f) ? memoit_cache[f] :
memoit_cache[f]=Dict()
    haskey(c, p) ? c[p] : c[p] = f(p)
end
```

4. Now we implement our Fibonacci function to utilize this:

```julia
function fib2(n)
    n <= 2 ? 1 : memoit(fib2, n-1) + memoit(fib2, n-2)
end
```

5. Let's see how it performs:

```julia
julia> fib2(4)
3
julia> @time fib2(40)
  0.000188 seconds (58 allocations: 2.328 KiB)
102334155
```

We can see that the code now runs considerably faster.

6. It is evident that the preceding code with the memo function has worse readability, so let's introduce a macro to overcome this:

```julia
macro memo(e)
    println("macro @memo is run: ", e, " ", e.args)
    (!(typeof(e) <: Expr) || !(e.head == :call)) &&
```

```
        error("wrong @memo params")
    return quote # we handle only functions with a single parameter
        memoit($(esc(e.args[1])), $(esc(e.args[2])))
    end
end
```

7. The function can now be implemented with this new `macro` (this time we show the output):

```
julia> function fib3(n)
            n <= 2 ? 1 : (@memo fib3(n-1)) + (@memo fib3(n-2))
        end

macro @memo is run: fib3(n - 1) Any[:fib3, :(n - 1)]
macro @memo is run: fib3(n - 2) Any[:fib3, :(n - 2)]
fib3 (generic function with 1 method)
```

8. Check the new `fib3` function using the `@memo` macro:

```
julia> fib3(4)
3

julia> @time fib3(40)
  0.000191 seconds (58 allocations: 2.328 KiB)
102334155
```

We can see that execution speed remains the same as using the `fib2` function. Note that, in this example, we created a macro to cache function calls. However, it is also possible to create a memoization macro that can be used as a decorator to a function—such functionality has been implemented in the `Memoize.jl` package.

Loop unrolling with the @generated macro

Consider a scenario where we need to calculate an aggregated value for the same field for heterogeneous objects (for example, calculating a total sum of a field `.x` in a set of `struct` objects having different types):

1. We could implement it as the following function:

```
function sumx1(objs...)
    isempty(objs) && return 0
    total=objs[1].x
    for i in 2:length(objs)
        total += objs[i].x
```

```
        end
        total
    end
```

2. Let's create two `struct`s for testing purposes:

```
struct A x::Int end
struct B x::Float64 end
```

3. We can see that the function properly evaluates sums and that the result type is contingent on the values of the x fields:

```
julia> sumx1(A(5), B(7))
12.0
julia> sumx1(A(5), A(17))
22
```

4. However, the preceding function iterates over a set of parameters that have unknown types. The performance could be increased by generating the code for a specific set of parameter types and unrolling the loop inside of the sumx1 function. Take a look at an alternative function:

```
@generated function sumx2(objs...)
    isempty(objs) && return 0 # default where no arguments were
given
    total = :(objs[1].x)
    for i in 2:length(objs)
        total = :($total + objs[$i].x)
    end
    total
end
```

5. Firstly, we check for functional equivalence between the two implementations:

```
julia> sumx2(A(5), B(7)) == sumx1(A(5), B(7))
true
julia> sumx2(A(5), A(17)) == sumx1(A(5), A(17))
true
```

6. Then we test the performance:

```
julia> using BenchmarkTools

julia> const valsx = ([A(i) for i=1:10]..., [B(i) for i=1:10]...);

julia> typeof(valsx)
Tuple{A,A,A,A,A,A,A,A,A,A,B,B,B,B,B,B,B,B,B,B}
```

```
julia> @btime sumx1(valsx...)
  638.725 ns (38 allocations: 3.56 KiB)
110.0

julia> @btime sumx2(valsx...)
  1.706 ns (0 allocations: 0 bytes)
110.0
```

We can see that the `@generated` function runs almost 400 times faster and requires four times less memory. Hence, using the `@generated` macro is highly recommended in cases where the performance depends on the types of arguments.

How it works...

The `memoit` function creates a global cache storage for function calls. Since the recursive calculation of Fibonacci numbers requires evaluating the same values of `fib(n)` many times over, it greatly speeds up the computations.

In order to ensure a convenient usage of the `memoit` function, we wrap it in a `@memo` macro. A Julia macro takes any Julia expression (`Expr`), literal value, or symbol as its parameter, performs transformations on it, and returns an `Expr` object. Since a macro is expected to return an object of type `Expr`, we use a `quote` block to create such an object. Note that `quote` blocks support the interpolation operator, `$`, similarly to `Strings`. Since the arguments passed to the macro might contain some expression (and we want to retain that expression in the generated code), we need to use the escaping function `esc` to properly pass the parameters. More precisely, variables contained in expressions escaped by the `esc` function are evaluated in caller scope. Here is a simple example showing you the difference:

```
julia> macro example(v)
           :(($v, $(esc(v))))
       end
@example (macro with 2 methods)

julia> function f()
           x = 1
           @example x
       end
f (generic function with 1 method)

julia> x = 10
10
```

```
julia> f()
(10, 1)
```

You can simply check what is the expression returned by a macro using the @macroexpand macro. In our example we get the following:

```
julia> @macroexpand @example x
:((Main.x, x))
```

In order to better show how macros work, we added a `println` statement to the `memo` macro. One thing to note is that the macro is only executed when a new function is defined (at compile time)—it performs processing of the code given as its argument. A Julia macro is not executed at runtime—at this stage, the code making a `fib3` function call is already within the call to the `memoit` function.

We can use the `macroexpand` function to illustrate what our macro produces. In this case, we need to parse the macro call as an `Expr` object in Julia (here created with the `:()` operator):

```
julia> n=5
5
julia> macroexpand(Main, :(@memo fib3(n-1)))
macro executes fib3(n - 1) Any[:fib3, :(n - 1)]
quote
    #= REPL[2]:5 =#
    (Main.memoit)(fib3, n - 1)
end
```

We see that executing `@memo fib3(4)` creates a call to the previously defined `memoit` function with the parameters being parsed.

In the second part of the recipe, we have utilized the power of metaprogramming to unroll a loop within a function. Please note that the `sumx2` function returns a Julia `Expr` that can generate the `total` rather than the actual `total` value itself. This function is processed by the `@generated` macro. Whenever a call to a different set of parameters is made the function body executes and a new `Expr` is generated. Note the usage of interpolation operator, `$`—it is similar to how `String` syntax in Julia supports interpolation. Here we use it to place the index value in the generated code and to join subsequent Julia statements.

There's more...

Julia offers an `@code_lowered` macro that allows you to understand how its code is being processed by the compiler. Let's use this to investigate the underlying differences between the `sumx1` and `sumx2` functions:

```
julia> @code_lowered sumx2(A(1), B(2))
CodeInfo(
2 1 ─ %1 = (Base.getindex)(objs, 1)          │ │ macro expansion
  │    %2 = (Base.getproperty)(%1, :x)        │ │
  │    %3 = (Base.getindex)(objs, 2)          │ │
  │    %4 = (Base.getproperty)(%3, :x)        │ │
  │    %5 = %2 + %4                           │ │
  └──        return %5                        │ │
)
```

We can see that the code is compiled into a short set of instructions. Moreover, the types of all arguments are known:

```
julia> @code_warntype sumx2(A(1), B(2))
Body::Float64
2 1 ─ %1 = (Base.getfield)(objs, 1, true)::A      │ │ │       macro expansion
  │    %2 = (Base.getfield)(%1, :x)::Int64         │ │ │        getproperty
  │    %3 = (Base.getfield)(objs, 2, true)::B      │ │ │        getindex
  │    %4 = (Base.getfield)(%3, :x)::Float64       │ │ │        getproperty
  │    %5 = (Base.sitofp)(Float64, %2)::Float64    │ │ │ │ │ │ │    promote
  │    %6 = (Base.add_float)(%5, %4)::Float64      │ │ │ │            +
  └──        return %6          │ │
```

It is apparent that in the generated code of function `sumx2`, the type of all parameters is known. Note the horizontal dash lines at the end of each line. The number of lines indicates the level of code nesting, with a half-size line (╷) indicating the start of a variable scope and a full-size line (│) indicating a continuing scope. Finally, line thickness shows the level of the scope name that is printed on the right. More information can be found in source code documentation at https://github.com/JuliaLang/julia/blob/master/base/compiler/ssair/show.jl#L170.

In the case of the `sumx1` function, the type of arguments is not known and this results in much more code being generated:

```
julia> @code_warntype sumx1(A(1), B(2))
Body::Union{Float64, Int64}
2 1 ──        goto #3 if not false                      │
  2 ──        nothing                                    │
3 3 ── %3  = (Base.getfield)(objs, 1, true)::A       │ │      getindex
  │    %4  = (Base.getfield)(%3, :x)::Int64          │ │      getproperty
```

```
 4 |              (Base.ifelse)(true, 2, 1)         | |  | |     Colon
   |      %6  = (Base.slt_int)(2, 2)::Bool          | |  | |       isempty
   └────              goto #5 if not %6
... omitted output lines ....
  12   %31 = φ (#8 => %22, #10 => %27)::Union{Float64, Int64}
   |        %32 = (isa)(%15, Float64)::Bool          |
   |        %33 = (isa)(%31, Float64)::Bool          |
   |        %34 = (and_int)(%32, %33)::Bool          |
... omitted output lines ....
  26 ─ %80 = φ (#24 => %68, #6 => %4)::Union{Float64, Int64}
   └────              return %80                     |
```

Notice how `Union{Float64, Int64}` within the output of the `@code_warntype` macro is marked in red. It means that the compiler does not know the exact type of the variables. Also running `sumx1` involves executing a loop at run time. These two factors explain the significant difference in speed between these two functions.

See also

The technique presented for speeding up computations is called **memoization**. For production uses of the memoization, we recommend the Julia package `Memoize.jl` available at `https://github.com/simonster/Memoize.jl`.

More documentation on Julia macros and generated functions can be found at Julia's metaprogramming tutorial `https://docs.julialang.org/en/v1/manual/metaprogramming/`.

Defining your own types – linked list

A linked list is a basic data structure in programming. In this recipe, we will show how you can implement it in Julia.

Getting ready

A **linked list** is a collection of elements, where each element points to the next. Together, the elements represent a sequence. The simplest representation of one element of a linked list consists of two fields—one holding data and one holding a reference (link) to the next node in the sequence.

In the GitHub repository for this recipe, you will find
the `commands.txt` file that contains the presented sequence of shell and
Julia commands. Additionally, in the `11.jl` file you can find the
definitions of the linked list type and related methods used in this recipe.

Now open your favorite terminal to execute the commands.

How to do it...

In order to define a linked list, first define an appropriate data structure and then specify
functions that allow you to manipulate it. The following definitions given can be found in
the `11.jl` file.

We start with defining the required types and one additional outer constructor:

```
struct ListNode{T}
    value::T
    next::Union{ListNode{T}, Nothing}
end

mutable struct LinkedList{T}
    head::Union{ListNode{T}, Nothing}
end

LinkedList(T::Type) = LinkedList{T}(nothing)
```

We want our `LinkedList` to support iteration, so we define the `iterate` function:

```
Base.iterate(ll::LinkedList) = ll.head === nothing ? nothing :
(ll.head.value, ll.head)
Base.iterate(ll::LinkedList{T}, state::ListNode{T}) where T =
    state.next === nothing ? nothing : (state.next.value, state.next)
```

Finally, we define several basic functions that operate on our `LinkedList` type:

```
function Base.getindex(ll::LinkedList, idx::Integer)
    idx < 1 && throw(BoundsError("$idx is less than 1"))
    for v in ll
        idx -= 1
        idx == 0 && return v
    end
    throw(BoundsError("index beyond end of linked list"))
end

function Base.pushfirst!(ll::LinkedList{T}, items::T...) where T
```

```
    for item in reverse(items)
        ll.head = ListNode{T}(item, ll.head)
    end
    ll
end

Base.show(io::IO, ll::LinkedList{T}) where T =
    print(io, "LinkedList{$T}[" * join(ll, ", ") * "]")

Base.eltype(ll::LinkedList{T}) where T = T

Base.length(ll::LinkedList) = count(v -> true, ll)

Base.firstindex(ll::LinkedList) = 1
Base.lastindex(ll::LinkedList) = length(ll)
```

Execute the contents of ll.jl file by running the include("ll.jl") command in the Julia command line. Now you can test the newly defined type:

```
julia> charlist = LinkedList(Char)
LinkedList{Char}[]

julia> pushfirst!(charlist, collect("12345")...)
LinkedList{Char}[1, 2, 3, 4, 5]

julia> collect(charlist)
5-element Array{Char,1}:
 '1'
 '2'
 '3'
 '4'
 '5'

julia> charlist[1], charlist[5]
('1', '5')

julia> charlist[0]
ERROR: BoundsError: attempt to access "0 is less than 1"
Stacktrace:
 [1] getindex(::LinkedList{Char}, ::Int64)
 [2] top-level scope at none:0

julia> charlist[6]
ERROR: BoundsError: attempt to access "index beyond end of linked list"
Stacktrace:
 [1] getindex(::LinkedList{Char}, ::Int64)
 [2] top-level scope at none:0
```

```
julia> charlist[end]
'5': ASCII/Unicode U+0035 (category Nd: Number, decimal digit)
```

How it works...

In this recipe, we define two types: `ListNode{T}` and `LinkedList{T}`. Both types are generic and take the parameter `T`, which is the type of data stored in the linked list. This means that, by default, only constructors that are passed the type `T` in curly braces are defined; for example, you can construct `ListNode{Int}(12)` or `LinkedList{Float64}(nothing)`. Therefore, we provide a special outer constructor that creates an empty `LinkedList` taking the type of contained data as an argument.

Also, observe in the definition of both types that the `next` and `head` fields can either have a value of type `ListNode{T}` or be of type `Nothing`. Such small unions are efficiently handled by Julia.

Next, we make our `LinkedList{T}` follow the iteration protocol. For this, we define a method for the `iterate` function, which will allow `LinkedList{T}` to be used in `for` loops. The definition of the `iterate` function must obey two rules:

- A single argument version should accept the collection and return either a tuple of the first item and initial state, or `Nothing` if the collection is empty.
- The two-argument version should accept the collection and its state and return either a tuple of the next item and the next state, or `Nothing` if no items remain in the collection.

Finally, we define methods for the following standard functions from `Base` to work with `LinkedList{T}`:

- `getindex` allows accessing elements of the defined type by their index using square braces (note that this is an $O(n)$ operation though)
- `pushfirst!` adds items at the beginning of the collection
- `show` provides a custom display of our `LinkedList{T}` type
- `eltype` allows us to get the type stored in our `LinkedList`
- `length` returns the length of the collection
- `firstindex` and `lastindex` return the first and last valid index, respectively, in our `LinkedList`; defining the `lastindex` method allows `charlist[end]` to work correctly

At the end of the example, we create a simple instance of `LinkedList{Char}`. Observe that the `collect` function works on our type without having to define a custom method for it.

Note that in this recipe when we want to define a method for some function from `Base` we have to prepend it with `Base.`. If we omitted this step a new function in module Main would get defined (or the definition would fail if a given function is earlier invoked or referenced to during the Julia command line session) and the recipe would fail to work.

There's more...

If we wanted a fully functional linked list type, we could make it a subtype of `AbstractArray` and define additional functions required by the indexing and array protocols:

- **Indexing protocol**: `setindex!` (You should probably change the `ListNode` type to `mutable struct` if you want to support assignment).
- **Array protocol**: `size` (defined underneath), `setindex!`, `similar`.

Here is an example of how the `size` method from the iteration protocol can be defined:

```
Base.size(ll::LinkedList) = (length(ll),)
Base.size(ll::LinkedList, dim::Int) =
    if dim == 1
        length(ll)
    elseif dim > 1
        1
    else
        throw(ArgumentError("negative dimension"))
    end
end
```

See also

The iteration protocol is defined here `https://docs.julialang.org/en/latest/manual/interfaces/#man-interface-iteration-1`.

The index protocol is defined here `https://docs.julialang.org/en/latest/manual/interfaces/#Indexing-1`.

The abstract array protocol is defined here `https://docs.julialang.org/en/latest/manual/interfaces/#man-interface-array-1`.

Defining primitive types

In Julia, you are able to define your own composite types, as explained in the previous recipe. However, you can also define your own raw-bytes type, like `Float64` or `UInt32`.

Getting ready

ARGB (see `https://en.wikipedia.org/wiki/RGBA_color_space#ARGB_(word-order)`) is a method of encoding the color of a pixel, where **A** (α) stands for **pixel opacity**, and **R** (**red**), **G** (**green**), and **B** (**blue**) are the components of its color. Each component takes eight bits, making 32 bits in total. In this recipe, we will create a custom primitive type that facilitates working with ARGB-encoded data.

 In the GitHub repository for this recipe, you will find the `commands.txt` file that contains the presented sequence of shell and Julia commands. Additionally, in the `argb.jl` file you can find the definitions of the `ARGB` type and related methods used in this recipe.

Now open your favorite terminal to execute the commands.

How to do it...

Start by inspecting the contents of the `argb.jl` file. First, we define the new type:

```
primitive type ARGB 32 end
```

Next, we add its basic constructors:

```
ARGB(c::UInt32) = reinterpret(ARGB, c)
ARGB(c) = ARGB(UInt32(c))
ARGB(α::UInt8, red::UInt8, green::UInt8, blue::UInt8) =
    ARGB(UInt32(α) << 24 + UInt32(red) << 16 +
        UInt32(green) << 8 + UInt32(blue))
ARGB(α, red, green, blue) = ARGB(UInt8(α), UInt8(red),
                                UInt8(green), UInt8(blue))
```

We also add a constructor allowing ARGB objects to be created from a string:

```
function ARGB(c::AbstractString)
    if !occursin(r"^#[0-9a-fA-F]{8}$", c)
        throw(DomainError("wrong color string: $c"))
    end
    ARGB(parse(UInt32, c[2:end], base=16))
end

macro ARGB_str(s) ARGB(s) end
```

Next comes the functions allowing us to extract components of the ARGB type:

```
α(c::ARGB)::UInt8 = (UInt32(c) >> 24) & 0x000000FF
red(c::ARGB)::UInt8 = (UInt32(c) >> 16) & 0x000000FF
green(c::ARGB)::UInt8 = (UInt32(c) >> 8) & 0x000000FF
blue(c::ARGB)::UInt8 = UInt32(c) & 0x000000FF
```

Finally, we define methods allowing for conversions between the ARGB type and the UInt32 and String types:

```
Base.UInt32(c::ARGB) = reinterpret(UInt32, c)
convert(UInt32, c::ARGB) = UInt32(c)
convert(ARGB, c::UInt32) = ARGB(c)
Base.String(c::ARGB) = "#" * lpad(string(UInt32(c), base=16), 8, "0")
convert(String, c::ARGB) = String(c)
convert(ARGB, c::AbstractString) = ARGB(c)
```

In order to test our newly defined type, first execute the contents of the argb.jl file by running the command include("argb.jl") in the Julia command line. Now you can create an instance of ARGB type and work with it using the following commands:

```
julia> ARGB(10,11,12,13)
ARGB(0x0a0b0c0d)

julia> c = ARGB"#12345678"
ARGB(0x12345678)

julia> [f(c) for f in [α, red, green, blue]]
4-element Array{UInt8,1}:
 0x12
 0x34
 0x56
 0x78

julia> UInt32(c)
0x12345678
```

```
julia> String(c)
"#12345678"
```

How it works...

It is simple to define a primitive type; you just need to specify its name and the number of bits it should accept. The tricky part is defining how to operate on it. The key function that allows this is `reinterpret`, which takes a block of memory and changes its interpretation to the desired type. Using this function, we create a two-way mapping between our ARGB type and UInt32 type.

In the recipe, we provide several constructors of the ARGB type. One thing to note is that for constructors taking four arguments, we define their versions performing conversion of an argument to the required type. This approach is similar to how a default constructor for `struct` or `mutable struct` would behave.

We also provide a constructor taking a string with a standard form #XXXXXXXX and which accepts hexadecimal digits. In particular, we define a simple macro that allows the user to create ARGB objects using the ARGB"#XXXXXXXX" notation.

Finally, one last thing to observe is that when we define the `convert` methods, they fall back to constructors since this is the recommended approach for defining a new type in Julia.

There's more...

When you define a primitive type, it is good to have an easy way to perform a two-way conversion between this type and some standard type that consists of bits. In our example, this standard type is UInt32. This allows you to simply add methods for working on a new type. For instance, if we wanted to write a function that would zero the alpha channel of our ARGB type, this would be one way to do it:

```
julia> zeroalpha(c::ARGB) = ARGB(UInt32(c) & 0x00FFFFFF)
```

And we can see that we convert to UInt32 and back to ARGB, taking advantage of the fact that & is defined for the UInt32 type.

It is important to know that the Julia compiler handles such conversions very efficiently, as can be seen in the following example:

```
julia> c = ARGB"#12345678"
```

```
ARGB(0x12345678)

julia> zeroalpha(c)
ARGB(0x00345678)

julia> @code_native zeroalpha(c)
        .text
; Function zeroalpha {
; Location: REPL[21]:1
        pushq %rbp
        movq %rsp, %rbp
; Function &; {
; Location: int.jl:297
        andl $16777215, %ecx # imm = 0xFFFFFF
;}
        movl %ecx, %eax
        popq %rbp
        retq
        nop
;}
```

Evidently, there is no overhead from using the ARGB type here.

See also

The documentation of primitive types in Julia is provided at https://docs.julialang. org/en/v1.0/manual/types/#Primitive-Types-1.

Understanding the structure of Julia numeric types with introspection

Julia has a wealth of built-in numeric types, which users can make use of in order to achieve maximum time and memory efficiency of computations. Also, when writing methods, it is advisable to choose the most general numeric type to which a given method applies. However, it is hard to easily grasp the entire hierarchy of types. In this recipe, we show how you can explore the entire tree of base numeric types in Julia. Additionally, you will learn how to work with the type hierarchy in Julia.

The recipe is generic and can be applied to any other type.

Getting ready

Numeric types are the basic building blocks of any program. Julia provides a vast range of integer and floating-point numbers. In this recipe, you will inspect their hierarchy.

 In the GitHub repository for this recipe, you will find the commands.txt file that contains the presented sequence of shell and Julia commands. Additionally, in the types.jl file you can find the definitions of methods used in this recipe.

Now open your favorite terminal to execute the commands.

How to do it...

Firstly, define and inspect the following contents of the types.jl file the:

```
function printsubtypes(T, indent=0)
    sT = subtypes(T)
    println(" "^indent, T, isempty(sT) ? "" : ":")
    for S in sT
        printsubtypes(S, indent + 1)
    end
end

function supertypes(T)
    print(T)
    if T != Any
        print(" <: ")
        S = supertype(T)
        supertypes(S)
    end
end
```

The first function prints all subtypes of a given type, and the second prints all its supertypes.

The base type of the entire numeric type hierarchy in Julia is Number, so we now call printsubtypes, passing this type as an argument. In order to do it, first execute the types.jl file by running the command include("types.jl") in the Julia command line. Now we can test the functions it defines:

```
julia> printsubtypes(Number)
Number:
 Complex
```

```
    Real:
     AbstractFloat:
      BigFloat
      Float16
      Float32
      Float64
     AbstractIrrational:
      Irrational
     Integer:
      Bool
      Signed:
       BigInt
       Int128
       Int16
       Int32
       Int64
       Int8
      Unsigned:
       UInt128
       UInt16
       UInt32
       UInt64
       UInt8
     Rational

julia> supertypes(Bool)
Bool <: Integer <: Real <: Number <: Any
```

How it works...

The output shows us that Number has two subtypes: Complex and Real. Most of the types are self-explanatory for a programmer with moderate experience. However, it is worth highlighting here that the Irrational type is reserved for such mathematical constants as π or the Euler constant. Also, note that Bool is a subtype of Integer. If Boolean values are used in numeric computations, true is converted to 1 and false to 0. Additionally, if you want to perform arbitrary precision arithmetic, you can use BigInt and BigFloat types, albeit at the cost of considerable performance degradation. Finally, the Rational type allows you to work with fractions without loss of precision of computations.

The supertypes function does the inverse operation—it starts from a given type and walks up the type hierarchy to reach the root type, which is called Any. In the formatting of output, we use the <: symbol because it is used in Julia as a subtype operator; that is, $T <: S$ is true if all values of type T are also values of type S.

The `printsubtypes` function takes two arguments: the type for which we want to list its subtypes, and the indentation level for printing (defaulting to 0).

First, we call the `subtypes` function, which returns a vector of subtypes of a given type.

In the line `println(" "^indent, T, isempty(sT) ? "" : ":")`, we show several features of Julia:

- `" "^indent` repeats the `" "` string `indent` times so that we can clearly see the hierarchy of types
- `isempty(sT) ? "" : ":"` means that if `sT` is not empty (type `T` has subtypes), a colon will be printed at the end of the line
- Finally, we see that the `println` function can take several arguments that will be printed consecutively

We traverse the elements of `sT` using a `for` loop and recursively call `printsubtypes` while increasing the indentation by one level. Note that this recursion is not invoked if `sT` is empty (that is, a given type has no subtypes).

The `supertypes` function is simpler. It recursively moves to a supertype of a given type by calling the `supertype` function until we reach the root type, `Any`. At this point, we have to break the recurrence as the call `supertype(Any)` itself returns `Any`.

There's more...

It is important to highlight that concrete types (types that can have objects of their type) may not have subtypes. For example, `Integer` has subtypes and so it is impossible to create variables of this type. Such types are called **abstract**. You can check if a type is abstract using the `isabstracttype` function. Such types, as mentioned earlier, are typically used in function signatures to indicate that some function accepts any concrete type that is a subtype of `Integer`.

Another thing you may have noticed in the Julia code is that a type with the name `Int` is used, yet it is not present in our list. The solution to this puzzle is that it is an alias for `Int32` on 32-bit machines and for `Int64` on 64-bit machines. Here it is worth adding that integer literals, such as `123`, are interpreted as having type `Int` by default. There is also a similar type, `UInt`, that is unsigned.

The other noteworthy issue is that some of the types in a given hierarchy are actually parametric—that is, they define the full range of concrete types and their instances have an additional parameter. For example, complex numbers can be defined over any `Real` type:

```
julia> typeof(1 + 1im)
Complex{Int64}

julia> typeof(1.0 + 1.0im)
Complex{Float64}
```

See also

See the *Ensuring type stability of your code* recipe in this chapter for more examples of working with numeric types in Julia.

Using static arrays

The `StaticArrays.jl` package provides an interface and tools for the creation and manipulation of statically-sized arrays in Julia. Compared to a normal `Array` type, in a `StaticArray` the array size is part of the data type definition. The `StaticArrays.jl` package supports the creation of immutable as well as immutable arrays. The usage of statically-sized arrays in many scenarios leads to huge performance benefits since the array size is known to the compiler. This is particularly visible for small arrays (up to 100 elements). In this recipe, we show `StaticArrays.jl` can be used to boost the performance of Julia code.

Getting ready

For this recipe, you need to install the `StaticArrays.jl` package. In the Julia command line (REPL), press the] key to start the Julia package manager and run the command:

```
(v1.0) pkg> add StaticArrays
```

This will install the `StaticArrays.jl` library and all its dependencies.

Additionally, to measure the performance of static arrays, we will use the
BenchmarkTools.jl package:

(v1.0) pkg> add BenchmarkTools

 In the GitHub repository for this recipe, you will find the commands.txt
file that contains the presented sequence of shell and Julia commands.

How to do it...

In this example, we will test various array operations where StaticArray is used as a
drop-in replacement for the standard Julia Array in order to increase execution speed:

1. We start by importing the StaticArrays.jl package, along with the
    BenchmarkTools and Random modules that we will use for testing:

    ```
    using StaticArrays
    using BenchmarkTools
    using Random
    ```

2. We will simulate the profits of a small business that purchases goods with a very
    short life-span (for example, flowers or food products)— the company buys *s*
    items in the morning and sells *min(s,d)*, where *d* is the observed demand. We
    assume that *s* and *d* are uniformly distributed in the range *[0,100]*. The profits
    from such trading could be represented by the following function:

    ```
    function profit(demand, prices_sale, purchases, prices_purchase)
        sales = min.(purchases,demand)
        sum(sales .* prices_sale .- purchases .* prices_purchase)
    end
    ```

    The preceding function calculates profits for a given demand level.

3. Now we define the values that will be used for our computations:

    ```
    Random.seed!(0);
    demand, prices_sale, purchases, prices_purchase =
        (rand(10).*100, 300:10:390, rand(10).*100, 100:10:190);
    ```

4. We define the same values using data types available in the `StaticArrays.jl` package (we assumed that the number of products that we use to calculate the profit is fixed while running these computations):

```
Random.seed!(0);
demand_s, prices_sale_s, purchases_s, prices_purchase_s =
    (((@SVector rand(10)).*100, SVector{10}(300:10:390),
    (@SVector rand(10)).*100, SVector{10}(100:10:190));
```

5. Let's now compare the execution times for the `profit` function with both parameter sets:

```
julia> @btime profit($demand, $prices_sale,
                     $purchases, $prices_purchase)
  135.780 ns (2 allocations: 320 bytes)
11056.395760776286

julia> @btime profit($demand_s, $prices_sale_s,
                     $purchases_s, $prices_purchase_s)
  34.290 ns (0 allocations: 0 bytes)
11056.395760776286
```

We can see that for the same function the execution times are around four times shorter when static-sized arrays are used in place of regular arrays.

How it works...

The `StaticArrays.jl` package enables information about the dimensions of an array to be stored and uses a series of `@generated` functions that statically iterate over the array elements. Since the size of the array is known at compile time, the Julia compiler system can perform several types of code optimizations, including loop unrolling (representing a loop as a series of statements—see https://en.wikipedia.org/wiki/Loop_unrolling). The resulting lowered code (that can be observed by running the `@code_lowered` macro) can be greatly optimized when compiled by the LLVM, including greater ability (compared to regular `Arrays`) to utilize the **SIMD** (short for **single instruction multiple data**) feature of Intel's processor. Hence, when the size of an array is known and the array size is not large (see the *There's more...* section of this recipe), the `StaticArrays.jl` package is the recommended way to handle numerical operations.

There's more...

In the preceding examples we have used the SVector type, representing a statistically-sized immutable vector. Let's take a look at a similar example with a statically-sized matrix.

Consider the following code:

```julia
julia> a=rand(5, 5);

julia> b=rand(5, 5);

julia> @btime $a*$b;
  259.765 ns (1 allocation: 336 bytes)

julia> as=rand(SMatrix{5,5});
julia> bs=rand(SMatrix{5,5});

julia> @btime $as*$bs;
  36.020 ns (0 allocations: 0 bytes)
```

In the preceding scenario, we can see that matrix multiplication is over seven times faster with StaticArrays.jl.

Since the package speed is achieved by internally using a lot of @generated functions for each static array type, the usage of the package is recommended for arrays up to 100 elements. Note that in our example, the compiler time required to generate a 100 element static array (in the following example code SMatrix{1,100}) is 2.34 seconds, and that it doubles with each additional 100 elements:

```julia
julia> @time m1 = rand(SMatrix{1,10});
  0.065490 seconds (129.97 k allocations: 5.778 MiB)

julia> @time m1 = rand(SMatrix{1,100});
  2.340947 seconds (304.61 k allocations: 15.495 MiB, 0.57% gc time)

julia> @time m1 = rand(SMatrix{1,200});
  7.003616 seconds (602.77 k allocations: 37.473 MiB, 0.87% gc time)

julia> @time m1 = rand(SMatrix{1,500});
  63.653265 seconds (1.50 M allocations: 147.813 MiB, 0.07% gc time)
```

However, once the static type has been generated, the subsequent calls to the library are very fast; for example:

```julia
julia> @time m1 = rand(SMatrix{1,500});
  0.000069 seconds (36 allocations: 6.125 KiB)
```

The preceding test demonstrates that when using `StaticArrays`, there is a tradeoff between the performance gain achieved in the runtime versus extended compilation times.

See also

The documentation for the `StaticArrays.jl` package is available at `https://github.com/JuliaArrays/StaticArrays.jl`.

The efficiency of mutable versus immutable types

Julia allows the user to define mutable and immutable types. In this recipe, we will show how their performance compares in a process of simulating a two-dimensional random walk.

Getting ready

Consider a process starting from a point, $x_t = (x_{1,0}, x_{2,0}) = (0,0)$, and updated following the rule: $x_{t+1} = x_t + (r_{1,t}, r_{2,t})$, where $r_{1,t}$ and $r_{2,t}$ are sequences of independent random variables taking values 1 and -1 with probability $1/2$.

Our objective is to generate two values:

- The maximum distance reached from the origin point during the simulation measured as $\max\limits_{t\in\{0,1,\ldots,10^6\}} |x_{1,t}| + |x_{2,t}|$
- A vector containing the path of the random walk

We will model this random walk process using a Monte Carlo simulation.

 In the GitHub repository for this recipe, you will find the `commands.txt` file that contains the presented sequence of shell and Julia commands. Additionally, in the `walk.jl` and `work.jl` files you can find the definitions of the types and related methods used in this recipe.

Now open your favorite terminal to execute the commands.

How to do it...

We will define the simulation in two distinct ways. In the first we use an immutable type, and in the second we use a mutable type.

All the definitions are contained in the `walk.jl` file, so please inspect it now. We start with defining the types:

```
abstract type AbstractPoint end

struct PointI <: AbstractPoint
    x::Int
    y::Int
end

mutable struct PointM <: AbstractPoint
    x::Int
    y::Int
end

PointM(p::PointM) = PointM(p.x, p.y)
```

Now we define two functions, one for calculating the sum of absolute values of the position of the point, and one that moves the point:

```
d(p::AbstractPoint) = abs(p.x) + abs(p.y)
move(p::PointI, d::PointI) = PointI(p.x+d.x, p.y+d.y)
move(p::PointM, d::PointM) = (p.x += d.x; p.y += d.y; p)
```

We are ready to define the simulation, calculating the maximum distance traveled from the starting point . We do it in two variants—immutable and mutable:

```
function simI()
    maxd = 0
    x = PointI(0, 0)
    @inbounds for i in 1:10^6
```

```
            x = move(x, PointI(2rand(Bool)-1, 2rand(Bool)-1))
            curd = d(x)
            maxd = max(maxd, curd)
        end
        maxd
    end

function simM()
    maxd = 0
    x = PointM(0, 0)
    m = PointM(0, 0)
    @inbounds for i in 1:10^6
        m.x, m.y = 2rand(Bool)-1, 2rand(Bool)-1
        move(x, m)
        curd = d(x)
        maxd = max(maxd, curd)
    end
    maxd
end
```

In order to check the performance of both approaches, first execute the walk.jl file using the command include("walk.jl") in the Julia command line.

We now check that their performance is very similar (you need the BenchmarkTools.jl package installed for this example to work; if it is not installed, run the following commands using Pkg; Pkg.add("BenchmarkTools") in the Julia command line):

```
julia> using BenchmarkTools

julia> @benchmark simI()
BenchmarkTools.Trial:
  memory estimate: 0 bytes
  allocs estimate: 0
  --------------
  minimum time: 5.231 ms (0.00% GC)
  median time: 5.465 ms (0.00% GC)
  mean time: 6.254 ms (0.00% GC)
  maximum time: 37.677 ms (0.00% GC)
  --------------
  samples: 799
  evals/sample: 1

julia> @benchmark simM()
BenchmarkTools.Trial:
  memory estimate: 0 bytes
  allocs estimate: 0
  --------------
```

```
minimum time: 5.291 ms (0.00% GC)
median time: 5.527 ms (0.00% GC)
mean time: 6.268 ms (0.00% GC)
maximum time: 16.900 ms (0.00% GC)
--------------
samples: 797
evals/sample: 1
```

Now we move to define functions for collecting the entire path of the random walk. The codes can be also found in the `walk.jl` file:

```
function simI2()
    path = PointI[]
    x = PointI(0, 0)
    @inbounds for i in 1:10^6
        push!(path, x)
        x = move(x, PointI(2rand(Bool)-1, 2rand(Bool)-1))
    end
    path
end

function simM2()
    path = PointM[]
    x = PointM(0, 0)
    m = PointM(0, 0)
    @inbounds for i in 1:10^6
        push!(path, PointM(x))
        m.x, m.y = 2rand(Bool)-1, 2rand(Bool)-1
        move(x, m)
    end
    path
end
```

When we benchmark them, we observe a significant performance difference:

```
julia> @benchmark simI2()
BenchmarkTools.Trial:
  memory estimate: 17.00 MiB
  allocs estimate: 20
  --------------
  minimum time: 32.483 ms (0.00% GC)
  median time: 33.773 ms (0.00% GC)
  mean time: 36.740 ms (7.84% GC)
  maximum time: 49.264 ms (32.69% GC)
  --------------
  samples: 127
  evals/sample: 1
```

```
julia> @benchmark simM2()
BenchmarkTools.Trial:
  memory estimate: 39.52 MiB
  allocs estimate: 1000020
  --------------
  minimum time: 43.856 ms (29.56% GC)
  median time: 57.796 ms (40.67% GC)
  mean time: 61.260 ms (44.41% GC)
  maximum time: 213.813 ms (73.62% GC)
  --------------
  samples: 82
  evals/sample: 1
```

How it works...

We first create two concrete types—one immutable and one mutable, which are subtypes of a common abstract type. Importantly, it is convenient for the mutable version to define an outer constructor that takes PointM and creates a new PointM with the same coordinates. We typically would not need it for an immutable type, as such a constructor would simply be an identity function.

Next, the d function that calculates the distance from the origin is generically defined over an abstract type. However, the move function has two separate methods. For an immutable type, a new object is created with a new location. On the other hand, for a mutable type, we can update the object in place (this is not possible for immutable types).

As demonstrated earlier, the simI and simM functions have very similar performance. The reason for this is that we are able to use two instances of a PointM type that are only mutated. Such an operation will be as equally fast as using an immutable type in this case.

However, we can see that if we want to store the entire path of a random walk, as we do in simI2 and simM2, the situation is significantly different and the mutable type is less efficient. The reason, in this case, is that we have to make a copy of the PointM object, and this creates a significant amount of allocations and slows down execution.

There's more...

There are cases when working with mutable structures will be more efficient than immutable. This happens in situations when the data structure has a big memory footprint and only a small part of it needs to be mutated. Here is an example code setup (you can find it in the work.jl file):

```
struct T1
    x::NTuple{1000, Int}
    y::Int
end

mutable struct T2
    x::NTuple{1000, Int}
    y::Int
end

function worker1()
    p = T1(ntuple(x->1, 1000), 0)
    for i in 1:10^6
        p = T1(p.x, p.y+1)
    end
    p
end

function worker2()
    p = T2(ntuple(x->1, 1000), 0)
    for i in 1:10^6
        p.y += 1
    end
    p
end
```

And the results of benchmarks (in order to run the tests first execute the command include("work.jl") in the Julia command line):

```
julia> @benchmark worker1()
BenchmarkTools.Trial:
  memory estimate: 31.75 KiB
  allocs estimate: 6
  --------------
  minimum time: 404.016 μs (0.00% GC)
  median time: 435.274 μs (0.00% GC)
  mean time: 455.677 μs (1.88% GC)
  maximum time: 69.270 ms (99.34% GC)
  --------------
  samples: 10000
```

```
  evals/sample: 1

julia> @benchmark worker2()
BenchmarkTools.Trial:
  memory estimate: 39.69 KiB
  allocs estimate: 7
  --------------
  minimum time: 32.190 µs (0.00% GC)
  median time: 33.124 µs (0.00% GC)
  mean time: 38.904 µs (6.03% GC)
  maximum time: 17.854 ms (99.73% GC)
  --------------
  samples: 10000
  evals/sample: 1
```

See also

If you are interested in fast implementations of arrays, you can check out the *Using static arrays* recipe, which discusses the static array type.

Ensuring type stability of your code

In this recipe, we discuss how to detect problems with the type stability of Julia code and how to solve them. In particular, we concentrate on exploring type stability in closures.

Getting ready

You will work with a function for calculating the roots of a quadratic equation:

$ax^2 + bx + c = 0$ using the well-known formula $x_{1,2} = \dfrac{-b \pm \sqrt{b^2 - 4ac}}{2a}$ if $a \neq 0$.

 In the GitHub repository for this recipe, you will find the commands.txt file that contains the presented sequence of shell and Julia commands. Additionally, in the quad.jl file you can find the definitions of methods used in this recipe.

Now open your favorite terminal to execute the commands.

How to do it...

Start by running the command include("quad.jl"), which defines the following two functions for calculating the desired roots of the quadratic equation:

```
function quadratic1(a, b, c)
    t(s) = (-b + s*sqrt(Δ))/(2a)
    a == 0 && error("a must be different than zero")
    Δ = Complex(b^2-4*a*c)
    t(1), t(-1)
end

function quadratic2(a, b, c)
    Δ = Complex(b^2-4*a*c)
    t(s) = (-b + s*sqrt(Δ))/(2a)
    a == 0 && error("a must be different than zero")
    t(1), t(-1)
end
```

Although they seemingly perform the same work, when we benchmark them, it turns out that they have significantly different performance characteristics (you need to have the BenchmarkTools.jl package installed for this code to work; if it is not installed, add it using the commands using Pkg; Pkg.add("BenchmarkTools") in the Julia command line):

```
julia> using BenchmarkTools

julia> @benchmark quadratic1(1,2,3)
BenchmarkTools.Trial:
  memory estimate: 384 bytes
  allocs estimate: 12
  --------------
  minimum time: 545.941 ns (0.00% GC)
  median time: 560.835 ns (0.00% GC)
  mean time: 663.809 ns (9.55% GC)
  maximum time: 276.220 μs (99.67% GC)
  --------------
  samples: 10000
  evals/sample: 188

julia> @benchmark quadratic2(1,2,3)
BenchmarkTools.Trial:
  memory estimate: 0 bytes
  allocs estimate: 0
  --------------
  minimum time: 81.643 ns (0.00% GC)
  median time: 83.043 ns (0.00% GC)
```

```
mean time: 87.307 ns (0.00% GC)
maximum time: 192.678 ns (0.00% GC)
--------------
samples: 10000
evals/sample: 1000
```

This is puzzling, so let's first check the code with the @inferred macro from the Test module:

```julia
julia> using Test

julia> @inferred quadratic1(1,2,3)
ERROR: return type Tuple{Complex{Float64},Complex{Float64}} does not match
inferred return type Tuple{Any,Any}
Stacktrace:
 [1] error(::String) at .\error.jl:33
 [2] top-level scope at none:0

julia> @inferred quadratic2(1,2,3)
(-1.0 + 1.4142135623730951im, -1.0 - 1.4142135623730951im)
```

It seems that the quadratic1 function is not type-stable, while quadratic2 is. We can investigate further using the @code_warntype macro:

```julia
julia> @code_warntype quadratic1(1,2,3)
Body::Tuple{Any,Any}
2 1 ─ %1 = new(Core.Box)::Core.Box │ │ Type
  │   %2 = new(getfield(Main, Symbol("#t#11")){Int64,Int64}, %%a, %%b,
%1)::getfield(Main, Symbol("#t#11")){Int64,Int64}
3 │   %3 = Base.:===(%%a, 0)::Bool │ │ ==
  └──      goto 4 if not %3 │
  2 ─ %5 = new(Core.ErrorException, "a must be different than
zero")::ErrorException │ │ │ Type
  │   Base.throw(%5) │ │
  └──      unreachable │ │
  3 ─ φ () │
  └──      unreachable │
4 4   %10 = Base.mul_int(%%b, %%b)::Int64 │ │ │ literal_pow
  │   %11 = Base.mul_int(4, %%a)::Int64 │ │ │ *
  │   %12 = Base.mul_int(%11, %%c)::Int64 │ │ │
  │   %13 = Base.sub_int(%10, %12)::Int64 │ │ -
  │   %14 = new(Complex{Int64}, %13, 0)::Complex{Int64} │ │ │ │ Type
  │   Core.setfield!(%1, :(:contents), %14) │
5 │   %16 = invoke %2(1::Int64)::Any │
  │   %17 = invoke %2(-1::Int64)::Any │
  │   %18 = Core.tuple(%16, %17)::Tuple{Any,Any} │
  └──      return %18 │
  5 ─ goto 4 │
```

```
julia> @code_warntype quadratic2(1,2,3)
Body::Tuple{Complex{Float64},Complex{Float64}}
2 1 ─ %1  = Base.mul_int(%%b, %%b)::Int64 | | | literal_pow
  │ %2  = Base.mul_int(4, %%a)::Int64 | | | *
  │ %3  = Base.mul_int(%2, %%c)::Int64 | | |
  │ %4  = Base.sub_int(%1, %3)::Int64 | | ─
4 │ %5  = Base.:===(%%a, 0)::Bool | | ==
  └── goto 4 if not %5 |
  2 ─ %7  = new(Core.ErrorException, "a must be different than
zero")::ErrorException | | | Type
  │ Base.throw(%7) | |
  └── unreachable | |
  3 ─ φ () |
  └── unreachable |
5 4 %12 = Base.neg_int(%%b)::Int64 | | | t
  │ %13 = Base.sitofp(Float64, %4)::Float64 | | | | | | sqrt
  │ %14 = Base.sitofp(Float64, 0)::Float64 | | | | | float
  │ %15 = new(Complex{Float64}, %13, %14)::Complex{Float64} | | | | | Type
  │ %16 = invoke Base.sqrt(%15::Complex{Float64})::Complex{Float64} | | |
  │ %17 = Base.getfield(%16, :(:re))::Float64 | | | | | real
  │ %18 = Base.mul_float(1.0, %17)::Float64 | | | | | *
  │ %19 = Base.getfield(%16, :(:im))::Float64 | | | | | getproperty
  │ %20 = Base.mul_float(1.0, %19)::Float64 | | | | | *
  │ %21 = Base.sitofp(Float64, %12)::Float64 | | | | | | | | +
  │ %22 = Base.add_float(%21, %18)::Float64 | | | | | +
  │ %23 = Base.mul_int(2, %%a)::Int64 | | | *
  │ %24 = Base.sitofp(Float64, %23)::Float64 | | | | | | | | /
  │ %25 = Base.div_float(%22, %24)::Float64 | | | | | /
  │ %26 = Base.sitofp(Float64, %23)::Float64 | | | | | | | | promote
  │ %27 = Base.div_float(%20, %26)::Float64 | | | | | /
  │ %28 = new(Complex{Float64}, %25, %27)::Complex{Float64} | | | | | Type
  │ %29 = Base.neg_int(%%b)::Int64 | | | ─
  │ %30 = Base.sitofp(Float64, %4)::Float64 | | | | | | | float
  │ %31 = Base.sitofp(Float64, 0)::Float64 | | | | | | float
  │ %32 = new(Complex{Float64}, %30, %31)::Complex{Float64} | | | | | | Type
  │ %33 = invoke Base.sqrt(%32::Complex{Float64})::Complex{Float64} | | |
  │ %34 = Base.getfield(%33, :(:re))::Float64 | | | | | real
  │ %35 = Base.mul_float(-1.0, %34)::Float64 | | | | | *
  │ %36 = Base.getfield(%33, :(:im))::Float64 | | | | | getproperty
  │ %37 = Base.mul_float(-1.0, %36)::Float64 | | | | | *
  │ %38 = Base.sitofp(Float64, %29)::Float64 | | | | | | | | +
  │ %39 = Base.add_float(%38, %35)::Float64 | | | | | +
  │ %40 = Base.mul_int(2, %%a)::Int64 | | | *
  │ %41 = Base.sitofp(Float64, %40)::Float64 | | | | | | | | /
  │ %42 = Base.div_float(%39, %41)::Float64 | | | | | /
  │ %43 = Base.sitofp(Float64, %40)::Float64 | | | | | | | | promote
  │ %44 = Base.div_float(%37, %43)::Float64 | | | | | /
  │ %45 = new(Complex{Float64}, %42, %44)::Complex{Float64} | | | | | Type
```

```
 |  %46 = Core.tuple(%28, %45)::Tuple{Complex{Float64},Complex{Float64}} |
 └── return %46  |
5 ─ goto 4
```

We provide a detailed explanation of the difference between these two functions in the following section.

How it works...

The reason for the slow performance of the quadratic1 function is that it is not type-stable. In Julia, this means that the compiler is generally unable to determine the types of all variables used in the body of the function. There are two possible reasons for this. One is that the type of the variable changes during execution of the function, and the other is that there is some obstacle preventing type inference from working (at least at the current stage of the Julia compiler).

In this recipe, we discuss the second problem, as it is subtler. The first one (changing of the variable type) is much simpler and is explained in detail in the Julia manual at https://docs.julialang.org/en/v1.0/manual/performance-tips/#Avoid-changing-the-type-of-a-variable-1.

We want to figure out why quadratic1 has type stability problems. The reason is that the inner function t is defined unconditionally, but variable Δ is defined only if a is not equal to 0. This means, at least given the present capabilities of the Julia compiler, that when Julia compiles the quadratic1 function, it is not able to unconditionally decide the type of Δ (if we had a branch of code where a==0 and called t from there, then the type may indeed be different).

The simple solution in quadratic2 is to move the definition of Δ before the branching statement. The other solution would be to pass Δ as an argument to t, like this:

```
julia> function quadratic3(a, b, c)
           t(s,Δ) = (-b + s*sqrt(Δ))/(2a)
           a == 0 && error("a must be different than zero")
           Δ = Complex(b^2-4*a*c)
           t(1,Δ), t(-1,Δ)
       end
quadratic3 (generic function with 1 method)

julia> @benchmark quadratic3(1,2,3)
BenchmarkTools.Trial:
  memory estimate: 0 bytes
  allocs estimate: 0
  --------------
```

```
minimum time: 81.643 ns (0.00% GC)
median time: 83.043 ns (0.00% GC)
mean time: 87.886 ns (0.00% GC)
maximum time: 177.282 ns (0.00% GC)
--------------
samples: 10000
evals/sample: 1000
```

And we see that `quadratic3` has the same performance as `quadratic2`.

In the recipe we used the `@inferred` macro from the `Test` module. This macro is useful when you want to check if the call expression returns a value of the same type as is inferred by the compiler. If this macro throws an error it typically is a signal that the function we test has problems with type stability.

See also

We highly recommend reading the performance issues section in the Julia manual that can be found at `https://docs.julialang.org/en/v1.0/manual/performance-tips/`.

7
Handling Analytical Data

In this chapter, we take a deep dive into the `DataFrames.jl` package ecosystem, which allows you to conveniently perform the most common data transformation tasks. In particular, we cover the following topics:

- Converting between `DataFrame` and `Matrix`
- Investigating the contents of `DataFrame`
- Reading CSV data from the internet into `DataFrame`
- Working with categorical data
- Handling missing data
- Applying the split-apply-combine pattern to `DataFrame`
- Converting `DataFrame` between wide and narrow formats
- Comparing two data frames for identity
- Applying complex transformations to rows of `DataFrame`
- Creating pivot tables by chaining operations on data frames

Introduction

Working with tabular data is the most basic and common task in a typical workflow in data science projects. In this chapter, you will learn how support for working with such data is provided in the Julia language by the `DataFrame.jl` package. We will discuss how to read data into `DataFrame`, how to export it, how to inspect the contents of `DataFrame`, and finally how to perform transformations of objects of `DataFrame` type.

Converting data between DataFrame and Matrix

The DataFrames.jl package provides a vast array of procedures that allow you to manipulate tabular data with rows of heterogeneous types. However, you often have your data stored initially in a matrix. In this recipe, we discuss how you can convert such data to DataFrame. We also show how you can perform the reverse procedure, that is, transform the data from DataFrame to a value of a standard Matrix type available in Julia.

Getting ready

Make sure that you have the DataFrames.jl package installed. You can check this by writing this in the Julia command line:

```
julia> using DataFrames
```

If this command fails, then add the DataFrames.jl package, in accordance with the instructions in the *Managing packages* recipe in Chapter 1, *Installing and Setting Up Julia*:

```
julia> using Pkg; Pkg.add("DataFrames")
```

 In the GitHub repository for this recipe, you will find the commands.txt file, which contains the presented sequence of shell and Julia commands.

Now, open your favorite terminal to execute the commands.

How to do it...

Here is a list of the steps that we follow:

1. We start by creating a matrix to work with, in order to show how to create DataFrame from Matrix:

```
julia> mat = [x*y for x in 1:3, y in 1:4]
3×4 Array{Int64,2}:
 1  2  3   4
 2  4  6   8
 3  6  9  12
```

2. Convert our matrix `mat` into `DataFrame` by calling the `DataFrame` constructor:

```julia
julia> df = DataFrame(mat)
3×4 DataFrame
| Row | x1    | x2    | x3    | x4    |
|     | Int64 | Int64 | Int64 | Int64 |
|-----|-------|-------|-------|-------|
| 1   | 1     | 2     | 3     | 4     |
| 2   | 2     | 4     | 6     | 8     |
| 3   | 3     | 6     | 9     | 12    |
```

Notice how Julia created the default column names, `x1`, `x2`.

3. If you want specific column names, then this is easy to do; simply pass the desired column names to the `DataFrame` constructor:

```julia
julia> df = DataFrame(mat, [:a, :b, :c, :d])
3×4 DataFrame
| Row | a     | b     | c     | d     |
|     | Int64 | Int64 | Int64 | Int64 |
|-----|-------|-------|-------|-------|
| 1   | 1     | 2     | 3     | 4     |
| 2   | 2     | 4     | 6     | 8     |
| 3   | 3     | 6     | 9     | 12    |
```

Note that column names are passed as `Symbol`.

4. It is equally straightforward to convert `DataFrame` back to a matrix by using the `Matrix` function:

```julia
julia> Matrix(df)
3×4 Array{Int64,2}:
 1  2  3   4
 2  4  6   8
 3  6  9  12
```

How it works...

There are a wide number of methods that can be used to create `DataFrame`. Here are some of the most frequently used methods:

- By using keyword arguments, for example, `DataFrame(a=[1, 2], b = "s")` (the scalar in column `:b` will be converted to a vector of appropriate length)

- By passing column types, column names, and number of rows; for example, `DataFrame([Int, String], [:a, :b], 2)` will create a data frame with two columns that are uninitialized

- By passing a vector of data vectors and, optionally, column names, for example, `DataFrame([[1, 2], ["a", "b"]], [:a, :b])`

An important feature of `DataFrame` constructors is that if you pass a vector of data as a column, this vector is not copied. In other words, a variable is passed by a reference rather than by its value. Please have a look at the following example:

```julia
julia> vals = [1, 2];

julia> df = DataFrame(a=vals, b=["x", "y"])
2×2 DataFrame
| Row | a     | b      |
|     | Int64 | String |
|-----|-------|--------|
| 1   | 1     | x      |
| 2   | 2     | y      |

julia> df.a[1] = 8
8

julia> vals
2-element Array{Int64,1}:
 8
 2
```

Finally, note that when converting `DataFrame` to `Matrix`, you can optionally specify the type of element of a target matrix you request, for example, `Matrix{Float64}(df)`.

There's more...

Conversion to `Matrix` from `DataFrame` allocates a new data structure. Sometimes you might want to extract all the columns of `DataFrame` into a vector of data vectors without copying them. In this case, you can use the following code:

```julia
julia> getindex.(eachcol(df), 2)
4-element Array{Array{Int64,1},1}:
 [1, 2, 3]
 [2, 4, 6]
 [3, 6, 9]
 [4, 8, 12]
```

In future releases of the DataFrames.jl package, you will be able to get a vector like a read-only view into the columns of DataFrame by simply writing columns(df).

See also

In *Investigating the contents of a data frame* recipe, we discuss how you can inspect the contents of the created DataFrame.

Investigating the contents of a data frame

Understanding how to check the contents of DataFrame after creating it is an essential aspect of working with data. In this recipe, we explain what features of the DataFrames.jl package make this task easy.

Getting ready

Make sure that you have the DataFrames.jl package installed. If it is missing, install it by running the commands using Pkg; Pkg.add("DataFrames") in the Julia command line.

In the GitHub repository for this recipe, you will find the commands.txt file, which contains the presented sequence of shell and Julia commands.

Now, open your favorite terminal to execute the commands.

How to do it...

Here is a list of steps to be followed:

1. Create a random DataFrame so that its contents can be inspected later:

```julia
julia> using DataFrames, Random

julia> Random.seed!(1);

julia> df = DataFrame(rand(1000, 100));
```

2. Confirm the `DataFrame` that was created is too large to be displayed, as it contains `1000` rows and `100` columns by using the `nrow`, `ncol`, and `size` functions:

```julia
julia> nrow(df), ncol(df), size(df)
(1000, 10, (1000, 10))
```

3. Take a closer look at the contents of this `DataFrame`. The key function here is `describe`:

```julia
julia> describe(df[1:3])
3×8 DataFrame. Omitted printing of 3 columns
| Row   | variable | mean      | min         | median   | max       |
|       | Symbol   | Float64   | Float64     | Float64  | Float64   |
|-------|----------|-----------|-------------|----------|-----------|
| 1     | x1       | 0.488644  | 0.000576032 | 0.476469 | 0.999954  |
| 2     | x2       | 0.509981  | 0.00288489  | 0.512756 | 0.997931  |
| 3     | x3       | 0.508213  | 0.00109271  | 0.535656 | 0.999943  |
```

An important feature of the `describe` function is that it returns `DataFrame`, which means that it is easy to perform subsequent work using this data structure.

4. See a description of your `DataFrame` that consists only of those columns with an even number between 10 and 20 in their name by filtering the `desc` data frame and selecting only the rows that match the desired pattern:

```julia
julia> filter(x -> occursin(r"1[13579]$", String(x[:variable])),
              describe(df))
5×8 DataFrame. Omitted printing of 3 columns
| Row   | variable | mean     | min         | median   | max      |
|       | Symbol   | Float64  | Float64     | Float64  | Float64  |
|-------|----------|----------|-------------|----------|----------|
| 1     | x11      | 0.504936 | 0.000827051 | 0.520504 | 0.999032 |
| 2     | x13      | 0.500973 | 0.00115659  | 0.505368 | 0.998485 |
| 3     | x15      | 0.510734 | 0.000727684 | 0.531603 | 0.999445 |
| 4     | x17      | 0.503683 | 0.000417392 | 0.503093 | 0.999452 |
| 5     | x19      | 0.505176 | 0.0010843   | 0.515455 | 0.999975 |
```

How it works...

`describe` is a very flexible function, allowing you to calculate a number of useful summary statistics of rows. You can pass a `stats` keyword argument to it and provide a vector listing the desired statistic, selected from the following: `:mean`, `:std`, `:min`, `:q25`, `:median`, `:q75`, `:max`, `:eltype`, `:nunique`, `:first`, `:last`, and `:nmissing`.

When selecting only a subset of rows from the result of describe(df), it was necessary to take into account the fact that column names are Symbol, so we had to convert them first to String type. Next, the occursin function was used to check this string against a regular expression.

There's more...

There are several other useful functions that let you inspect DataFrame:

- names: Returns a vector of column names of DataFrame

- eltypes: Allows you to get a vector of the types of columns in DataFrame

- head and tail: Allow you to peek at the first few (six by default) rows of a DataFrame

See also

The describe function produces the nmissing column, which holds the number of rows with missing data. In the *Handling missing data* recipe, we discuss how you can work with missing values in your dataset.

Reading CSV data from the internet

Often, you need to fetch data in CSV format from the internet. In this recipe, you will discover a simple way of fetching such data and reading it into DataFrame using the CSV.jl package. Then, we will look at how you can save this data back to a CSV file.

Getting ready

We will use a classic dataset called Iris, which is available for download here: https://archive.ics.uci.edu/ml/machine-learning-databases/iris/iris.data.

The citation is as follows:

> *@misc{R.A. Fisher ,*
> *author = "R.A. Fisher ",*
> *year = "2017",*
> *title = "{UCI} Machine Learning Repository",*
> *url = "http://archive.ics.uci.edu/ml",*
> *institution = "University of California, Irvine, School of Information and Computer*
> *Sciences" }*

Start your Julia command line and make sure that you do not have a file named iris.csv in your working directory. Also, make sure that you have the DataFrames.jl and the CSV.jl packages installed. If they are missing, then install them by running the commands using Pkg; Pkg.add("DataFrames"); Pkg.add("CSV") in the Julia command line.

 In the GitHub repository for this recipe, you will find the commands.txt file, which contains the presented sequence of shell and Julia commands. The iris.csv file is also stored in the repository, in case you have problems with downloading it.

Now, open your favorite terminal to execute the commands.

How to do it...

Here is a list of steps to be followed:

1. Firstly, download the sample data file from the internet and then load it into a data frame:

```
julia>
download("https://archive.ics.uci.edu/ml/machine-learning-databases
/iris/iris.data",
                    "iris.csv")
"iris.csv"

julia> isfile("iris.csv")
true

julia> readline("iris.csv")
"5.1,3.5,1.4,0.2,Iris-setosa"
```

The `isfile` function confirms that the file has been properly downloaded, and then `readline` shows that it is comma delimited, that dot is a decimal separator, and that it does not have a header.

2. With this information to hand, read in the data using the `CSV.read` function and check the contents of the resulting data frame:

```julia
julia> using CSV, DataFrames

julia> df = CSV.read("iris.csv",
                     header=["PetalLength", "PetalWidth",
                             "SepalLength", "SepalWidth",
"Class"]);

julia> describe(df)
```
```
5×8 DataFrame
5×8 DataFrame. Omitted printing of 3 columns
| Row | variable    | mean     | min          | median   | max            |
|     | Symbol      | Union... | Any          | Union... | Any            |
| --- | ----------- | -------- | ------------ | -------- | -------------- |
| 1   | PetalLength | 5.84333  | 4.3          | 5.8      | 7.9            |
| 2   | PetalWidth  | 3.054    | 2.0          | 3.0      | 4.4            |
| 3   | SepalLength | 3.75867  | 1.0          | 4.35     | 6.9            |
| 4   | SepalWidth  | 1.19867  | 0.1          | 1.3      | 2.5            |
| 5   | Class       |          | Iris-setosa  |          | Iris-virginica |
```

3. Inspect the last six rows of your data frame:

```julia
julia> tail(df)
```
```
6×5 DataFrame. Omitted printing of 1 columns
| Row | PetalLength | PetalWidth | SepalLength | SepalWidth |
|     | Float64     | Float64    | Float64     | Float64    |
| --- | ----------- | ---------- | ----------- | ---------- |
| 1   | 6.7         | 3.0        | 5.2         | 2.3        |
| 2   | 6.3         | 2.5        | 5.0         | 1.9        |
| 3   | 6.5         | 3.0        | 5.2         | 2.0        |
| 4   | 6.2         | 3.4        | 5.4         | 2.3        |
| 5   | 5.9         | 3.0        | 5.1         | 1.8        |
| 6   | missing     | missing    | missing     | missing    |
```

```julia
julia> eltypes(df)
```
```
5-element Array{Type,1}:
 Union{Missing, Float64}
 Union{Missing, Float64}
 Union{Missing, Float64}
 Union{Missing, Float64}
 Union{Missing, String}
```

It turns out that the last row of data consists only of missing values (this is due to an extraneous newline in the input data file).

4. To get around this problem, remove the missing values from the data frame by stripping out the final row, and change the column types so that they do not allow missing values:

```julia
julia> df = disallowmissing!(df[1:end-1, :]);

julia> eltypes(df)
5-element Array{Type,1}:
 Float64
 Float64
 Float64
 Float64
 String
```

5. With confirmation that the data is now clean, it can be saved back to a CSV file:

```julia
julia> CSV.write("iris2.csv", df);
```

How it works...

The download function fetches a file from a URL. Though this function is very simple, it suffices in most typical situations. Take note that it depends on the availability of external tools (for example, curl, wget, or fetch) to actually get the file, so take care to ensure that you have them installed before running the download function.

The CSV.read function can be used to read in a file in CSV format and store its contents in DataFrame. Some of its more useful keyword arguments are the following:

*   delim: Specifies a field delimiter (, by default).
*   quotechar: Specifies which character is used for quoting fields (" by default).
*   escapechar: The character escaping quotechar in quoted fields (\ by default).

- `missingstring`: Indicates how missing values are represented (`""` by default).
- `decimal`: Specifies what constitutes a decimal point character (`.` by default).
- `header`: Specifies column names as strings (useful if your file is missing them, as in our example).
- `allowmissing`: Specifies if the columns produced should allow `missing` values. `:all` (the default) makes them all accept `missing` values, `:none` makes them require non-missing values, and `:auto` tries to autodetect if the column contains `missing` values.
- `categorical`: If `true` (the default), it will store the data as categorical if there is a low number of unique values in the column.
- `footerskip`: Specifies the number of rows to skip at the end of the file. We could have used this parameter to skip the last empty line when reading the original file.

Finally, a useful function presented in this recipe is `disallowmissing!`, which ensures that the columns of `DataFrame` do not allow `missing` values. Its use has two potential benefits:

- The operations on such columns can be slightly faster
- We can be sure that Julia raises an error if we want to assign a `missing` value to such a column

The latter is desirable if we are sure that the `missing` values must not be accepted.

There's more...

There are several other packages that provide functionality for reading CSV files in Julia, for example, `CSVFiles.jl` and `TextParse.jl`.

See also

To learn more about the handling of `missing` values, see *Handling missing data* recipe.

Categorical values are discussed in the *Working with categorical data* recipe.

Working with categorical data

In Julia, the type of data often carries important information about how the information stored should be interpreted. However, in some cases, working with categorical data can be tricky. In this recipe, we explain how you can refer to an order defined in a categorical vector to filter its contents.

Getting ready

Start the Julia command line. Make sure that you have the `DataFrames.jl` package installed. If it is missing, then install it by running the commands `using Pkg;` `Pkg.add("DataFrames")` in the Julia command line.

 In the GitHub repository for this recipe, you will find the `commands.txt` file, which contains the presented sequence of shell and Julia commands.

Now, open your favorite terminal to execute the commands.

How to do it...

In this recipe, we create a simple data frame containing categorical data, which we will later filter. Here is a list of steps to be followed:

1. Firstly, load the `DataFrames.jl` package and define a vector of possible grades from F to A+:

```
julia> using DataFrames

julia> grade_levels = ["F"; [x*y for x in 'D':-1:'A' for y in ["-",
"", "+"]]]
13-element Array{String,1}:
 "F"
 "D-"
 "D"
 "D+"
 "C-"
```

```
"C"
"C+"
"B-"
"B"
"B+"
"A-"
"A"
"A+"
```

2. Use the vector to generate random grades for 100 students and store them in DataFrame. Grades are stored in a categorical variable, grades:

```julia
julia> using Random

julia> Random.seed!(1);

julia> grades = categorical(rand(grade_levels, 100), ordered=true);

julia> levels!(grades, grade_levels);

julia> df = DataFrame(id=eachindex(grades), grades = grades);
```

3. Check that our grades variable is an ordered categorical type and inspect the order of its levels:

```julia
julia> isordered(grades)
true

julia> levels(grades)
13-element Array{String,1}:
 "F"
 "D-"
 "D"
 "D+"
 "C-"
 "C"
 "C+"
 "B-"
 "B"
 "B+"
 "A-"
 "A"
 "A+"

julia> describe(df, stats=:eltype)
2×2 DataFrame
| Row | variable | eltype   |
|     | Symbol   | DataType |
```

```
| ----- | ---------- | ------------------------------ |
|   1   | id         | Int64                          |
|   2   | grades     | CategoricalString{UInt32}      |
```

Now comes the key part of the recipe. Assume that we want to select all students whose grade is better than A-.

4. Here is how you can do it:

```
julia> filter(x -> x.grades > "A-", df)
15×2 DataFrame
| Row | id    | grades         |
|     | Int64 | Categorical... |
| ----- | ------- | --------------- |
|   1   | 6     | A              |
|   2   | 9     | A+             |
|   3   | 13    | A+             |
|   4   | 15    | A              |
|   5   | 23    | A+             |
|   6   | 26    | A              |
|   7   | 40    | A              |
|   8   | 44    | A              |
|   9   | 47    | A              |
|   10  | 48    | A              |
|   11  | 49    | A              |
|   12  | 63    | A              |
|   13  | 70    | A              |
|   14  | 75    | A+             |
|   15  | 93    | A              |
```

How it works...

CategoricalArray is a type that can store nominal (unordered) or ordinal (ordered) categories.

A categorical array is typically created using the categorical function, which optionally allows a keyword argument, ordered, to specify whether it is nominal (ordered=false; the default) or ordinal (ordered=true).

Each categorical array has two important properties:

- If it is ordered, it can be checked using the isordered function
- A list of its levels, which can be checked using the levels function

A categorical array can be constructed from an array of any type, but strings have special treatment. They are always stored as `String` internally and such categorical values can be worked with as if they were normal strings. For example, consider adding a `"grade"` string to the first ten entries of the `grades` vector:

```julia
julia> grades[1:10] .* " grade"
10-element Array{String,1}:
 "D grade"
 "B- grade"
 "D- grade"
 "C grade"
 "D grade"
 "A grade"
 "D grade"
 "D+ grade"
 "A+ grade"
 "C- grade"
```

However, when we compare a string to a categorical string, then the ordering of levels of the categorical string is used. Therefore, for instance, the `grades[1] > "X"` comparison will throw an exception because `"X"` is not a valid level of the `grades` vector.

There's more...

A categorical array not only adds a structure to your data but it is also memory efficient. The reason is that each unique element of the array is stored only once as a level, and the array itself holds references to those levels.

You can simply check how much memory you save using the following code:

```julia
julia> x = repeat(["a"^20, "b"^20], 1000);

julia> y = categorical(x);

julia> Base.summarysize(x)
72040

julia> Base.summarysize(y)
8912
```

We can see that y is a categorical version of x and it uses almost 90% less memory.

See also

You can find more details about how to work with categorical arrays on the
`CategoricalArrays.jl` package website at `http://juliadata.github.io/`
`CategoricalArrays.jl/latest/`.

Handling missing data

In this recipe, you will find out how to create a correlation matrix from `DataFrame` of
numbers whose entries can contain missing values.

Getting ready

Make sure you have the `CSV.jl` and `DataFrames.jl` packages installed. If they are
missing, add them using the following commands:

```julia
julia> using Pkg

julia> Pkg.add("DataFrames")

julia> Pkg.add("CSV")
```

Also, download the following file and load it into a variable called `df` by using the
following commands:

```julia
julia> download("https://openmv.net/file/class-grades.csv",
                "grades.csv")

julia> using CSV, DataFrames, Statistics

julia> df = CSV.read("grades.csv");
```

 In the GitHub repository for this recipe, you will find
the `commands.txt` file, which contains the presented sequence of shell
and Julia commands. An additional example related to this recipe can be
found in the `cor.jl` file. The `grades.csv` file is also stored in the
repository, in case you have problems with downloading it.

Now, continue working in the Julia command line to execute the commands.

How to do it...

Before calculating the correlation, take a look at the data frame you just created:

1. Start by inspecting the summary statistics of the data contained in your data frame:

```julia
julia> summary(df)
"99×6 DataFrame"
```

```julia
julia> describe(df, stats=[:min, :max, :nmissing])
6×4 DataFrame
```

| Row | variable | min | max | nmissing |
	Symbol	Real	Real	Int64
1	Prefix	4	8	0
2	Assignment	28.14	100.83	0
3	Tutorial	34.09	112.58	0
4	Midterm	28.12	110.0	0
5	TakeHome	16.91	108.89	1
6	Final	28.06	108.89	3

The data has been read in correctly, although the file is malformed.

2. We can check this using the CSV.validate function:

```julia
julia> CSV.validate("grades.csv")
ERROR: CSV.TooManyColumnsError("row=21, col=6: expected 6 columns
then a newline or EOF, but parsing encountered another delimiter:
','; parsed row: '8.0,63.4,86.21,63.12,72.78,missing'")
```

A closer inspection of the grades.csv file reveals that in several lines (namely 22, 40, and 62), it contains one comma too many at the end of the line. The CSV.read function silently ignores the additional columns.

We observe that all the data is numeric and the two last columns contain missing data.

3. Now, try to calculate the correlations using the cor function from the Statistics.jl package from the standard library:

```julia
julia> [cor(df[i], df[j]) for i in axes(df, 2), j in axes(df, 2)]
6×6 Array{Union{Missing, Float64},2}:
  1.0         0.0224759  0.431078  -0.0625435  missing  missing
  0.0224759   1.0        0.440115   0.215868   missing  missing
  0.431078    0.440115   1.0        0.135597   missing  missing
 -0.0625435   0.215868   0.135597   1.0        missing  missing
```

```
missing    missing    missing    missing    missing  missing
missing    missing    missing    missing    missing  missing
```

Unfortunately, we obtain `missing` as a result when calculating the correlation with a column that contains at least one missing value. There are two ways to solve this problem.

4. The first approach is to calculate the correlations by removing all rows that contain `missing` values from the data frame:

```
julia> df2 = dropmissing(df);

julia> describe(df2, stats=:nmissing)
6×2 DataFrame
| Row | variable    | nmissing   |
|     | Symbol      | Int64      |
|-----|-------------|------------|
| 1   | Prefix      | 0          |
| 2   | Assignment  | 0          |
| 3   | Tutorial    | 0          |
| 4   | Midterm     | 0          |
| 5   | TakeHome    | 0          |
| 6   | Final       | 0          |

julia> [cor(df2[i], df2[j]) for i in axes(df2, 2), j in axes(df2,
2)]
6×6 Array{Float64,2}:
  1.0 0.0484327 0.434525 -0.0586403 -0.0689997 0.0881758
  0.0484327 1.0 0.459001 0.200715 0.483206 0.286304
  0.434525 0.459001 1.0 0.148637 0.238167 0.23987
 -0.0586403 0.200715 0.148637 1.0 0.42719 0.724478
 -0.0689997 0.483206 0.238167 0.42719 1.0 0.474231
  0.0881758 0.286304 0.23987 0.724478 0.474231 1.0
```

5. The other approach is to remove the missing rows pairwise. Here is how to do it:

```
julia> function cor2(x, y)
           df = dropmissing(DataFrame([x, y]))
           cor(df[1], df[2])
       end
cor2 (generic function with 1 method)

julia> [cor2(df[i], df[j]) for i in axes(df, 2), j in axes(df, 2)]
6×6 Array{Float64,2}:
  1.0        0.0224759  0.431078  -0.0625435  -0.0916684  0.0902548
  0.0224759  1.0        0.440115   0.215868    0.492297   0.291232
  0.431078   0.440115   1.0        0.135597    0.209513   0.240551
 -0.0625435  0.215868   0.135597   1.0         0.442408   0.725121
```

-0.0916684	0.492297	0.209513	0.442408	1.0	0.474231
0.0902548	0.291232	0.240551	0.725121	0.474231	1.0

The obtained results are similar but not identical. In the pairwise method, the part of the correlation matrix that corresponds to a pair of columns that originally did not contain `missing` values remains identical to the original calculation.

How it works...

In our dataset, any missing values were represented as empty strings, so by default the `CSV.read` command reads in those values as `missing`.

As we saw in an earlier recipe, the `dropmissing` function (from the `DataFrames.jl` package) removes rows containing missing values from a `DataFrame` object.

The following functions are most useful when working with missing data:

- `ismissing`: Checks if a value passed to it is missing.

- `coalesce`: Takes a sequence of arguments and returns the first non-missing item. It is useful for the replacement of `missing` values. For example, `coalesce.([missing,2,missing,5],0)` creates a vector, replacing all `missing` values in with zero and in the result you get as `[0, 2, 0, 5]`.

- `completecases`: Takes `DataFrame` and returns the indices of rows that do not contain `missing` values.

Finally, many functions have defined behavior when they receive a `missing` value as an argument, for example:

```julia
julia> sin(missing)
missing

julia> 1 + missing
missing
```

However, if you encounter a function that does not handle `missing` values, then you can use the following pattern:

```
julia> s = ["a", "bb", missing, "dddd"]
4-element Array{Union{Missing, String},1}:
 "a"
 "bb"
 missing
 "dddd"

julia> (x -> isequal(x, missing) ? missing : length(x)).(s)
4-element Array{Union{Missing, Int64},1}:
 1
 2
  missing
 4
```

We have used `isequal` instead of `==` for comparison. The reason is that `==` and standard comparisons like `<` support three-valued logic:

```
julia> 1 == missing
missing

julia> missing == missing
missing

julia> 1 < missing
missing
```

On the other hand, the `isequal` and `isless` functions are guaranteed to return a `Bool` result:

```
julia> isequal(1, missing)
false

julia> isequal(missing, missing)
true

julia> isless(1, missing)
true
```

In comparisons by the means of the `isless` function, a `missing` value is considered greater than any other value:

```
julia> isless(Inf, missing)
true
```

There's more...

Actually, we could write a function that handles all three cases described like this (the contents of this script can be found in the cor.jl file):

```julia
using Statistics

abstract type CorMethod end
struct CorAll <: CorMethod end
struct CorComplete <: CorMethod end
struct CorPairwise <: CorMethod end

function Statistics.cor(df::DataFrame; method::CorMethod=CorAll())
    cor1(i, j) = nrow(df2) == 0 ? missing : cor(df2[i], df2[j])

    function cor2(i, j)
        x = dropmissing(DataFrame([df2[i], df2[j]]))
        nrow(x) == 0 ? missing : cor(x[1], x[2])
    end

    use_cor = method == CorPairwise() ? cor2 : cor1
    df2 = method == CorComplete() ? dropmissing(df) : df

    m = Matrix{Union{Float64, Missing}}(undef, ncol(df), ncol(df))
    for i in 1:ncol(df), j in i:ncol(df)
        m[i, j] = use_cor(i, j)
        m[j, i] = m[i, j]
    end
    m
end
```

Observe that we assume that the function always returns `Matrix{Union{Float64, Missing}}` because we want it to type stable. Additionally, we explicitly handle the case of zero rows in `DataFrame` by returning a `missing` value and avoiding calculation of the correlation twice for each pair of indices. Here is how the method can be applied to the data frame defined in the recipe:

```julia
julia> include("cor.jl");

julia> cor(df)
6×6 Array{Union{Missing, Float64},2}:
  1.0         0.0224759  0.431078   -0.0625435  missing  missing
  0.0224759   1.0        0.440115    0.215868   missing  missing
  0.431078    0.440115   1.0         0.135597   missing  missing
 -0.0625435   0.215868   0.135597    1.0        missing  missing
  missing     missing    missing     missing    missing  missing
  missing     missing    missing     missing    missing  missing
```

```
julia> cor(df, method=CorComplete())
6×6 Array{Union{Missing, Float64},2}:
   1.0         0.0484327   0.434525   -0.0586403   -0.0689997   0.0881758
   0.0484327   1.0         0.459001    0.200715     0.483206    0.286304
   0.434525    0.459001    1.0         0.148637     0.238167    0.23987
  -0.0586403   0.200715    0.148637    1.0          0.42719     0.724478
  -0.0689997   0.483206    0.238167    0.42719      1.0         0.474231
   0.0881758   0.286304    0.23987     0.724478     0.474231    1.0

julia> cor(df, method=CorPairwise())
6×6 Array{Union{Missing, Float64},2}:
   1.0         0.0224759   0.431078   -0.0625435   -0.0916684   0.0902548
   0.0224759   1.0         0.440115    0.215868     0.492297    0.291232
   0.431078    0.440115    1.0         0.135597     0.209513    0.240551
  -0.0625435   0.215868    0.135597    1.0          0.442408    0.725121
  -0.0916684   0.492297    0.209513    0.442408     1.0         0.474231
   0.0902548   0.291232    0.240551    0.725121     0.474231    1.0
```

You can see that we have obtained the same results.

See also

More details about handling `missing` values are described in the Julia manual at `https://docs.julialang.org/en/latest/manual/missing/` and in the `DataFrames.jl` package documentation at `http://juliadata.github.io/DataFrames.jl/latest/man/missing.html`.

Split-apply-combine in DataFrames

Split-apply-combine is a basic pattern in data analytics that allows you to obtain aggregated information about your dataset. In this recipe, we demonstrate how you can perform this task using the `DataFrames.jl` package.

Getting ready

Make sure you have the `iris.csv` file in your working directory, which was downloaded in the *Reading CSV data from the internet* recipe. Open the Julia command line and install the `DataFrames.jl` and `CSV.jl` packages if required, using the following commands:

```
julia> using Pkg

julia> Pkg.add("DataFrames")

julia> Pkg.add("CSV")
```

 In the GitHub repository for this recipe, you will find the `commands.txt` file, which contains the presented sequence of shell and Julia commands. The `iris.csv` file contains the data that we will analyze.

Now, continue to execute the commands in the Julia command line.

The citation is as follows:

@misc{R.A. Fisher ,
author = "R.A. Fisher ",
year = "2017",
title = "{UCI} Machine Learning Repository",
url = "http://archive.ics.uci.edu/ml",
institution = "University of California, Irvine, School of Information and Computer Sciences" }

How to do it...

Here are the steps that you should follow:

1. Before aggregating the data, load the Iris dataset from disk:

```
julia> using CSV, DataFrames

julia> df = CSV.read("iris.csv", footerskip=1,
                    header=["PetalLength", "PetalWidth",
                            "SepalLength", "SepalWidth",
"Class"]);

julia> describe(df, stats=[:mean, :nmissing])
5×3 DataFrame
```

```
| Row | variable    | mean      | nmissing |
|     | Symbol      | Union...  | Int64    |
|-----|-------------|-----------|----------|
| 1   | PetalLength | 5.84333   | 0        |
| 2   | PetalWidth  | 3.054     | 0        |
| 3   | SepalLength | 3.75867   | 0        |
| 4   | SepalWidth  | 1.19867   | 0        |
| 5   | Class       |           | 0        |
```

2. Now, calculate the number of observations in each `Class` along with the `mean` and the standard deviation of `SepalWidth`:

```julia
julia> using Statistics

julia> by(df, :Class) do x
           DataFrame(n = nrow(x),
                     mean = mean(x.SepalWidth),
                     std = std(x.SepalWidth))
       end
3×4 DataFrame
| Row | Class           | n     | mean     | std      |
|     | String          | Int64 | Float64  | Float64  |
|-----|-----------------|-------|----------|----------|
| 1   | Iris-setosa     | 50    | 0.244    | 0.10721  |
| 2   | Iris-versicolor | 50    | 1.326    | 0.197753 |
| 3   | Iris-virginica  | 50    | 2.026    | 0.27465  |
```

How it works...

The `by` function has two signatures:

- `by(function, dataframe, grouping columns, sort)`

- `by(dataframe, grouping columns, function, sort)`

They perform the same tasks and only differ in the location of the `function` argument. The first form is useful with a `do` block, as shown in this recipe. Observe that the function should accept a data frame and return a data frame to control the column names of the result. The data frame passed to this function is a subset of rows for the given unique values of a grouping column. As a result, the function should return a data frame with the aggregated data. We can check this by running the `by` function with the `describe` function as an argument:

```
julia> by(df, :Class, x -> describe(x, stats=[:mean, :nunique]))
15×4 DataFrame
| Row | Class           | variable    | mean     | nunique  |
|     | String          | Symbol      | Union... | Union... |
|-----|-----------------|-------------|----------|----------|
| 1   | Iris-setosa     | PetalLength | 5.006    |          |
| 2   | Iris-setosa     | PetalWidth  | 3.418    |          |
| 3   | Iris-setosa     | SepalLength | 1.464    |          |
| 4   | Iris-setosa     | SepalWidth  | 0.244    |          |
| 5   | Iris-setosa     | Class       |          | 1        |
| 6   | Iris-versicolor | PetalLength | 5.936    |          |
| 7   | Iris-versicolor | PetalWidth  | 2.77     |          |
| 8   | Iris-versicolor | SepalLength | 4.26     |          |
| 9   | Iris-versicolor | SepalWidth  | 1.326    |          |
| 10  | Iris-versicolor | Class       |          | 1        |
| 11  | Iris-virginica  | PetalLength | 6.588    |          |
| 12  | Iris-virginica  | PetalWidth  | 2.974    |          |
| 13  | Iris-virginica  | SepalLength | 5.552    |          |
| 14  | Iris-virginica  | SepalWidth  | 2.026    |          |
| 15  | Iris-virginica  | Class       |          | 1        |
```

Note that in the `do` block, we have used the `x.SepalWidth` construct, which gets the `SepalWidth` column from the `x` data frame.

There's more...

Another function that can be used to quickly summarize the columns of a data frame by certain grouping columns is `aggregate`. It applies the same function (or functions) to all columns that are not grouping columns, for example:

```
julia> adf = aggregate(df, :Class, maximum);

julia> describe(adf, stats=:mean)
5×2 DataFrame
| Row | variable             | mean     |
|     | Symbol               | Union... |
|-----|----------------------|----------|
```

```
  | 1   | Class                |         |
  | 2   | PetalLength_maximum  | 6.9     |
  | 3   | PetalWidth_maximum   | 3.86667 |
  | 4   | SepalLength_maximum  | 4.63333 |
  | 5   | SepalWidth_maximum   | 1.63333 |
```

```
julia> summary(adf)
"3×5 DataFrame"
```

See also

You can also use the DataFramesMeta.jl package, which provides convenient macros that aid in transforming DataFrame, as described in the *Creating pivot tables by chaining transformations of data frames* recipe.

Converting a data frame between wide and narrow formats

There are two typical approaches to storing data in a data frame:

- **The wide format**: Each row of a data frame contains one observation, possibly consisting of several measurements

- **The long format** (sometimes called the **entity-attribute-value model**): Each row of a data frame contains one measurement, a single observation can span across several rows of a data frame

Both formats can be useful in statistical analysis; therefore, the DataFrames.jl package provides functionality allowing data frames to be converted from one format to another.

Getting ready

In this recipe, we use the Iris data set that we already used in the *Reading CSV data from the internet* recipe.

Make sure you have the CSV.jl and DataFrames.jl packages installed. If they are missing, add them using the following commands:

```
julia> using Pkg

julia> Pkg.add("DataFrames")

julia> Pkg.add("CSV")
```

Before we begin, start the Julia command line and load the iris.csv file into a data frame called df by using the following commands:

```
julia> using CSV, DataFrames

julia> df = CSV.read("iris.csv", footerskip=1,
                    header=["PetalLength", "PetalWidth",
                        "SepalLength", "SepalWidth", "Class"]);
```

 In the GitHub repository for this recipe, you will find the commands.txt file, which contains the presented sequence of shell and Julia commands. The iris.csv file contains the data that we will analyze.

Now, continue working in the Julia command line to execute the commands.

The citation is as follows:

@misc{R.A. Fisher ,
author = "R.A. Fisher ",
year = "2017",
title = "{UCI} Machine Learning Repository",
url = "http://archive.ics.uci.edu/ml",
institution = "University of California, Irvine, School of Information and Computer Sciences" }

How to do it...

The Iris dataset is stored in a wide format, as one observation is represented by one row of data. It can be converted to the narrow format using the `stack` function:

1. Before doing this, it is good practice to add a unique identifier to each row of the data frame. This tells us which rows in the narrow format represent the same observation:

```
julia> df.id = axes(df, 1);

julia> sdf = stack(df)
600×4 DataFrame
```

Row	variable Symbol	value Float64	Class String	id Int64
1	PetalLength	5.1	Iris-setosa	1
2	PetalLength	4.9	Iris-setosa	2
3	PetalLength	4.7	Iris-setosa	3
.				
.				
.				
597	SepalWidth	1.9	Iris-virginica	147
598	SepalWidth	2.0	Iris-virginica	148
599	SepalWidth	2.3	Iris-virginica	149
600	SepalWidth	1.8	Iris-virginica	150

```
julia> describe(sdf, stats=[:min, :max])
4×3 DataFrame
```

Row	variable Symbol	min Any	max Any
1	variable	PetalLength	SepalWidth
2	value	0.1	7.9
3	Class	Iris-setosa	Iris-virginica
4	id	1	150

We can see that after converting to the narrow format, the resulting data frame has four columns: the `variable` and `value` columns represent key-value pairs, and `Class` and `id` are columns allowing us to identify the observation a specific row represents.

2. We can convert the narrow format to wide format using the `unstack` function:

```julia
julia> udf = unstack(sdf, :variable, :value);

julia> names(udf)
6-element Array{Symbol,1}:
 :Class
 :id
 :PetalLength
 :PetalWidth
 :SepalLength
 :SepalWidth
```

We can see that the data frame now contains the same columns as the original data frame (though in a different order).

3. In order to make sure that the data frames actually contain exactly the same information, run the following commands:

```julia
julia> permutecols!(udf, names(df));

julia> df == udf
true
```

The comparison check confirms that the `df` and `udf` data frames, after the reordering of the columns, are now identical.

One specific use of the narrow format is the aggregation of numeric data. If we have many numerical columns on which we want to perform the same aggregation operation, then it can be conveniently achieved in narrow format, while in the wide format we would have to specify all the columns to be transformed explicitly.

4. Here is an example showing that the end results of aggregating the narrow and the wide data formats yield the same results:

```julia
julia> using Statistics

julia> agg = by(sdf, [:Class, :variable],
                x -> DataFrame(value=mean(x.value), n = nrow(x)))
12×4 DataFrame
│ Row │ Class           │ variable    │ value   │ n     │
│     │ String          │ Symbol      │ Float64 │ Int64 │
│─────│─────────────────│─────────────│─────────│───────│
│ 1   │ Iris-setosa     │ PetalLength │ 5.006   │ 50    │
│ 2   │ Iris-versicolor │ PetalLength │ 5.936   │ 50    │
│ 3   │ Iris-virginica  │ PetalLength │ 6.588   │ 50    │
```

```
| 4  | Iris-setosa    | PetalWidth  | 3.418 | 50 |
| 5  | Iris-versicolor| PetalWidth  | 2.77  | 50 |
| 6  | Iris-virginica | PetalWidth  | 2.974 | 50 |
| 7  | Iris-setosa    | SepalLength | 1.464 | 50 |
| 8  | Iris-versicolor| SepalLength | 4.26  | 50 |
| 9  | Iris-virginica | SepalLength | 5.552 | 50 |
| 10 | Iris-setosa    | SepalWidth  | 0.244 | 50 |
| 11 | Iris-versicolor| SepalWidth  | 1.326 | 50 |
| 12 | Iris-virginica | SepalWidth  | 2.026 | 50 |

julia> agg2 = unstack(agg, :Class, :variable, :value);

julia> agg3 = by(df, :Class) do x
 DataFrame(PetalLength=mean(x.PetalLength),
 PetalWidth=mean(x.PetalWidth),
 SepalLength=mean(x.SepalLength),
 SepalWidth=mean(x.SepalWidth));
 end;

julia> agg2 == agg3
true
```

How it works...

The `stack` function is used to convert a data frame from wide format to narrow format. Its general signature accepts three arguments:

- `df`: A data frame to be converted
- `measure_vars`: A list of variable names containing measurements
- `id_vars`: A list of variable names containing identifier columns

You can omit specifying `id_vars`. In this case, it is assumed that all variables not included in `measure_vars` are in this list. Additionally, you can also omit specifying `measure_vars`. In this case, it is assumed that all columns of a data frame that contain floating point values are `measure` variables. This is exactly the format we have used in our recipe, where the `stack(df)` call used numeric variables as measures and all other variables as identifiers.

Additionally, you can pass two keyword arguments to the `stack` function, `variable_name` and `value_name`, which allow you to specify the names of columns that should store variable names and variable values, respectively.

A converse operation to `stack` is performed by the `unstack` function. It accepts three arguments:

- `rowkeys`: Specifies a unique key for a column (can be omitted, in which case all columns other than `colkey` and `value` will be used as `rowkeys`)
- `colkey`: Holds variable names (`:variable` by default)
- `value`: Holds values of variables (`:value` by default)

If you specify the `colkey` argument, you must also specify the `value` argument.

At the end of the recipe, we used the `permutecols!` function. It can be used to reorder the columns of a data frame in place. You have to pass a data frame and the desired new order of columns as arguments to this function.

There's more...

There is also the `melt` function, which works exactly like the `stack` function but has the `measure_vars` and `id_vars` arguments reversed in order (sometimes it is easier to list `id_vars` than `measure_vars`, especially when there are a lot of them).

Finally, there are the `stackdf` and `meltdf` functions, which work exactly like the `stack` and `melt` functions but return a view of the original data frame (`stack` and `melt` perform copying of data). They can be useful when working with very large data frames.

See also

You can find more information about the split-apply-combine pattern in the *Split-apply-combine in DataFrames* recipe.

Comparing data frames for identity

In this recipe, we show you how to check if two data frames are identical and if they contain unique rows.

Getting ready

In this recipe, we will use the grades dataset, which we have already employed in the *Working with categorical data* recipe.

Make sure you have the CSV.jl and DataFrames.jl packages installed. If they are missing, add them using the following commands:

```julia
julia> using Pkg

julia> Pkg.add("DataFrames")

julia> Pkg.add("CSV")
```

Before we begin, start the Julia command line and load the grades.csv file into a data frame, using the following commands:

```julia
julia> using CSV, DataFrames

julia> df1 = CSV.read("grades.csv")
99x6 DataFrame
```

| Row | Prefix | Assignment | Tutorial | Midterm | TakeHome | Final |
	Int64	Float64	Float64	Float64	Float64	Float64
1	5	57.14	34.09	64.38	51.48	52.5
2	8	95.05	105.49	67.5	99.07	68.33
3	8	83.7	83.17	30.0	63.15	48.89
.						
.						
96	7	85.34	80.54	41.25	93.7	39.72
97	8	89.94	102.77	87.5	90.74	87.78
98	7	95.6	76.13	66.25	99.81	85.56
99	8	63.4	97.37	73.12	72.78	77.22

In the GitHub repository for this recipe, you will find the commands.txt file, which contains the presented sequence of shell and Julia commands. The grades.csv file is also stored in the repository.

Now, continue working in the Julia command line to execute the commands.

How to do it...

Here is a list of steps that we follow:

1. First, create another data frame, df2, which has reordered rows and columns so that we can then perform the comparison:

```julia
julia> using Random

julia> Random.seed!(1);

julia> df2 = df1[shuffle(axes(df1, 1)), shuffle(axes(df1, 2))];
```

2. Next, verify that the df1 and df2 data frames contain unique and identical rows by using the following join function:

```julia
julia> res = join(df1, df2, kind=:outer,
                  on=union(names(df1), names(df2)),
                  indicator=:check, validate=(true, true));

julia> unique(res.check)
1-element Array{String,1}:
 "both"
```

The result returned by the call to the unique function indicates that all rows are found in both tables.

3. Now, check what would happen if we removed one row from the df1 and df2 data frames:

```julia
julia> res = join(df1[1:end-1,:], df2[2:end,:], kind=:outer,
                  on=union(names(df1), names(df2)),
                  indicator=:check, validate=(true, true));

julia> by(res, :check, nrow)
3×2 DataFrame
```

Row	check	x1
	Categorical…	Int64
1	both	97
2	left_only	1
3	right_only	1

We see, as expected, that there is one row that is found only in the left table and one row that is only in the right table.

Additionally, if both tables did not have the same columns, then `join` would throw an error because we used `union(names(df1), names(df2))` as the on keyword argument. Similarly, because we have set the `validate` keyword argument to `(true, true)`, we would get an error if any of the tables contained duplicates.

How it works...

The `DataFrames.jl` package allows you to perform a `join` operation on two data frames. The following join types specified by the `kind` keyword argument are supported: `:inner` (the default), `:outer`, `:left`, `:right`, `:semi`, `:anti`, and `:cross` (which represents a full Cartesian product of two tables).

For all joins except `:cross`, you need to specify the on keyword argument, which indicates on which columns a join is to be performed. The names of the columns passed in the on argument must be present in both data frames.

Additionally, you can specify three keyword arguments in the call to `join`:

- `makeunique` (`false` by default): If `true`, then duplicate column names other than on will be made unique; if `false`, an error is thrown when duplicates are encountered.
- `indicator`: If present, the name of an extra column to be created will be indicated that will hold information about whether a given row contains data from the left, the right, or both data frames.
- `validate`: A tuple of `Bool` that indicates if the `join` function should check columns specified by the on keyword argument for uniqueness in the left and right data frame, respectively.

There's more...

We could have performed the check presented in this recipe without `join` by using the `countmap` function from the `StatsBase.jl` package (if it is missing, then install it by executing the following commands `using Pkg; Pkg.add("StatsBase")` in the Julia command line), for instance:

```
julia> using StatsBase

julia> df_id(df) = countmap(collect(eachrow(df[sort(names(df))])))
df_id (generic function with 1 method)

julia> df_id(df1) == df_id(df2)
true
```

The `df_id` function creates a dictionary that contains the number of times each unique row is present in a data frame with sorted column names. A subtle property of dictionaries (and similarly sets) that we use here is that they allow missing values to be present in keys and the `==` operator still returns `true`/`false` on them (as opposed to an array comparison).

See also

We discuss standard rules for the comparison of `missing` values in the *Handling missing data* recipe.

We explain how the `eachrow` function works in the *Transforming rows of a DataFrame* recipe.

Transforming rows of DataFrame

Performing a transformation on a set of columns in a `DataFrame` object is one of the most common operations. In this recipe, we describe how you can perform complex transformations on rows in `DataFrame`.

Getting ready

In this recipe, we use the `grades` dataset, which we have already used in the *Working with categorical data* recipe.

Assume there are the following grading rules in this course:

- If Final is missing or less than *50*, then the grade is *fail*
- If Final is greater than or equal to *50* but less than *75*, and both Midterm and TakeHome are missing or less than *50*, then the grade is *fail*
- In all other cases, the grade is *pass*

Make sure you have the CSV.jl and DataFrames.jl packages installed. If they are missing, add them using the following commands:

```julia
julia> using Pkg

julia> Pkg.add("DataFrames")

julia> Pkg.add("CSV")
```

Before we begin, start the Julia command line and load the grades.csv file into a data frame, using the following commands:

```julia
julia> using CSV, DataFrames

julia> df = CSV.read("grades.csv");
```

 In the GitHub repository for this recipe, you will find the commands.txt file, which contains the presented sequence of shell and Julia commands. The grades.csv file is also stored in the repository.

Now, continue working in the Julia command line to execute the commands.

How to do it...

In this recipe, we present two approaches to calculating the final grade:

1. In the first approach, we start by defining a function that is used to calculate the grade:

```julia
julia> function get_grade(final, midterm, takehome)
           (ismissing(final) || final < 50) && return "fail"
           if final < 75 && coalesce(midterm, 0) < 50 &&
coalesce(takehome, 0) < 50
               "fail"
           else
               "pass"
```

```
            end
        end
get_grade (generic function with 1 method)
```

2. Then, we can define a new column in our data frame:

```
julia> df.grade = get_grade.(df.Final, df.Midterm, df.TakeHome);
```

3. Another approach is to use the `eachrow` iterator, which returns data frame-like objects along with the `map` function and the `do` block, like this:

```
julia> df.grade2 = map(eachrow(df)) do r
        coalesce(r.Final, 0) < 50 && return "fail"
        if r.Final < 75 && coalesce(r.Midterm, 0) < 50 &&
coalesce(r.TakeHome < 50)
            "fail"
        else
            "pass"
        end
    end;
```

4. Finally, check that both methods of grade calculation return the same result:

```
julia> df.grade == df.grade2
true
```

How it works...

Simple transformations of data frame columns can usually be achieved using broadcasting. For instance, if we wanted to use just the `Final` variable test to indicate which students failed, we could write this:

```
df.failed = coalesce.(df.Final, 0) .< 50
```

In our recipe, the required transformation is relatively complex. Therefore, in this case, the most convenient approach is to define a new function that we apply to our data, either using broadcasting (the first approach) or map (the second approach).

Please note that in the second approach (using the `eachrow` iterator), the function defined in the `do` block receives a `DataFrameRow` object, which behaves as a view of one row of the parent data frame. In particular, you can access its columns using names or numbers.

Also, notice how the `coalesce` function is used in the example. It is needed here because comparison operators such as < return `missing` when at least one of their arguments is `missing`. Using `coalesce`, we say that `missing` is equivalent to 0 points for the purposes of grading.

There's more...

Similarly to the `eachrow` iterator, there is the `eachcol` iterator, which allows you to process all columns of a data frame sequentially.

See also

In the *Creating pivot tables by chaining transformations of data frames* recipe, we discuss how you can perform transformations of data frames using the `DataFramesMeta.jl` package.

Creating pivot tables by chaining transformations of data frames

Often in data analysis, you have to perform multiple steps on transformations of your data frame. In this recipe, we show how you can conveniently perform those operations using the `DataFramesMeta.jl` package, with an example of preparing a pivot table, one of the most basic methods of summarizing data.

Getting ready

Make sure you have the `iris.csv` file in your working directory, which was downloaded in the *Reading CSV data from the internet* recipe. Open the Julia command line and install the `DataFrames.jl`, `DataFramesMeta.jl`, and `CSV.jl` packages if required, using the following commands:

```
julia> using Pkg

julia> Pkg.add("DataFrames")

julia> Pkg.add("DataFramesMeta")

julia> Pkg.add("CSV")
```

In the GitHub repository for this recipe, you will find the `commands.txt` file, which contains the presented sequence of shell and Julia commands. The `iris.csv` file contains the data that we will analyze.

Before we begin, start the Julia command line and load the `iris.csv` file into the data frame, `df`, using the following commands:

```
julia> using DataFrames, DataFramesMeta, CSV, Statistics

julia> df = CSV.read("iris.csv", footerskip=1,
                header=["PetalLength", "PetalWidth",
                    "SepalLength", "SepalWidth", "Class"]);
```

We will want to get the mean of the `SepalLength` column, grouped by the `PetalLength` and `SepalWidth` columns, only for `Class` equal to `"Iris-setosa"`, and then present it using a pivot table.

Now, continue to execute the commands in the Julia command line.

The citation is as follows:

@misc{R.A. Fisher ,
author = "R.A. Fisher ",
year = "2017",
title = "{UCI} Machine Learning Repository",
url = "http://archive.ics.uci.edu/ml",
institution = "University of California, Irvine, School of Information and Computer Sciences" }

How to do it...

The code for this recipe is very terse, as we can perform the preceding transformations in one command, as follows:

```
julia> @linq df |>
        where(:Class .== "Iris-setosa") |>
        by([:PetalLength, :SepalWidth], meanSL = mean(:SepalLength)) |>
        unstack(:SepalWidth, :meanSL)
15×7 DataFrame. Omitted printing of 3 columns
| Row | PetalLength  | 0.1      | 0.2      | 0.3      |
|     | Float64      | Float64  | Float64  | Float64  |
| --- | ------------ | -------- | -------- | -------- |
| 1   | 4.3          | 1.1      | missing  | missing  |
```

2	4.4	missing	1.33333	missing
3	4.5	missing	missing	1.3
4	4.6	missing	1.3	1.4
5	4.7	missing	1.45	missing
6	4.8	1.4	1.7	1.4
7	4.9	1.5	1.4	missing
8	5.0	missing	1.42	1.3
9	5.1	missing	1.5	1.45
10	5.2	1.5	1.45	missing
11	5.3	missing	1.5	missing
12	5.4	missing	1.6	missing
13	5.5	missing	1.35	missing
14	5.7	missing	missing	1.7
15	5.8	missing	1.2	missing

Note that in your terminal you will probably see more columns printed, as in the preceding output Julia has omitted printing three columns of the resulting data frame.

How it works...

`DataFramesMeta.jl` is a package that allows you to simplify working with `DataFrame` objects in two ways:

- You do not need to qualify column names with the data frame object name when you reference them; it is enough to pass them as a symbol.
- You can chain transformations of `DataFrame` using the `@linq` macro; you can mix operations built into the `DataFramesMeta.jl` package and other functions. The `DataFramesMeta.jl` package assumes that the first argument to all operations is the `DataFrame` package you are working on and you do not have to write that name when specifying them. We see both features in action in our recipe.

The `where` and `by` operations are macros defined in the `DataFramesMeta.jl` package. Normally, you would call them in the following forms:

- `@where(data_frame, condition)` to filter rows of the `data_frame` with the given condition

- `@by(data_frame, columns, aggregations...)` to aggregate the `data_frame` by the `columns` and calculate the `aggregations` on them

In our case, these macros are invoked inside the @linq macro chain using the |> operator. Therefore, we do not have to write @ in front of them, nor pass their first argument. Also, we see that the unstack function, which is not defined in the DataFramesMeta.jl package, can be called as normal, but still without passing its first argument (a data frame object).

As a result of all these operations, we see that we have obtained a pivot table with rows defined by the PetalLength variable, columns defined by the SepalWidth variable, and in the intersection, we get the mean of SepalLength, or a missing value in cases where no observations are present in the intersection of the dimensions.

There's more...

The DataFramesMeta.jl package defines the following basic operations relating to data frames:

- @with allows column names to be referenced as symbols
- @where filters rows
- @select selects and transforms columns
- @transform adds new columns
- @by_row performs row-wise operations
- @orderby sorts rows
- @by performs aggregation of groups in a data frame
- @based_on performs aggregation of a grouped data frame
- @linq allows for chaining of data frame operations

You can find more details about these functions at https://github.com/JuliaStats/DataFramesMeta.jl.

See also

In the *Split-apply-combine in DataFrames* recipe, we show how you can perform the split-apply-combine cycle using the functions built into the DataFrames.jl package.

In *Converting a data frame between wide and narrow formats*, we discuss the use of the unstack function in detail.

8

Julia Workflow

In this chapter, we will cover the following topics:

- Julia development workflow with `Revise.jl`
- Benchmarking code
- Profiling Julia code
- Setting up logging in your code
- Calling Python from Julia
- Calling R from Julia
- Managing project dependencies

Introduction

In this chapter, we present several recipes with hints and tips on organizing workflows with Julia.

We start with `Revise.jl`, an essential package in any larger Julia project, which automatically reloads function definitions in packages that have changed. Next, we explain how to benchmark and profile your code. For some scenarios, Julia alone might not be enough to achieve your data science/analytical goals efficiently and hence a need arises to use other programming languages. We show how to configure and mix Julia code with code and libraries from the two most popular data science languages: Python and GNU R. Finally, we present a standard template for a Julia project.

Julia development workflow with Revise.jl

In this recipe, we describe how to organize the module development process in Julia using the Revise.jl package. A Julia program contains several functions that are normally aggregated into **modules**. On one hand, the process of module development and testing usually involves experimenting with the code in the Julia command line. However, every time a change is made in one of the functions within a module, it requires reloading the entire module. This is inconvenient because as well as having to remember to reload the module, you will need to do it after every single change to your code. Additionally, for large modules, reloading an entire module may take a significant amount of time. A remedy for this problem is the Revise.jl package.

Getting ready

In this recipe, we assume that you have configured your favorite programming environment.

Revise can simply be installed with the Julia package manager. In the Julia command line, press the] key and run the following command:

```
(v1.0) pkg> add Revise
```

This will install the Revise.jl library and all its dependencies. Additionally, for the examples presented in this recipe, we will use the HTTP.jl library:

```
(v1.0) pkg> add HTTP
```

 In the GitHub repository for this recipe, you will find the commands.txt file, which contains the presented sequence of Julia commands and the Module1.jl file containing the sample module definition.

How to do it...

In this example, a module for collecting data on Bitcoin cryptocurrency prices from coindesk.com will be created. Please follow these steps:

1. Create a file, `Module1.jl`, with the following content. Note that this code is assembled into a module:

```
module Module1

using HTTP
using JSON

export getcoinprices

function getcoinprices(dateFrom::String,dateTo::String)
    url =
string("https://api.coindesk.com/v1/bpi/historical/close.json?curre
ncy=USD&start=",
                dateFrom, "&end=", dateTo)
    res = HTTP.request("GET", url ,verbose=0)
    dat = JSON.parse(join(readlines(IOBuffer(res.body)), " "))
    haskey(dat, "bpi") ? dat["bpi"] : Dict()
end

end # module
```

In order to use the preceding module, you need to make sure that the file is located in the same directory as working directory of the Julia command line.

2. Use the `pwd()` command to check the current directory. If you want to switch directories, use the `cd("enter_new_directory_here")` command. Once you have made sure the directories are correct, run the following commands:

```
push!(LOAD_PATH, ".")
using Revise
using Module1
```

3. Now, test the module by running the following code:

```
julia> getcoinprices("2018-06-20", "2018-06-22")
Dict{String,Any} with 3 entries:
  "2018-06-22" => 6053.9
  "2018-06-20" => 6758.38
  "2018-06-21" => 6717.2
```

Please be aware that since the returned result is a `Dict` object, you might get a different result order.

4. Add an incorrect date range and observe what happens:

```
julia> getcoinprices("2018-06-23", "2018-06-22")
ERROR: HTTP.ExceptionRequest.StatusError(404,
HTTP.Messages.Response:
"""
HTTP/1.1 404 Not Found
   ...(more errors here)...
```

We shall update the implementation of the `getcoinprices` function in order to avoid throwing an error for such date ranges, and instead return an empty `Dict` object.

5. Open the `Module1.jl` file in any text editor and add the following line at the beginning of the `getcoinprices(dateFrom::String, dateTo::String)` function. Remember to save the file:

```
dateFrom > dateTo && return Dict()
```

6. Now, run the same function again:

```
julia> getcoinprices("2018-06-23", "2018-06-22")
Dict{Any,Any} with 0 entries
```

Please note that the function definition has been automatically updated by `Revise.jl`; we did not need to relaunch Julia nor reload the module, `Module1`.

How it works...

`Revise.jl` works by continuously scanning the source code for changes. Special event handling for command-line Terminals (including the Julia command line and Juno) is added. Whenever a change in function implementation is discovered, this function is automatically passed to the Julia interpreter. Please note that `Revise.jl` does not reload the entire module; only those functions that have changed are reloaded.

Revise.jl is able to track most code changes, with two exceptions. Firstly, when a type definition is changed (for example, a new field is added to struct), the Julia interpreter needs to be reloaded (that is, you need to execute the exit() command and start the Julia interpreter again). Secondly, module or file renaming is not supported; again, if you decide to rename modules or files, you should restart the Julia command line.

 Revise.jl only provides automatic tracking out of the box for files that have been included within the namespace, either by executing a using or an import statement. However, it is possible to manually add files to the tracking system by executing the push!(LOAD_PATH, "/path/to/the/file/that/will/be/tracked") command. Files loaded by include can also be tracked by explicitly using Revise.track(filename).

There's more...

When working in Juno, please makes sure that your Julia is set to **Cycler Boot Mode**. In this way, when you eventually need to restart the Julia command line due to type definition changes, for instance, you will not be left waiting for a new Julia Terminal to start up (there will always be one Julia process waiting in the background for you).

The Julia workflow guidelines are given at https://docs.julialang.org/en/latest/manual/workflow-tips/.

See also

Have a look at the Julia style guide to find more information on how to organize your Julia code at https://docs.julialang.org/en/latest/manual/style-guide/.

Benchmarking code

In this recipe, we will explain how you can benchmark your code and how code benchmarking can be used to improve its efficiency.

Getting ready

We will show how to benchmark a simple function that takes a single argument in the form of an integer, n, creates a random 10 x 10 matrix of floats, A, and then calculates the norm of a product of this matrix by a random vector, x. The sampling of x should be performed n times and the result of the function should be an n-element vector of calculated norms.

Before we start, please make sure that you have the BenchmarkTools package installed. If it is missing, then add it using the following commands: using Pkg; Pkg.add("BenchmarkTools").

> In the GitHub repository for this recipe, you will find the commands.txt file, which contains the presented sequence of shell and Julia commands.

Now, open your favorite terminal to execute the commands.

How to do it...

We will implement the required functionality using two different approaches in the f1 and f2 functions, and then we will show you how to compare their performance:

1. Our first approach starts by defining the requested function:

```
julia> function f1(n::Integer)
           n > 0 || error("n must be a positive number")
           A = rand(10,10)
           [A*rand(10) for i in 1:n]
       end
f1 (generic function with 1 method)
```

2. Measure how much time the function takes to run by invoking it with the @time macro twice:

```
julia> @time f1(10^6);
  0.887396 seconds (2.51 M allocations: 338.263 MiB, 21.45% gc time)

julia> @time f1(10^6);
  0.537961 seconds (2.00 M allocations: 312.806 MiB, 27.33% gc time)
```

3. A more precise estimate of function performance can be obtained using the @benchmark macro from the BenchmarkTools package:

```
julia> using BenchmarkTools
julia> @benchmark f1(10^6)
BenchmarkTools.Trial:
  memory estimate: 312.81 MiB
  allocs estimate: 2000007
  --------------
  minimum time: 370.117 ms (0.00% GC)
  median time: 597.999 ms (30.58% GC)
  mean time: 714.208 ms (43.69% GC)
  maximum time: 1.280 s (71.83% GC)
  --------------
  samples: 7
  evals/sample: 1
```

4. Now, let's examine an alternative implementation that avoids reallocation of x in each iteration but tries to reuse it by using the rand! function instead:

```
julia> using Random

julia> function f2(n::Integer)
           n > 0 || error("n must be a positive number")
           A = rand(10,10)
           x = rand(10)
           [A*rand!(x) for i in 1:n]
       end
f2 (generic function with 1 method)

julia> @benchmark f2(10^6)
BenchmarkTools.Trial:
  memory estimate: 160.22 MiB
  allocs estimate: 1000009
  --------------
  minimum time: 344.432 ms (0.00% GC)
  median time: 437.508 ms (0.00% GC)
  mean time: 486.926 ms (23.38% GC)
  maximum time: 989.181 ms (65.77% GC)
  --------------
  samples: 12
  evals/sample: 1
```

We can see that the f2 function is faster and allocates less memory than f1, as expected.

How it works...

The @time macro reports the time taken by a passed expression to run, in addition to memory allocations and the percentage of garbage collection time. Observe that in our example, the first invocation of f1(10^6) with the @time macro took longer than in the second run. The reason is that on the first run, the method of f1 specialized for the argument type Int had to be compiled.

We can check which function would be compiled by using the @which macro:

```
julia> @which f1(10^6)
f1(n::Integer) in Main at REPL[1]:2
```

 Note that functions that are called inside f1 have to be compiled by Julia before running them.

Observe that the @time macro prints its result to the console. Therefore, we use ; at the end of the expression to suppress printing the expression's value after timing information is printed. If we wish to get the value for the elapsed time when running an expression, we can use the @elapsed macro. Similarly, to get memory allocation information, we can use the @allocated macro:

```
julia> @elapsed f1(10^6)
0.421779857

julia> @allocated f1(10^6)
328001072
```

Now we did not use ;, as both macros do not print anything but return the requested value.

In simple situations, running the @time macro is good enough to get a rough understanding of the performance of a function. However, sometimes we want to run comprehensive benchmarks of code execution time. In such situations, the BenchmarkTools package is the recommended method for analyzing your function. The simplest way to use this package is with the @benchmark macro, which runs the function multiple times and outputs the collected statistics from running the code.

In our example, we can see that f2 is faster than f1 and allocates less memory, because the rand! function reuses the x vector without having to allocate memory for it in each iteration of the loop inside the comprehension.

The `BenchmarkTools` package also offers the `@btime` and `@belapsed` macros, which work similarly to `@time` and `@elapsed`, with the difference that they collect statistics exactly like `@benchmark` and return `minimum` observed values.

One important thing to keep in mind when using the `BenchmarkTools` package is that if one uses global variables for benchmarking, they should be interpolated into the expression passed to the `@benchmark` macro with a `$` sign:

```
julia> x = 10
10

julia> @benchmark rand(x)
BenchmarkTools.Trial:
  memory estimate: 160 bytes
  allocs estimate: 1
  --------------
  minimum time: 95.181 ns  (0.00% GC)
  median time: 98.632 ns  (0.00% GC)
  mean time: 121.989 ns  (7.53% GC)
  maximum time: 47.540 µs  (99.70% GC)
  --------------
  samples: 10000
  evals/sample: 946

julia> @benchmark rand($x)
BenchmarkTools.Trial:
  memory estimate: 160 bytes
  allocs estimate: 1
  --------------
  minimum time: 83.748 ns  (0.00% GC)
  median time: 86.588 ns  (0.00% GC)
  mean time: 106.827 ns  (8.40% GC)
  maximum time: 46.464 µs  (99.76% GC)
  --------------
  samples: 10000
  evals/sample: 986
```

This effect will be particularly apparent in functions whose execution time is low.

There's more...

The `BenchmarkTools.jl` package allows you to control the sampling procedure used. You can read the details at `https://github.com/JuliaCI/BenchmarkTools.jl/blob/master/doc/manual.md`, but the parameters that are most often useful are the following:

- `samples`: Number of samples to take (`10000` by default).
- `seconds`: Time in seconds allowed for benchmarking (`5` by default). It is guaranteed that at least one sample will be taken. The actual execution time can be a bit longer, as Julia will wait until the last sample has started before the seconds time finishes.

They should be passed as keyword arguments to the macros defined in the `BenchmarkTools` package, or can be set globally for a session by updating an appropriate field in the `BenchmarkTools.DEFAULT_PARAMETERS` object.

See also

If you find that the performance of your code in execution is sub-par, the most probable reason is that your functions are not type stable. This issue is explained in detail in the *Ensuring type stability of your code* recipe.

Code profiling is explained in the next recipe.

Profiling Julia code

The goal of code profiling (`https://en.wikibooks.org/wiki/Introduction_to_Software_Engineering/Testing/Profiling`) is to identify bottlenecks (critical parts) of the code that have a considerable effect on its performance. Once the most time-consuming code sections have been identified, additional code optimization can be considered. From the standpoint of computation time, it makes sense to only optimize those code fragments that take a significant time to run. Julia offers a simple, yet useful, built-in sampling profiler.

Getting ready

The sampling profiler is built into Julia. However, in order to visualize profiling results, the ProfileView.jl package is recommended, which can be installed with the Julia package manager. In the Julia command line, press the *J* key and run the following command:

```
(v1.0) pkg> add ProfileView
```

We will also show how to perform profiling using Juno's Juno.@profile macro. This macro is built into Juno and hence no installation is required.

 In the GitHub repository for this recipe, you will find the commands.txt file, which contains the presented sequence of Julia commands and the profiletest.jl file containing the sample code that will be profiled.

How to do it...

In order to see how profiling works, please perform these steps:

1. Start with defining a function that we will use for profiling. You will also need to include the following contents within the profiletest.jl file:

```
using Statistics
function timeto1(mv)
    x = Int[]
    while true
        push!(x, rand(1:mv))
        1 in x && return length(x)
    end
end
agg(f, mv, rep) = mean(f(mv) for i in 1:rep)
```

2. Measure the execution times for the preceding specified function:

```
julia> include("profiletest.jl");

julia> @time agg(timeto1, 1000, 10_000);
   6.422435 seconds (627.43 k allocations: 254.511 MiB, 0.95% gc
time)
julia> @time agg(timeto1, 1000, 10_000);
   5.710283 seconds (96.25 k allocations: 223.124 MiB, 0.76% gc
time)
```

3. Check how much memory is used by the analyzed function call. Note that this information (in a different format) was also visible in the results of the @time macro:

```
julia> @allocated agg(timeto1, 1000, 10_000)
236393040
```

4. Load the profiler and ProfileViewer and set the measuring intervals to half a millisecond:

```
using Profile
using ProfileView
Profile.init(delay=0.0005)
```

5. Run the profiler to collect the code execution statistics:

```
Profile.clear()
Profile.@profile agg(timeto1, 1000, 10_000);
```

6. Use the Profile.print() command to visualize profiling results. Please note that in order to increase readability, we have removed most of the profile listing and replaced it with [...]. Additionally note that the following command has been run from the Atom Juno IDE (running from a console outside of Atom will yield slightly different output; however, it will lead to the same conclusions):

```
julia> Profile.print()
1527 .\task.jl:85; (::getfield(Atom,
Symbol("##116#121"))){Dict{String,Any}})()
[ ... ]
 135 profiletest.jl:5; timeto1(::Int64)
 46 .\array.jl:856; push!
 46 .\array.jl:814; _growend!
 4 .\array.jl:857; push!
 4 .\array.jl:769; setindex!
 85
...64\build\usr\share\julia\stdlib\v1.0\Random\src\Random.jl:222;
```

```
rand
 [ ... ]
1145 profiletest.jl:6; timeto1(::Int64)
 351 .\operators.jl:0; in
 152 .\operators.jl:954; in
 152 .\array.jl:707; iterate
 642 .\promotion.jl:425; in
 [ ... ]
```

Each line in the code profile listing represents a line in Julia code (identified by filename and line number). The number in front of the line shows how many times the profiler recorded the given function as being executed. The listing shows the entire execution tree; the numeric values at the start of a line at each branch sum up to its sub-branches. For example, the fifth line of the profiletest.jl file (that is, push!(x, rand(1:mv))) was executed during 135 out of 1527 total measurements. We can see that around 63% of its time was consumed by generating random numbers, while 33% of the time was used to extend the array. Underneath, we have measurements for the sixth line of the profiletest.jl file. We see that this line consumes a significant amount of the total execution time (1154 out of 1527 measurements). Furthermore, we realize that the extended execution time is caused by the use of the in function. As a result, one idea for the improvement of the code presented is to use Set for searching rather than an Array.

7. The profiling results can also be presented using the ProfileView module to show an interactive plot of the execution times:

```
julia> ProfileView.view()
```

Once the preceding command is executed, you will see a graphical profiler window similar to the one that follows. The width of the blocks represents the percentage of times they were running when measured by the profiler. The higher the block, the deeper it was found in the execution stack. Hence, the big red block at the bottom is the Julia command line. Hovering over the orange block, we notice that the most significant part of the execution time is related to finding elements in the array (the `in` function):

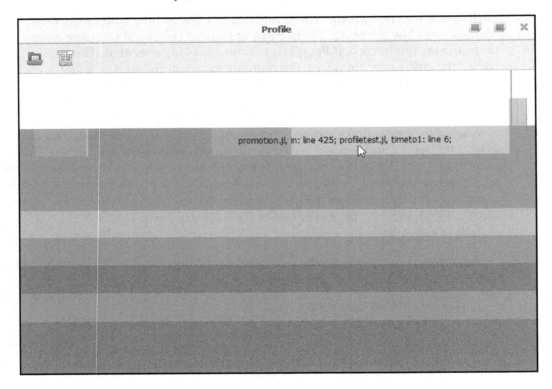

8. We can now use this knowledge to improve the code. In order to avoid pushing the elements, replace `Array` with `Set`, as follows:

```
function timeto2(mv)
    x = Set{Int}()
    while true
        push!(x, rand(1:mv))
        1 in x && return length(x)
    end
end
```

It can be seen that the execution time has decreased by over eight times, while memory consumption has slightly increased (Set is less memory efficient data storage than Array):

```
julia> @time agg(timeto2, 1000, 10_000);
  0.0,65833029 seconds (597.52 k allocations: 280.118 MiB, 9.18% gc
time)

julia> @time agg(timeto2, 1000, 10_000);
  0.658473 seconds (139.72 k allocations: 255.847 MiB, 10.86% gc
time)

julia> @allocated agg(timeto2, 1000, 10_000)
268906688
```

How it works...

The @profile macro runs the code and performs frequent checks of which functions are currently running. The data is collected and statistics are generated (that is why the sampling profiler is also called the **statistical profiler**).

By default, the Julia sampling profiler polls for function information every one millisecond on Linux/Unix platforms and every 10 milliseconds on Windows platforms. This frequency can easily be changed using the Profile.init function with a delay parameter. Please note that every time the profiler is run, new statistics are added to the existing ones. That is why the Profile.clear() command is usually executed before actually running the @profile macro.

There's more...

The Julia profiler is integrated with Juno. When running code inside Juno, simply execute the following command:

```
Juno.@profiler agg(timeto1, 1000, 10_000);
```

The preceding command can be executed either by pressing *Ctrl + Enter* in the Juno editor or by running it inside the REPL console in Juno. The `Juno.@profiler` runs a profiler in a similar manner to `@profile`. Once the macro has been run, an interactive graphical profiler output will be presented, resembling the one created by the `ProfileView.jl` library. Note that by hovering over the large main block at the bottom, we can easily find out that the main reason for the long execution time is the use of the `in` function (see the picture). Moreover, clicking on the block in the Profiler graph opens the relevant code with the Atom Juno editor:

Finally, bear in mind that there is even more room for improvement in the preceding example by using `BitSet`. Take a look at the following example:

```julia
julia> function timeto3(mv)
    x = BitSet()
    while true
        push!(x, rand(1:mv))
        1 in x && return length(x)
    end
end
timeto3 (generic function with 1 method)

julia> @time agg(timeto3, 1000, 10_000);
  0.330514 seconds (449.19 k allocations: 24.903 MiB, 4.81% gc time)

julia> @time agg(timeto3, 1000, 10_000);
  0.134365 seconds (39.98 k allocations: 5.010 MiB)
```

See also

We have discussed here the default Julia profiler, which is a statistical profiler. Currently, an instrumenting profiler is also being developed for Julia. The instrumenting profiler is executed with every function call within a running program (and hence adds a significant overhead) but on the other hand, it allows every function call to be captured. If you need instrumenting profiling, you can look at `IProfile.jl`, available at https://github.com/timholy/IProfile.jl.

For a further discussion of Julia performance optimization, take a look at the Julia performance tips, available at https://docs.julialang.org/en/latest/manual/performance-tips/. Some additional useful performance-related insights on how to organize your Julia code can be found in the Julia style guide at https://docs.julialang.org/en/latest/manual/style-guide/.

Setting up logging in your code

In simple workflows, users often use the print family of functions to report the state of their programs, for example, for debugging purposes. However, in Julia 1.0, we have built-in functionality enabling diagnostic messages from a program to be handled using custom loggers.

In this recipe, we will explain how you can use loggers to control what is reported by your application. In particular, we will explain how you can add debugging information to your application, yet only enable it on demand.

Getting ready

Now, open your favorite terminal to execute the commands.

 In the GitHub repository for this recipe, you will find the commands.txt file, which contains the presented sequence of shell and Julia commands.

How to do it...

Here is a list of steps to be followed:

1. First, load the Logging module and then define a function that performs some operations on sets:

```julia
julia> using Logging

julia> function f(x)
           y = Set(x)
           for v in x
               pop!(y, v)
           end
       end
f (generic function with 1 method)
```

The intention is that the function should silently finish execution as we create a set from a collection and then iteratively remove elements of that collection from the set.

2. Run the function for sample data:

```julia
julia> f([1,2,3])

julia> f([1,2,1,3])
ERROR: KeyError: key 1 not found
Stacktrace:
 [1] pop!(::Dict{Int64,Nothing}, ::Int64) at .\dict.jl:581
 [2] pop! at .\set.jl:49 [inlined]
 [3] f(::Array{Int64,1}) at .\REPL[2]:4
 [4] top-level scope at none:0
```

3. Use the @debug macro to investigate what is going on inside our function:

```julia
julia> function f(x)
           y = Set(x)
           for v in x
               @debug v, y, (v in y)
               pop!(y, v)
           end
       end
f (generic function with 1 method)
```

4. Run it again, but first enable the debugger output by setting it to the stderr stream :

```julia
julia> old = global_logger(ConsoleLogger(stderr, Logging.Debug));

julia> f([1,2,1,3])
┌ Debug: (1, Set([2, 3, 1]), true)
└ @ Main REPL[5]:4
┌ Debug: (2, Set([2, 3]), true)
└ @ Main REPL[5]:4
┌ Debug: (1, Set([3]), false)
└ @ Main REPL[5]:4
ERROR: KeyError: key 1 not found
Stacktrace:
 [1] pop!(::Dict{Int64,Nothing}, ::Int64) at .\dict.jl:581
 [2] pop! at .\set.jl:49 [inlined]
 [3] macro expansion at .\logging.jl:295 [inlined]
 [4] f(::Array{Int64,1}) at .\REPL[5]:4
 [5] top-level scope at none:0
```

5. Observe that element 1 was already removed from the set and we have its duplicate in the passed vector. Using this information, we can fix our function:

```julia
julia> function f(x)
           y = Set(x)
           for v in x
               if v in y
                   @debug v, y, (v in y)
                   pop!(y, v)
               else
                   @debug "$v not found"
               end
           end
       end
f (generic function with 1 method)
```

6. Run the function again. The output will be similar to what is shown here:

```julia
julia> f([1,2,1,3])
┌ Debug: (1, Set([2, 3, 1]), true)
└ @ Main REPL[11]:5
┌ Debug: (2, Set([2, 3]), true)
└ @ Main REPL[11]:5
┌ Debug: 1 not found
└ @ Main REPL[11]:8
┌ Debug: (3, Set([3]), true)
└ @ Main REPL[11]:5
```

Now, when you are sure that the function is correct, you can decide to deploy your code and disable the printing of debugging messages.

7. Therefore, reset the logger to `old` and run the function again:

```julia
julia> global_logger(old);

julia> f([1,2,1,3])
```

And observe that no debugging messages were printed.

How it works...

By default, Julia exposes four macros that allow you to insert logging information into your code. They are ordered by level of severity (lowest to highest) in the following way:

1. @debug
2. @info
3. @warn
4. @error

Each of these macros takes a string that will be logged and optional values or key-value pairs that are to be reported. For instance, in our f function in the @debug macro call, we pass the variables whose state we want to monitor.

By default, all messages except debug are logged. We changed this to print debugging information by replacing the global logger using the global_logger(ConsoleLogger(stderr, Logging.Debug)) call. Observe that the global_logger function returns the logger that is being replaced so that we can simply switch back to it, which we do at the end of the example.

There's more...

It is easy to totally disable logging by creating NullLogger, for instance, by running this:

```
julia> global_logger(NullLogger())
NullLogger()
```

This could be desired in circumstances where you move your code from development to a production environment, in cases where you want to achieve the maximum speed of execution for crucial parts of the application. Of course, you should ensure that disabling logging will not cause you to miss crucial information since even errors will not be reported under this logger:

```
julia> @error "Important error"

julia>
```

See also

You can find details about setting up more complex logging at `https://docs.julialang.org/en/latest/stdlib/Logging/#Logging-1`. In particular, you can explore the `@logmsg` macro, which allows you to change the logging level programmatically or use a custom logging level.

Calling Python from Julia

Python is a popular general-purpose programming language. From a Julia programmer's point of view, the main advantage of Python is having a large set of available libraries that can be seamlessly called and used within Julia.

In this recipe, we will use Python's `scrapy` package for parsing XML data.

Getting ready

In order to use Python from Julia, you should install and configure the `PyCall.jl` package. `PyCall` can be configured in one of two modes:

- Using Python Anaconda, which is automatically installed within Julia

- Using an external Python installation (for example, a separately installed Python Anaconda)

In this recipe, we use the second option (that is, using external Python), but we also provide comments for the built-in Julia Anaconda. Using a version of Anaconda that is separate from Julia makes it possible to use several Anaconda installations (though just one at a time) with a single Julia installation.

We assume that you have installed and configured Python Anaconda in the `~/anaconda3/` directory (for Windows users, for example, `C:\ProgramData\Anaconda3`; this recipe remains valid for both Windows and Linux).

To install `PyCall`, please follow these steps:

1. Download and install Python Anaconda (note that this recipe has been tested with Python 3.6.5 that was installed with Anaconda 5.2.0. Anaconda installer archive can be found at `https://repo.continuum.io/archive/`).

2. Set the `PYTHON` environment variable to point to the Python executable (we assume that Python 3 is used but the instructions that are followed will also work for Python 2):

   - The Julia command to execute on Windows is this:

     ```
     julia> ENV["PYTHON"]="C:\\ProgramData\\Anaconda3\\python.exe"
     ```

   - The Julia command to execute on Linux/macOS is this:

     ```
     julia> ENV["PYTHON"]="~/anaconda3/bin/python"
     ```

3. Install the `PyCall.jl` package by pressing the *]* key in the Julia command line (REPL) and executing the `add PyCall` command.

If you want to use Anaconda Python external to your Julia installation, it is crucial to configure the Anaconda Python executable and set the `ENV["PYTHON"]` variable **before** the installation of `PyCall`. If you reverse this order, since `PyCall` cannot find Anaconda Python, it will then download and install its own version inside the Julia folders.

Once you have installed `PyCall`, you might want to decide to use a different Python version. If this is the case, in the Julia command line, execute the following command:

```
julia> ENV["PYTHON"]="/new/Python/installation/directory/path"
```

Then, go to the Julia package manager (by pressing the *]* key in the Julia command line) and type the following:

```
(v1.0) pkg> build PyCall
```

This will reconfigure `PyCall` to use the new Python installation. Due to its ease of management, we always recommend Python Anaconda rather than different Python distributions.

In the GitHub repository for this recipe, you will find the `commands.txt` file, which contains the presented sequence of shell and Julia commands.

How to do it...

In this example, we will use Python's `scrapy` functionality to extract a given field from an HTML document. Scrapy is a set of Python tools for website scraping:

1. If `scrapy` is not installed in your Python Anaconda, run the following shell command:

   ```
   $ conda install scrapy
   ```

   Note that you might need to provide a full path to the `pip` package manager (for example, `~/anaconda3/bin/pip` on Linux or `C:\ProgramData\Anaconda3\Scripts\pip` on Windows).

   If you're using the built-in version of Anaconda, you can use the `Conda.jl` package to install `scrapy`:

   ```
   using Conda
   Conda.add("scrapy")
   ```

2. Start the Julia command line. In the first step, load the `PyCall` package:

   ```
   using PyCall
   ```

3. Now you are ready to work with Python, so import the package:

   ```
   @pyimport scrapy.selector as ssel
   ```

4. Create a variable containing some sample HTML on the command line:

   ```
   txt="""<html>
       <body>
         My favorite languages
         <ul>
           <li>Julia
           <li>Python
           <li>R
         </ul>
       </body>
   </html>"""
   ```

5. Extract the list of languages from the HTML document with the following command:

```julia
julia> s = ssel.Selector(text=txt)
PyObject <Selector xpath=None data='<html>\n<body>\n          My
favorite language'>

julia> [strip(e[:extract]()) for e in s[:xpath]("//li/text()")]
3-element Array{SubString{String},1}:
 "Julia"
 "Python"
 "R"
```

How it works...

`PyCall` provides a convenient framework for working with Python programs. The only noticeable difference between calling Python and Julia is that module functions, as well as the methods of attributes of Python's objects, are accessed with the `python_object[:function_name](parameters)` syntax. Apart from this exception, using Python libraries is as simple as using any Julia library.

In the example shown, for querying elements within HTML/XML documents, we have used the XPath language; the language specification can be found at https://www.w3.org/TR/1999/REC-xpath-19991116/. Please note that in the HTML presented earlier, the `<li>` items do not have a corresponding closing element (`</li>`). It is a very common situation in many web pages that the HTML does not pass validation. However, Python's `scrapy` library enables the processing of such malformed HTML documents.

Python provides seamless integration for `Array` data; have a look at the following example (the `pybuiltin` function from the `PyCall` package can be used to execute any built-in Python command):

```julia
julia> pybuiltin("sorted")([3,2,1])
3-element Array{Int64,1}:
 1
 2
 3
```

In the case of the `s[:xpath]("//li/text()")` command, an array of callable Python objects is returned and we use `scrapy`'s object `extract` method to get the actual text.

There's more...

If you decide that you need to use Python's `matplolib` to generate plots, you should use the `PyPlot.jl` library rather than calling `matplotlib` directly from `PyCall`. `PyPlot.jl` solves several graphical backend and cross-platform graphics compatibility issues between Julia and Python. A simple use of `PyPlot` is presented in the introductory recipe, *Displaying computation results in Julia,* in Chapter 1, *Installing and Setting Up Julia.* A more complicated use of `PyCall` along with `PyPlot` is presented in the *Building machine learning models with SciKitLearn.jl* recipe in Chapter 9, *Data Science.*

See also

For a complete reference for `PyCall`, see the project's website at `https://github.com/JuliaPy/PyCall.jl`.

Calling R from Julia

R is a powerful language for statistical computing and machine learning. It also offers very potent plotting possibilities via the `ggplot2` module. Julia offers seamless integration with R via the `RCall.jl` package.

Getting ready

`RCall` can simply be installed with the Julia package manager. In the Julia command line (REPL), just press the *]* key and run the following command:

```
(v1.0) pkg> add RCall
```

The `RCall` installer will search for your local R installation. If it is not found, `RCall` will automatically install R for you using the inbuilt Python Anaconda (the `RCall` installer uses the `Conda.jl` Julia module to install `r-base`—`https://anaconda.org/r/r-base`). Please note that the minimal required GNU R version for `RCall` is 3.4.0.

For ease of configuration and management, we recommend using an external R installation. The following three locations are checked when installing `RCall`:

- The `ENV["R_HOME"]` environment variable
- The `ENV["PATH"]` environment variable
- The Windows registry (on Windows platforms, the default settings write the R installation location to the registry)

Normally, on Windows and Linux platforms, R will be in the system path and no configuration is required. More detailed instructions can be found in the `RCall` documentation, available at `https://github.com/JuliaInterop/RCall.jl/blob/master/docs/src/installation.md`.

Please note that you can always change the location of R used by Julia. Simply execute the following command in the Julia command line:

```
julia> ENV["R_HOME"]="/new/R/installation/directory/path"
```

And subsequently, go to the Julia package manager (by pressing the *]* key in the Julia command line) and type the following:

```
(v1.0) pkg> build RCall
```

The preceding command will reconfigure `RCall` for a different R installation.

Additionally, in the following examples, we will use Julia's `Distributions` and `DataFrames` packages. If you have not yet installed them, then do this now by using the package manager:

```
(v1.0) pkg> add Ditributions
(v1.0) pkg> add DateFrames
```

Last, but not least, in this recipe we assume that the `ggplot2` package is included in your R installation. If not, open your GNU R console and run the following R command (depending on your R configuration, you might need to compile the `ggplot2` package; please check the R documentation):

```
R> install.packages("ggplot2")
```

In the GitHub repository for this recipe, you will find the `commands.txt` file, which contains the presented sequence of R and Julia commands.

How to do it...

In this example, we will show how to use R's `ggplot2` to plot data frames created in Julia:

1. Firstly, load the `RCall` package:

```
using RCall
```

2. Secondly, generate `DataFrame` that will later be visualized (these are two sets of normally distributed random values, correlated at `0.75`):

```
using Distributions
using DataFrames
using Random
Random.seed!(0);
dat = rand(MvNormal([1 0.75; 0.75 1]), 1000);
df = DataFrame(permutedims(dat))
```

Now, it is time to visualize the dataset. We consider the following four options:

- Calling R libraries from Julia
- Directly calling R from Julia with variable interpolation
- Using the R command line available inside Julia with variable interpolation
- Sending variables with their values to R

Option 1 – calling R libraries from Julia

Load an R library with the `@rlibrary` macro and it is available in Julia just like any other function:

```
julia> @rlibrary ggplot2
julia> ggplot(df,aes(x=:x1,y=:x2)) + geom_point()
```

Option 2 – directly calling R from Julia with variable interpolation

Another option for executing R code from Julia is to use the `R""` string macro. The `$` sign is used to pass values from Julia to R:

```
julia> R"library(ggplot2)"
julia> R"ggplot($df,aes(x=x1,y=x2)) + geom_point()"
```

Option 3 – using the R command line available inside Julia with variable interpolation

To start the R command line inside Julia's command line, press the $ key and this will change the prompt to R>. Now, execute the R command:

```
R> library(ggplot2)
R> ggplot($df,aes(x=x1,y=x2)) + geom_point()
```

Please note that the $ sign is used to pass the df value from Julia to R.

Once you finish executing the R commands, press the *Backspace* key to go back to the Julia REPL.

Option 4 – sending variables with their values to R

It is possible to avoid interpolation via sending a variable's value to R before executing a command:

```
julia> @rput df
```

Now, you can either use the R"" string macro or the R command line. The following example is for the string macro:

```
julia> R"library(ggplot2)"
julia> R"ggplot(df,aes(x=x1,y=x2)) + geom_point()"
```

For the R command line, press $ inside Julia's command line:

```
R> library(ggplot2)
R> ggplot(df,aes(x=x1,y=x2)) + geom_point()
```

How it works...

Julia attaches to the R environment via the shared library mechanism. Hence, R runs within a Julia process as a separate environment. The R environment running inside Julia has its own namespace; any variable can be transferred between those environments using the @rgetand and @rput macros. Another option for transferring data between Julia and R is to use the interpolation mechanism that works with R"" string macros, as well as with the R command line running inside Julia (R>), which can be accessed by typing $ in the console.

For most data visualization scenarios, the most convenient option is to use the `@rlibrary` macro and call R commands in the same way that Julia commands are called.

On the other hand, if one decides to use R for performing machine learning on large datasets, one needs to have full control over the process of sending the data to the R environment. This way, we can avoid constantly copying large datasets between R and Julia.

There's more...

When analyzing large datasets, it's important to have control over when the data is copied between Julia and R. Please consider the following simple example:

```
julia> using RCall
julia> a = 5;
julia> @rput a
5
julia> R"b = a*2"
RCall.RObject{RCall.RealSxp}
[1] 10
julia> @rget b
10.0
julia> b
10.0
```

Please note that the `@rget` and `@rput` macros actually transfer variables between the R and Julia environments. Additionally, the required data type conversions between Julia and R are being performed on the fly. `RCall` makes it possible to convert data between R and basic Julia data types. Conversion for Julia's statistics packages is supported including `DataFrames`, `DataArrays`, `NullableArrays`, `CategoricalArrays`, `NamedArrays`, and `AxisArrays`.

For the up-to-date conversion list, visit https://github.com/JuliaInterop/RCall.jl/blob/master/docs/src/conversions.md.

See also

The full documentation of the `RCall.jl` package is available at http://juliainterop.github.io/RCall.jl/stable/gettingstarted.

Managing project dependencies

In the *Managing packages* recipe in Chapter 1, *Installing and Setting Up Julia*, we explained how you can install and remove packages in the global environment.

However, when you develop your own application, you often need to have precise control over its dependencies. In this recipe, we explain how Julia supports this requirement.

Getting ready

Create a new folder on your computer and start the Julia command line in this folder. Running the pwd() command should return the path to the folder in which you want to create your project.

Make sure that the folder is empty. You can check it, for example, by running isempty(readdir()), which should return true.

Also, make sure that the StaticArrays package is **not** installed. Running the using StaticArrays command should throw the following error:

```
julia> using StaticArrays
ERROR: ArgumentError: Package StaticArrays not found in current path:
- Run `import Pkg; Pkg.add("StaticArrays")` to install the StaticArrays
package.
```

In the GitHub repository for this recipe, you will find the commands.txt file, which contains the presented sequence of shell and Julia commands.

Now, open your favorite terminal to execute the commands.

How to do it...

In this recipe, we will create a new project, which will have the StaticArrays package installed. This package will only be visible from within this project's scope:

1. Start with creating a new project by switching to the package manager with the *]* key in the Julia command line:

   ```
   (v1.0) pkg>
   ```

2. Now, write the following line to initialize a new project:

```
(v1.0) pkg> generate Project
Generating project Project:
    Project/Project.toml
    Project/src/Project.jl
```

3. Observe that it contains one file, `Project.toml`, which holds the description of your project, and a default project file, `src/Project.jl`.

4. Now, switch back to Julia mode by pressing the *Backspace* key and try loading the `StaticArrays` package. It should fail like this:

```
julia> using StaticArrays
ERROR: ArgumentError: Package StaticArrays not found in current
path:
- Run `Pkg.add("StaticArrays")` to install the StaticArrays
package.
```

5. Press the *]* key to switch to package manager mode and use the `activate` command to activate your local project, named `Project`:

```
(v1.0) pkg> activate Project

(Project) pkg>
```

6. Now, add the `StaticArrays` package to your project:

```
(Project) pkg> add StaticArrays
[output truncated]
```

Observe that a new file, `Manifest.toml`, is created. Together with `Project.toml`, it holds metadata about your project.

7. Now, go back to Julia mode and load the `StaticArrays` package:

```
julia> using StaticArrays

julia>
```

8. You can also check that your `Project.toml` file has this package as a dependency:

```
julia> print(read("Project/Project.toml", String))
name = "Project"
uuid = "c064c660-b08c-11e8-00d7-a9ab788e66a7"
authors = ["Bogumił Kamiński <bkamins@sgh.waw.pl>"]
version = "0.1.0"

[deps]
StaticArrays = "90137ffa-7385-5640-81b9-e52037218182"
```

9. Now, exit Julia using `exit()` and start it again using the `julia` command in the OS shell, to have a new session of the Julia command line.

10. When you switch to the package manager prompt with the] key, you will notice that you are back in the default environment:

```
(v1.0) pkg>
```

11. Switch back to Julia mode and try loading the `StaticArrays` package:

```
julia> using StaticArrays
ERROR: ArgumentError: Package StaticArrays not found in current
path:
- Run `Pkg.add("StaticArrays")` to install the StaticArrays
package.
```

12. It still gives an error—this package was not installed in the global environment. But if we activate our project again in package manager mode and switch back to Julia mode, it works correctly:

```
(v1.0) pkg> activate Project

julia> using StaticArrays

julia>
```

How it works...

In Julia, you can create multiple projects that have separate namespaces of visible packages. Which environments are searched for in the installed packages is governed by the LOAD_PATH variable. By default, its value is the following:

```
julia> LOAD_PATH
3-element Array{String,1}:
 "@"
 "@v#.#"
 "@stdlib"
```

This means that the primary environment (current project) is searched first for packages, then the default environment for the whole of Julia, and finally the standard library is scanned.

This has an important consequence. Notice that in our project we only installed the StaticArrays package. However, we can run the following command without a problem:

```
julia> using Pkg

julia>
```

Even though we did not install the Pkg package itself. The reason for this is that this package is in the standard library that is specified in the search path. So, now remove this entry from the search path, like so:

```
julia> pop!(LOAD_PATH)
"@stdlib"

julia> LOAD_PATH
2-element Array{String,1}:
 "@"
 "@v#.#"
```

Now, when trying to load Statistics, another package from the standard library will fail:

```
julia> using Statistics
ERROR: ArgumentError: Package Statistics not found in current path:
- Run `Pkg.add("Statistics")` to install the Statistics package.
```

Therefore, we see that environments stack on top of each other. Julia tries to find a package in consecutive locations, as specified in the LOAD_PATH variable, until it finds it or fails.

There's more...

The package manager provides much more functionality related to project and package management, such as testing, building, and pinning dependencies to concrete versions. You can find the details at `https://docs.julialang.org/en/latest/stdlib/Pkg/`.

See also

The basics of installing packages in Julia are described in the *Managing packages* recipe in `Chapter 1`, *Installing and Setting Up Julia*.

9
Data Science

In this chapter, we present the following recipes:

- Working with databases
- Optimization using JuMP
- Estimation using maximum likelihood
- Complex plotting with the `Plots.jl` package
- Building machine learning models with the `ScikitLearn.jl` package

Introduction

The goal of this chapter is to show how to use Julia for typical data science tasks.

We start by explaining how to use Julia with various types of relational databases and the full-text search engine Elasticearch. Next, we show how to construct optimization models in Julia. In addition to this, we discuss estimating models with the maximum likelihood function. Finally, we move on to complex plotting and machine learning models.

Working with databases in Julia

In this recipe, we show how to connect to various database engines with Julia. There are three ways to access database systems from Julia:

- Access databases directly from Julia, using packages provided with `https://github.com/JuliaDatabases/`
- Use Java's JDBC drivers to access databases via the `JDBC.jl` package built on top of the `JavaCall.jl` package
- Use Python's database drivers by loading packages in the `PyCall.jl` package

In this section, the first scenario will be discussed by presenting how to connect to MySQL and PostgreSQL with dedicated Julia packages. The second scenario will show how to connect to an Oracle database with **JDBC (Java Database Connectivity)** drivers provided by the JDBC.jl package. The third scenario will be discussed in the *There's more...* section by presenting ways of using the PyCall.jl package to open a connection to the Elasticsearch document database.

Getting ready

We will show how to set up the environments for working in Julia with three popular relational database systems—MySQL, PostgreSQL, and Oracle.

 In the GitHub repository for this recipe, you will find the commands.txt file that contains the presented sequence of shell and Julia commands.

Getting ready for MySQL

MySQL drivers can be installed with the following command:

```
(v1.0) pkg> add MySQL
```

Since version 8.0, MySQL uses a new authentication mechanism that is not yet supported by Julia's MySQL package. In order to be able to work with MySQL 8.0, you need to do two things:

- Edit the MySQL configuration file to use the previous authentication mechanism
- Set the root user authentication rules

The MySQL configuration file on Windows is found in the home data directory (for example, C:\ProgramData\MySQL\MySQL Server 8.0\my.ini), while on Linux it can usually be found at /etc/mysql/mysql.cnf. In this file, find the default_authentication_plugin parameter and set it to mysql_native_password:

```
default_authentication_plugin = mysql_native_password
```

If this parameter is not present in the file, add the preceding line to the [mysqld] section of the MySQL configuration file.

Additionally, in order to enable the MySQL native authentication mechanism, go to the MySQL console (for example, use MySQL Workbench or run `sudo mysql` in Linux; for further details check the MySQL documentation) and execute the following command:

```
ALTER USER 'root'@'localhost' IDENTIFIED WITH mysql_native_password BY
'type_password_here';
```

Now, you are ready to connect to MySQL from Julia.

Getting ready for PostgreSQL

The `LibPQ.jl` package provides PostgreSQL for Julia by wrapping the PostgreSQL `libpq` C package. Hence, you need to start with installing the `libpq` driver:

- On Ubuntu, use `sudo apt install libpq5` to install it, while on macOS you can use `brew install libpq`.
- On Windows, the `libpq.dll` file can be obtained together with the PostgreSQL installer. You might need to add a path to the `libpq.dll` file, for example:

  ```
  julia>  ENV["PATH"] = "C:\\Program
  Files\\PostgreSQL\\10\\lib;"*ENV["PATH"]
  ```

Now you are ready to install the `LibPQ` package:

```
(v1.0) pkg> add LibPQ
```

Please note that you need to know the `postgres` user password for PostgreSQL. On Windows, it can be entered into the graphical installer. On the other hand, on Linux\Ubuntu run the `sudo -i -u postgres psql` command and in the `psql` console run `\password postgres` to set up the password. The `psql` console can be exited by entering the `\q` command. In this recipe, we assume that the password for the `postgres` user is `type_password_here`.

Getting ready for JDBC and Oracle

We first show how to install `JDBC.jl`, and subsequently explain how to obtain Oracle drivers for JDBC.

Configuring JDBC in Julia

JDBC offers a standard interface for working with databases in Java. Since the Java language is very popular in business, all relational databases offer high-quality JDBC drivers.

The first step in configuring JDBC for Julia is to check whether Java is installed in your system. Start the system console and execute the java -version command. You should see output similar to the following one:

```
$ java -version
java version "1.8.0_151"
Java(TM) SE Runtime Environment (build 1.8.0_151-b12)
Java HotSpot(TM) 64-Bit Server VM (build 25.151-b12, mixed mode)
```

If instead you see a message such as 'java' is not recognized or java not found, you need to install Java.

In order to install Java, go to https://java.com/en/download/. From this website, you can download the Java installer for all major operating systems. However, if you use Linux/Ubuntu and Java is not installed, it might be easier to use the apt package manager and simply execute the sudo apt install default-jre command (please note that this apt command will install OpenJDK Java rather than Oracle Java, but it does not affect our example).

Once you know that Java is present on your system, JDBC can simply be installed with the Julia package manager. On the Julia command line, press the] key and run the following command:

```
(v1.0) pkg> add JDBC
```

This will install the JDBC.jl package and all its dependencies.

Getting Oracle JDBC drivers

In the Oracle examples in this chapter, we use Oracle **AWS RDS (Amazon Web Services Relational Database Service**; see https://aws.amazon.com/rds/oracle/). Cloud computing is the easiest and fastest option for launching an Oracle database server (note that Amazon RDS also offers MySQL and PostgreSQL databases). If you decide to run Julia examples against an Oracle database hosted with Amazon RDS, please make sure that the network connectivity between your Julia machine and Oracle machine is enabled (in particular, check the AWS security group settings for your Amazon RDS Oracle instance).

Regardless of which version of Oracle database you want to connect to, you need to obtain a JDBC driver from the Oracle website at https://www.oracle.com/technetwork/database/application-development/jdbc/downloads/index.html. Once you download the driver file (for example, ojdbc8.jar), simply place it in your Julia working folder (you can check the current Julia working folder with the pwd function or change it with the cd("/path/to/new/folder") Julia commands).

Finally, in this recipe we will use the DataFrames.jl package. If you do not have it installed yet, please add it using the following command:

```julia
julia> using Pkg; Pkg.add("DataFrames")
```

How to do it...

In this section, we look at recipes for several different databases and drivers. We will provide a script that creates a simple table, inserts two rows into it, and reads them back.

Connecting to MySQL Server with MySQL.jl

MySQL is a popular open source database often used by various web pages. The following commands show how to work with this database:

1. Execute the following commands to obtain a connection. For the "type_password_here" string, use your actual password. We will use the database named sys since it is present with a default MySQL installation for your project, you are recommended to create a separate database (for example, using a tool such as MySQL Workbench):

    ```julia
    julia> using DataFrames
    julia> using MySQL
    julia> conn = MySQL.connect("127.0.0.1", "root",
    "type_password_here",db="sys")
    MySQL Connection
    ------------
    Host: localhost
    Port: 3306
    User: root
    DB:   sys
    ```

2. Now, we can create a table:

```
julia> MySQL.execute!(conn, "CREATE TABLE mytable (col1 INT
AUTO_INCREMENT PRIMARY KEY, col2 VARCHAR(50), col3 INT)")
0
```

3. Insert some data into the table:

```
julia> st = MySQL.Stmt(conn, "INSERT INTO mytable(col2, col3)
VALUES (?,?)");
julia> MySQL.execute!(st, ["testdata",7]);
julia> MySQL.execute!(st, ["testdata2",8]);
```

4. Now, get the data out as `DataFrame`:

```
julia> df = MySQL.query(conn, "SELECT * FROM mytable") |> DataFrame
2×3 DataFrame
|       | Int32 | String    | Int32 |
| ----- | ----- | --------- | ----- |
| 1     | 1     | testdata  | 7     |
| 2     | 2     | testdata2 | 8     |
```

5. The data can be also obtained as `NamedTuple`:

```
julia> res = MySQL.query(conn, "SELECT * FROM mytable")
(col1 = Int32[1, 2], col2 = Union{Missing, String}["testdata",
"testdata2"], col3 = Union{Missing, Int32}[7, 8])
```

6. Remember to close the database connection:

```
julia> MySQL.disconnect(conn)
```

Please note that the `MySQL.jl` package is currently being re-engineered, and some changes to the API might occur. Please check the up-to-date documentation at `https://github.com/JuliaDatabases/MySQL.jl`.

Connecting to PostgreSQL with LibPQ.jl

In this recipe, we will use PostgreSQL. The PostgreSQL database is very suitable for data analytics and high-scale computational science owing to its flexibility, scalability, and programmability. Additionally, PostgreSQL is open source and available for free. Last but not least, PostgreSQL is offered as a managed database service by all major cloud providers (AWS, Microsoft, and Google). It's also worth noting that a popular data warehousing solution, AWS RedShift, is also PostgreSQL-based and hence compatible with the drivers discussed. The PostgreSQL database can be downloaded at https://www.postgresql.org/download/. Here is a list of steps to be followed:

1. Execute the following commands to obtain a connection. We connect within a local machine to the postgres default database, using postgres as the default username as well. In place of the string "type_password_here", use your actual password:

```
julia> using DataFrames
julia> using LibPQ
julia> conn = LibPQ.Connection("host=localhost dbname=postgres user=postgres password="type_password_here")
PostgreSQL connection (CONNECTION_OK) with parameters:
  user = postgres
  password = ********************
  dbname = postgres
  host = localhost
  port = 5432
  client_encoding = UTF8
  application_name = LibPQ.jl
  sslmode = prefer
  sslcompression = 1
  krbsrvname = postgres
  target_session_attrs = any
```

2. Now, we can create the table:

```
julia> LibPQ.execute(conn, "CREATE TABLE mytable (col1 SERIAL PRIMARY KEY NOT NULL, col2 VARCHAR(50), col3 INT)")
PostgreSQL result
```

3. Insert the data once the table has been created:

```
julia> st = LibPQ.prepare(conn, "INSERT INTO MYTABLE(col2, col3)
VALUES (\$1,\$2)")
PostgreSQL prepared statement named __libpq_stmt_0__ with query
INSERT INTO MYTABLE(col2, col3) VALUES ($1,$2)

julia> LibPQ.execute(st,["testdata",7])
PostgreSQL result

julia> LibPQ.execute(st,["testdata2",8])
PostgreSQL result
```

4. Now, let's fetch the inserted data. Firstly, the data can be retrieved as `DataFrame`:

```
julia> df = LibPQ.fetch!(DataFrame, LibPQ.execute(conn, "SELECT *
FROM mytable"))
2×3 DataFrame
| Row | col1  | col2      | col3  |
|     | Int32 | String    | Int32 |
|-----|-------|-----------|-------|
| 1   | 1     | testdata  | 7     |
| 2   | 2     | testdata2 | 8     |
```

5. You can also retrieve the data as `NamedTuple`:

```
julia> nt = LibPQ.fetch!(NamedTuple, LibPQ.execute(conn, "SELECT *
FROM mytable"))
(col1 = Union{Missing, Int32}[1, 2], col2 = Union{Missing,
String}["testdata", "testdata2"], col3 = Union{Missing, Int32}[7,
8])
```

6. After the job is done, we close the database connection:

```
julia> LibPQ.close(conn)
```

Connecting to Oracle with JDBC.jl

Since there is currently no Julia driver for the Oracle database, we will show how to connect using the JDBC driver as follows:

1. Execute the following commands to obtain a connection:

```
using DataFrames
using JDBC
```

```
JDBC.usedriver("ojdbc8.jar")
JDBC.init()
```

2. The next step is to open the connection. Please note that in this example we use the AWS RDS Oracle database that was available online when writing this recipe. You will need to provide a different database hostname; also, for the `"type_password_here"` string, use your actual password:

```
conn =
JDBC.DriverManager.getConnection("jdbc:oracle:thin:@ora.cez1pkekt7f
j.us-
east-2.rds.amazonaws.com:1521:ORCL",Dict("user"=>"orauser","passwor
d"=>"type_password_here"));
```

3. Once the connection is initialized, we can create the table:

```
st = JDBC.createStatement(conn);
JDBC.execute(st, "CREATE TABLE mytable (col1 INT GENERATED ALWAYS
AS IDENTITY NOT NULL,"
 * " col2 VARCHAR2(50), col3 INT, CONSTRAINT col1 PRIMARY KEY
(col1))");
```

4. Then, the data can be inserted. Simply execute the following Julia code:

```
pst = JDBC.prepareStatement(conn, "INSERT INTO mytable (col2, col3)
VALUES (:1,:2)")
JDBC.setString(pst,1,"testdata")
JDBC.setInt(pst,2,7)
JDBC.executeUpdate(pst)
JDBC.setString(pst,1,"testdata")
JDBC.setInt(pst,2,8)
JDBC.executeUpdate(pst)
JDBC.commit(conn)
```

5. Now, you can fetch the data from the table:

```
julia> rs = executeQuery(st, "select * from mytable");
julia> for r in rs
         println(JDBC.getInt(r,1),"|",
         JDBC.getString(r,2),"|",JDBC.getInt(r,3))
       end
1|testdata|7
2|testdata|8
```

6. For the next example, we will use a different `JDBC.jl` interface (which is called `JDBC.jl` **Julian Interface**), so we close the current connection:

```
julia> close(conn)
```

7. We can also get `DataFrame`, although it requires a different type of connection to the Oracle database:

```
julia> conn =
JDBC.Connection("jdbc:oracle:thin:@ora.cez1pkekt7fj.us-
east-2.rds.amazonaws.com:1521:ORCL",
        props=Dict("user"=>"orauser",
                    "password"=>"type_password_here"));
julia> csr=JDBC.Cursor(conn);

julia> df = JDBC.load(DataFrame, csr, "select * from mytable")
2×3 DataFrame
| Row | COL1     | COL2       | COL3     |
|     | Float64  | String     | Float64  |
| ----- | ---------- | ---------- | ---------- |
| 1   | 1.0      | testdata   | 7.0      |
| 2   | 2.0      | testdata   | 8.0      |

julia> nt = JDBC.load(NamedTuple, csr, "select * from mytable")
(COL1 = [1.0, 2.0], COL2 = Union{Missing, String}["testdata",
"testdata"], COL3 = Union{Missing, Float64}[7.0, 8.0])

julia> JDBC.close(csr)
```

8. Once you finish working with the Oracle database, close the connection:

```
julia> JDBC.close(conn)
```

How it works...

Julia has broad support for various database systems. The drivers are available under https://github.com/JuliaDatabases/.

In each discussed database scenario, we take the same approach:

1. Open a database connection
2. Create a table using a statement object
3. Write rows to the table with a precompiled `prepared` statement
4. Retrieve the data as `DataFrame` or `NamedTuple`
5. Close the database connection

To open the database connection, you need to know:

- The database server name (we use `localhost` in the first two examples and a remote AWS server in the Oracle example)
- Port (we always use default values and hence this parameter is skipped)
- Database name
- Username
- Password

Each package requires this information via slightly differently formatted function parameters. For creating a table, we use a statement object that represents an action performed on the database engine. However, when operations on the database are parametrized with user data (such as an `INSERT` statement), the recommended approach is to use a precompiled `prepared` statement object, a statement with parameters. This enables a complete separation between SQL queries and user data (malformed data will not affect query execution). Finally, we run a query against the data table. All Julia packages provide functionality to retrieve data, either as `DataFrame` or `NamedTuple`, for further processing. Once the work with the database is completed, the connection must be closed, so that it does not consume the server resources.

It is worth noting that JDBC drivers exist for virtually every relational database. Hence, we could also use it, for example, to connect to PostgreSQL (this requires obtaining the PostgreSQL JDBC driver, which can be downloaded from `https://jdbc.postgresql.org/`). Please take a look at the following example:

```
using JDBC
JDBC.usedriver("postgresql-42.2.4.jar")
JDBC.init()
conn = DriverManager.getConnection("jdbc:postgresql://localhost/postgres",
                        Dict("user"=>"postgres",
                             "password"=>"type_password_here"))
```

However, we expect that for most scenarios the native Julia drivers offer the best integration and highest throughput.

There's more...

While for many databases, direct Julia drivers are not supported, another alternative to JDBC is to connect to them with the `PyCall` Python driver package. In the *Calling Python from Julia* recipe in Chapter 8, *Julia Workflow*, we show how to use `PyCall` with any external Anaconda installation. Python drivers are currently available for virtually every database system that exists.

As an example, for many no-SQL databases, JDBC is not available (since JDBC is an API oriented toward relational databases). Let's consider Elasticsearch, one of the major products for storing and querying textual data. We will show how to use `PyCall` to connect and update data in an Elasticsearch database. This example assumes that `PyCall` is linked to an Anaconda installation that has the Python `elasticsearch` module and that Elasticsearch is configured and running with the default settings on a local machine. Elasticsearch configuration and management is beyond the scope of this recipe.

We start by importing `PyCall` and loading the Python `elasticsearch` library:

```
using PyCall
@pyimport elasticsearch
```

Let's now open a connection to Elasticsearch:

```
es = elasticsearch.Elasticsearch()
```

If the connection is successful, we can test it:

```
julia> es[:info]()
Dict{Any,Any} with 5 entries:
  "name" => "MYHOSTNAME"
  "tagline" => "You Know, for Search"
  "cluster_uuid" => "St2JmR8JRg-yqkzcmVz49Q"
  "cluster_name" => "elasticsearch"
  "version" => Dict{Any,Any}(Pair{Any,Any}("number", "6.2.4...
```

Now, let's use Elasticsearch to index some text data:

```
dat = Dict("col1"=>"some text","col2"=>"more text")
res = es[:index](index="data", doc_type="data", id="1", body=dat)
```

Once the data is present in the Elasticsearch database, we can query it (see the Elasticsearch manual for the query reference):

```
q=Dict("query"=>Dict("match"=>Dict("col1"=>Dict("query"=>"some text"))))
```

The query object has been defined as a Julia `Dict` query object. Now, the query can be run against the database:

```
julia> es[:search]("data",body=q)["hits"]["hits"]
1-element Array{Dict{Any,Any},1}:
 Dict{Any,Any}(Pair{Any,Any}("_id", "1"),Pair{Any,Any}("_score",
 0.575364),Pair{Any,Any}("_index", "data"),Pair{Any,Any}("_type",
 "data"),Pair{Any,Any}("_source", Dict{Any,Any}(Pair{Any,Any}("col2", "more
 text"),Pair{Any,Any}("col1", "some text"))))
```

More information on queries can be found in the Elasticsearch manual at
`https://www.elastic.co/guide/en/elasticsearch/reference/current/query-dsl.html`.

See also

A complete overview of all available database APIs can be found
at `https://github.com/svaksha/Julia.jl/blob/master/DataBase.md`.

More instructions on how to install dependencies for the PostgreSQL `LibPQ.jl` package
can be found at `https://github.com/invenia/LibPQ.jl`.

Optimization using JuMP

In this recipe, we will show how to define an optimization model with JuMP, and how to use the library with open source and commercial solvers. The recipe will be illustrated by solving a simple linear optimization model.

Getting ready

For this recipe, you need the following packages: JuMP.jl, Clp.jl, and Cbc.jl. These packages can be installed with the Julia package manager. In the Julia command line, press the *J* key and run the commands as follows:

```
(v1.0) pkg> add JuMP
(v1.0) pkg> add Clp
(v1.0) pkg> add Cbc
```

Please note that at the time of writing this book the Cbc.jl package fails to compile on Windows and hence can only be installed on the Linux operating system.

Additionally, we will show how to use a commercial solver named Gurobi. Firstly, you need to obtain a Gurobi license (free for academic use) from the Gurobi website, and secondly you need to download and install Gurobi.

Once you obtain a license from Gurobi, you need to configure it on your machine. A sample shell command could look like this (the actual command can be seen at the Gurobi website):

```
$ grbgetkey xxxxxxxx-xxxx-xxxx-xxxx-xxxxxxxxxxxx
```

Replace the row of x with an actual license number obtained from Gurobi. Please note that when you apply for a free academic license, you need to request the key to be connected through your university network (directly or via VPN).

Once Gurobi is installed, we need to add an appropriate library to Julia:

```
(v1.0) pkg> add Gurobi
```

If Julia fails to find Gurobi, you need to make sure that gurobi is in the executable path (system PATH variable) and you need to rebuild the Gurobi.jl package using the build Gurobi command that should be run from the Julia package manager.

 In the GitHub repository for this recipe, you will find the commands.txt file, which contains the presented sequence of shell and Julia commands.

How to do it...

Let's consider an optimization problem of a farm that has two types of fodder (1 and 2) which are used to feed its livestock. Each of these fodders has a different price (50 and 70 USD, respectively) and can be characterized by three nutritional characteristics (`calories`, `proteins`, and `vitamins`). The farm wants to provide livestock with the minimum required nutrition (9000, 300, and 60) at the lowest cost. This problem can be stated as follows:

```
Minimize: 50x₁ + 70x₂
Subject to conditions:
200x₁ + 2000x₂ >= 9000    #calories
100x₁ +   30x₂ >=  300    #proteins
9x₁   +   11x₂ >=   60    #vitamins
x₁ , x₂        >=    0    #values cannot be negative
```

This is a typical type of problem that can be solved by the linear optimization algorithm. To solve the problem, follow these steps:

1. We start by loading the `JuMP.jl` package:

   ```
   using JuMP
   using Clp
   ```

2. Now, we create an empty model (please note the use of the semicolon (`;`)—currently trying to show a JuMP model at console throws an error in Julia—you will need to use `println(m)` to see the model contents):

   ```
   m = Model(solver = ClpSolver());
   ```

3. Now, we add the variables (use the _1-*Tab* sequence to input subscripts):

   ```
   julia> @variable(m, x₁ >= 0)
   x₁

   julia> @variable(m, x₂ >= 0)
   x₂
   ```

4. Now, we define the objective function:

   ```
   julia> @objective(m, Min, 50x₁ + 70x₂)
   50 x₁ + 70 x₂
   ```

5. Finally, the constraints need to be defined:

```julia
julia> @constraint(m, 200x₁ + 2000x₂ >= 9000);
julia> @constraint(m, 100x₁ +   30x₂ >=  300);
julia> @constraint(m, 9x₁   +   11x₂ >=   60);
```

6. Now, we show our model:

```julia
julia> println(m)
Min 50 x₁ + 70 x₂
Subject to
 200 x₁ + 2000 x₂ >= 9000
 100 x₁ + 30 x₂ >= 300
 9 x₁ + 11 x₂ >= 60
 x₁ >= 0
 x₂ >= 0
```

7. Let's solve it:

```julia
julia> status = solve(m)
:Optimal
```

8. And we show the results:

```julia
julia> println("Cost:
$(getobjectivevalue(m))\nx₁=$(getvalue(x₁))\nx₂=$(getvalue(x₂))")
Cost: 388.1443298969072
x₁=1.701030927835052
x₂=4.329896907216495
```

We should buy 1.7 units of fodder 1 and 4.33 units of fodder 2.

Now, let's suppose that the quantity of fodder 2 needs to be bought in whole units (for example, the value of x_2 could represent the number of truckloads that need to be purchased). In this case, our problem turns out to be a mixed integer linear programming problem, and we need a different solver. Please follow these steps:

1. Redefine the optimization problem:

```
using JuMP
using Cbc
m = Model(solver = CbcSolver());
@variable(m, x₁ >= 0)
@variable(m, x₂ >= 0, Int)
@objective(m, Min, 50x₁ + 70x₂)
@constraint(m, 200x₁ + 2000x₂ >= 9000)
@constraint(m, 100x₁ +   30x₂ >=  300)
@constraint(m, 9x₁   +   11x₂ >=   60)
```

2. Now, let's solve the model:

```julia
julia> status = solve(m)
:Optimal

julia> println("Cost:
$(getobjectivevalue(m))\nx₁=$(getvalue(x₁))\nx₂=$(getvalue(x₂))")
Cost: 425.0
x₁=1.5
x₂=5.0
```

We can see that the solution with an integer constraint differs from the previous solution.

How it works...

The `JuMP.jl` package provides a powerful frontend for all major optimization solvers (the full list is available at `http://www.juliaopt.org/JuMP.jl/latest/installation/#Getting-Solvers-1`). This standardization enables efficient working with linear and nonlinear optimization models through a macro system. Hence, a user of the `JuMP.jl` package can define the problem once and test it against various optimization solvers.

The basic commands that we have used in this recipe are as follows:

- The `Model` constructor, which creates an object that will hold the optimization model
- The `@variable` macro, which adds a variable to the optimization model
- The `@objective` macro, which adds an objective function to the optimization model
- The `@constraint` macro, which adds a constraint to the optimization model
- The `solve` function, which invokes an external solver to find the optimum of the defined optimization problem
- The `getobjectivevalue` function, which returns the value of the objective function in the found optimum
- The `getvalue` function gets a value of a given variable in the found optimum

There's more...

Please note that available solvers can vary greatly by their performance and capabilities. For example, if we had used `Clp.jl` rather than `Cbc.jl` to solve the mixed integer linear programming model, we would have seen the following error:

```
julia> status = solve(m)
ERROR: Clp does not support integer variables
```

For large scale optimization, it is sometimes worth testing the performance of a commercial solver. One such solver engine is Gurobi, which can be used in Julia via the `Gurobi.jl` package.

One defines the Gurobi model similar to the other models:

```
using JuMP
using Gurobi
m = Model(solver = GurobiSolver());
@variable(m, x₁ >= 0)
@variable(m, x₂ >= 0, Int)
@objective(m, Min, 50x₁ + 70x₂)
@constraint(m, 200x₁ + 2000x₂ >= 9000)
@constraint(m, 100x₁ +   30x₂ >=  300)
@constraint(m, 9x₁   +   11x₂ >=   60)
```

And now, you can solve it:

```
julia> status = solve(m)
Academic license - for non-commercial use only
Optimize a model with 3 rows, 2 columns and 6 nonzeros
Variable types: 1 continuous, 1 integer (0 binary)

   [ ... the actual output was ommitted ... ]

Optimal solution found (tolerance 1.00e-04)
Best objective 4.250000000000e+02, best bound 4.250000000000e+02, gap
0.0000%
:Optimal

julia> println("Cost:
$(getobjectivevalue(m))\nx₁=$(getvalue(x₁))\nx₂=$(getvalue(x₂))")
Cost: 425.0
x₁=1.5
x₂=5.0
```

The answer is identical to the results from `Cbc.jl`. The actual choice of solver usually depends on the set of required features and performance. The `JuMP.jl` package enables overhead-free switching between solver engines.

Please note that Gurobi can, in fact, be accessed directly from Julia (without using JuMP); the full documentation can be found at `https://github.com/JuliaOpt/Gurobi.jl`.

See also

Detailed documentation of the `JuMP.jl` package is available at `http://www.juliaopt.org/JuMP.jl/latest/`. There are also projects extending JuMP's functionality for other optimization types, such as multiple criteria or robust optimization. For an overview of available packages, see `https://www.juliaopt.org/`.

Estimation using maximum likelihood

In this recipe, we discuss how you can perform the optimization of a likelihood function using Julia.

Getting ready

Maximum likelihood is one of the basic techniques for the estimation of the parameters of a statistical model; see `http://mathworld.wolfram.com/MaximumLikelihood.html` or `https://en.wikipedia.org/wiki/Maximum_likelihood_estimation` for a more detailed discussion. In this recipe, we estimate the mean and standard deviation of a sample coming from a normal distribution. In this case, an analytical solution to this optimization problem is known and the estimate of the mean is the mean of the sample $\bar{x} = \sum_{i=1}^{n} x_i / n$ and the estimate of standard deviation is $\sqrt{\sum_{i=1}^{n} (x_i - \bar{x})^2 / n}$, where n is the sample size and x_i are sample points.

We chose a problem whose analytical solution is known in order to compare whether the results using optimization and exact calculation are similar.

In this recipe, we will use the Optim.jl package. If you do not have it installed, please add it using these commands:

```julia
julia> using Pkg; Pkg.add("Optim")
```

 In the GitHub repository for this recipe, you will find the commands.txt file, which contains the presented sequence of shell and Julia commands. The functions defined in this recipe are contained in the opt.jl file.

Now, open your favorite terminal to execute the commands.

How to do it...

Here is a list of steps that we follow:

1. Here is the code that can be used to perform the desired optimization (you can find it in the opt.jl file):

```julia
using Optim
using Distributions

function loglik(x, μ, logσ)
    nd = Normal(μ, exp(logσ))
    -sum(logpdf(nd, v) for v in x)
end

function testoptim(x)
    res = optimize(par -> loglik(x, par[1], par[2]), zeros(2))
    display(res)
    res.minimizer[1], exp(res.minimizer[2])
end
```

2. The testoptim function is then used on a sample data set:

```julia
julia> include("opt.jl");

julia> using Random

julia> Random.seed!(1);

julia> x = randn(100);

julia> testoptim(x)
Results of Optimization Algorithm
```

```
 * Algorithm: Nelder-Mead
 * Starting Point: [0.0,0.0]
 * Minimizer: [-0.043288979878934694,0.015040192009564638, ...]
 * Minimum: 1.433977e+02
 * Iterations: 27
 * Convergence: true
    * √(Σ(yᵢ-ȳ)²)/n < 1.0e-08: true
    * Reached Maximum Number of Iterations: false
 * Objective Calls: 55
(-0.043288979878934694, 1.0151538648696379)

julia> mean(x), std(x)*sqrt(99/100)
(-0.04329512736686613, 1.0151523821496027)
```

How it works...

The `Optim.jl` package provides univariate and multivariate nonlinear optimization routines. It is used for addressing unconstrained optimization problems and finds the local minimum of a function.

In our recipe, the standard deviation of a distribution must be non-negative. However, the `optimize` procedure performs unbounded optimization by default. This means that it could test negative values of standard deviation. To solve this issue, we optimize over the logarithm of the standard deviation, which is defined over the entire domain of real numbers.

In the code, this variable is `logσ`. This means that when the optimization is finished, we have to transform the result using an exponential function to get the standard deviation back. This is done by the `exp(res.minimizer[2])` expression in the code.

Three additional practical issues in this code are worth noticing:

- It is more efficient numerically to optimize the sum of individual log-likelihoods than the product of individual likelihoods; in the code, we use the `logpdf` function from the `Distributions` package to achieve this
- By default, `optimize` minimizes a function, which is why we use a negative value of log likelihood in the `loglik` function
- Finally, we `display` the `res` object to obtain a quick summary of the statistics of the result of the optimization

There's more...

We have presented only a basic use of the `optimize` function here. In the package documentation, you can see that it actually provides many different solvers. In particular, you can do simple constrained optimization. The details are presented here: `http://julianlsolvers.github.io/Optim.jl/latest/#examples/generated/ipnewton_basics/`.

See also

If you are doing linear optimization or mixed integer optimization, you can use the examples given in the *Optimization using JuMP* recipe.

If you have to perform global optimization, you might consider using the `BlackBoxOptim.jl` package (`https://github.com/robertfeldt/BlackBoxOptim.jl`).

Complex plotting with Plots.jl

In this recipe, we show how to use Julia to generate various plots. The standard approach for graph visualization in Julia is the `Plots.jl` package. The package supports several graphical backends for the actual generation of figures. The most mature backends include `GR.jl` and `PyPlot.jl`. In this recipe, we show how to use `Plots.jl` with the `GR.jl` backend.

Getting ready

For this recipe, you need several packages for generating and manipulating the data, as well as for making the plot itself. All packages can simply be installed with the Julia package manager. In the Julia command line, simply press the *]* key and run the following commands:

```
(v1.0) pkg> add DataFrames
(v1.0) pkg> add Plots
(v1.0) pkg> add Distributions
(v1.0) pkg> add StatPlots
(v1.0) pkg> add CSV
```

This will install the packages and all their dependencies.

Here is the citation for the Iris dataset is as follows:

@misc{R.A. Fisher ,
author = "R.A. Fisher ",
year = "2017",
title = "{UCI} Machine Learning Repository",
url = "http://archive.ics.uci.edu/ml",
institution = "University of California, Irvine, School of Information and Computer
Sciences" }

 In the GitHub repository for this recipe, you will find
the commands.txt file, which contains the presented sequence of Julia
commands.

How to do it...

In this recipe, we will show various options for visualizing a dataset in Julia.

We start this example by loading all packages into the Julia session:

```
using Random
using DataFrames
using Plots
using Distributions
using StatPlots
```

Let's generate a test dataset with the first and third columns correlated with a degree of
ρ=0.8 (please note that the Distributions.jl package could be also used for that
purpose):

```
Random.seed!(0);
df = DataFrame(x1=randn(1000),x2=randn(1000));
ρ = 0.8
df.x3 = ρ*df.x1 + √(1-ρ*ρ)*df.x2;
```

Now, we set the graphics frontend:

```
julia> gr()
Plots.GRBackend()
```

We start by comparing x1 with x3 by presenting their values on overlapping histograms:

```
p = histogram(df.x1,nbins=25,labels="x1");
histogram!(p,df.x3,fillalpha=0.5,bar_width=0.3,labels="x3")
```

The preceding code generates the output as follows:

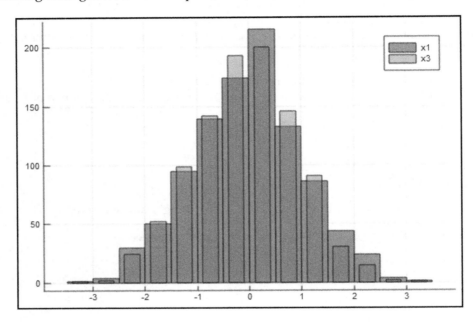

Let see how good the match of the x3 dataset is to the actual normal distribution:

```
p = histogram(df.x3,normed=true)
plot!(p,Normal(0,1),width=4)
```

The preceding code generates the output as follows:

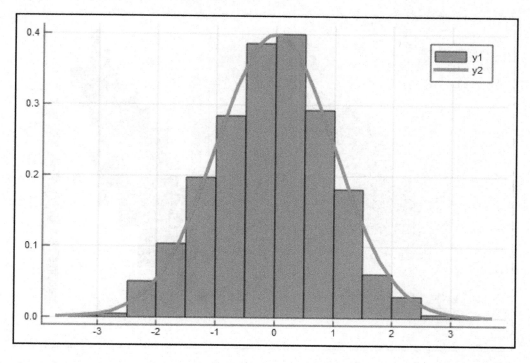

Now, let's show a scatterplot and a two-dimensional histogram to see the correlation pattern:

```
plot(scatter(df.x1,df.x3,legend=false),histogram2d(df.x1,df.x3),lay
out=Plots.GridLayout(1, 2),xlabel="x1",ylabel="x3" )
```

The following screenshot depicts the output:

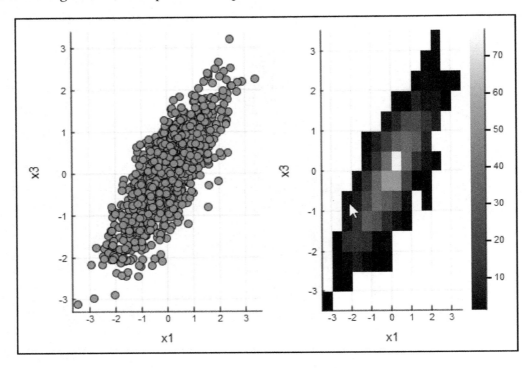

Another useful graph is a correlation plot:

```
corrplot(convert(Array, df), bins=25,labels=["x1","x2","x3"])
```

The following screenshot displays the output:

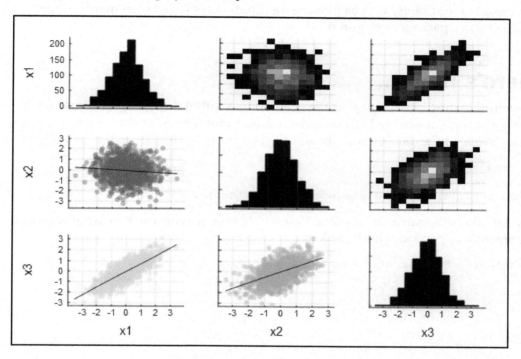

How it works...

The Plots.jl package provides a common frontend to several graphical backends implemented in Julia. The choice of the actual backend depends on the visualization needs. For static graphs, we recommend the GR backend for its speed and number of features. When some interaction with the graph is required, one should consider PyPlot.jl (which uses Python's matplotlib for visualization) or Plotly(JS) which renders interactive HTML/JavaScript plots. PyPlot.jl can also be used directly (without Plots.jl); this could be a good choice for people coming to Julia from Python. However, Plots.jl makes it much easier to switch between backends.

In our examples, we have selected the backend using the `gr()` command. Please note that for more advanced plots, such as plotting distributions or correlation matrices, the `StatPlots.jl` package is required.

There's more...

A powerful feature of `Plots.jl` is the generation of subplots. This allows visualizing several plots on one screen. Let's consider a scatter plot matrix for the very well-known Iris dataset. We load the dataset from the test file present in the `DataFrames.jl` package:

```
using CSV
iris =
CSV.read(joinpath(dirname(pathof(DataFrames)),"..","test/data/iris.csv"));
```

Now, let's create a matrix of subplots. Please note how we construct an array of plots that is subsequently appended within the loop:

```
font_h6 = Plots.font("Helvetica", 6)
plts = Plots.Plot[]
for i in 1:4, j in 1:4
    if i == j
        push!(plts,histogram(iris[i],group=iris[:Species],
            xlabel=names(iris)[j],ylabel="count",
            legend=false,fillalpha=0.5,
            guidefont=font_h6,tickfont=font_h6))
    else
        push!(plts,scatter(iris[j],iris[i],
            xlabel=names(iris)[j],ylabel=names(iris)[i],
            group=iris[:Species],legend=(i==4&&j==1),
            guidefont=font_h6,tickfont=font_h6,legendfont=font_h6,
            background_color_legend=RGBA(255,255,255,0.8),
            foreground_color_legend=nothing))
    end
end
p = plot(plts...,layout=Plots.GridLayout(4, 4))
```

Please have a look at the following screenshot for the output:

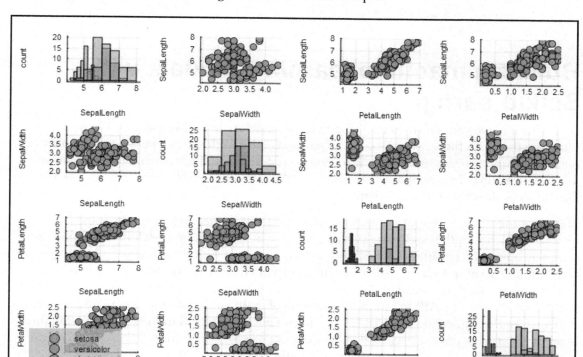

This type of plot made it possible to show all dependencies within the Iris dataset on a single picture. This pattern can be easily used to create other customized plot matrices.

See also

Depending on the requirements of your plot, it is worth looking at the plotting backend overview sections in the `Plots.jl` documentation (`https://docs.juliaplots.org/latest/backends/`).

When learning the framework, we suggest starting with the sample sections of a selected backend, and we recommend the GR for speed and functionality (`https://docs.juliaplots.org/latest/examples/gr/`). Those examples give a good overview of the `Plots.jl` functionality.

The `StatsPlots.jl` documentation is available at
`https://github.com/JuliaPlots/StatPlots.jl`.

Building machine learning models with ScikitLearn.jl

In this recipe, we show how to use Julia to create machine learning models. We will illustrate this with the `ScikitLearn.jl` package. Although our recipe focuses on how to create machine learning models in Julia, we do not focus on the business applications of machine learning. This recipe was inspired by the book *Python Machine Learning - Second Edition* by S. Raschka and V. Mirjalili.

Note that the `ScikitLearn.jl` package is not present in the package table of the `Preface` which is at the beginning of this book nor in the package installation scripts. We took this approach because on one hand `ScikitLearn.jl` is being developed continuously to map Python code to its Julia equivalent and on the other hand since the goal of this package is to mirror the Anaconda `scikit-learn` API we expect the `ScikitLearn.jl` API to be stable over time. Finally, at the moment, `ScikitLearn.jl` depends on the Anaconda `scikit-learn` package to be present in the Python installation used by Julia. This package will get installed as a `mlxtend` dependency. However, if you want to skip the `mlxtend` installation you should run the `Conda.add("scikit-learn")` command instead.

Getting ready

For this recipe, you need the following packages: `Conda.jl`, `CSV.jl`, `HTTP.jl`, `DataFrames.jl`, `ScikitLearn.jl`, and `PyCall.jl`, which can be installed with the Julia package manager. In the Julia command line, press the *]* key and run the command:

```
(v1.0) pkg> add Conda
(v1.0) pkg> add CSV
(v1.0) pkg> add HTTP
(v1.0) pkg> add DataFrames
(v1.0) pkg> add ScikitLearn
(v1.0) pkg> add PyCall
```

This will install the required packages and all their dependencies.

Additionally, we will use the Python `mlxtend` library for the visualization of classifiers. In Julia, the easiest way to install a Python library is to use the `Conda.jl` package. Since `mlxtend` is in the `conda-forge` repository, execute the following command:

```
using Conda
Conda.runconda(`install mlxtend -c conda-forge -y`)
```

In the GitHub repository for this recipe, you will find the `commands.txt` file, which contains the presented sequence of Julia commands.

How to do it...

In this example, we once again use the classic Iris dataset and show how to use `ScikitLearn` from Julia:

1. We start by loading the packages:

   ```
   using CSV, HTTP, DataFrames, ScikitLearn, Random, PyCall,
   Statistics
   ```

2. This time, we download the Iris dataset from the UCI machine learning repository:

   ```
   dat =
   HTTP.get("https://archive.ics.uci.edu/ml/machine-learning-databases
   /iris/iris.data")
   buf = IOBuffer(dat.body[1:end-1]) #cut-off trailing new line
   character
   iris = CSV.read(buf;header=false,allowmissing=:none)
   names!(iris,Symbol.(["SepalLength","SepalWidth","PetalLength","Peta
   lWidth","Class"]))
   ```

3. The `ScikitLearn.jl` package works only with arrays of numbers:

   ```
   ua = unique(iris[:Class])
   iris[:Class]=[findfirst(==(x), ua) - 1 for x in iris[:Class]]
   y = iris[:Class]
   X = Matrix(iris[1:4])
   ```

4. We start by splitting the data into training and test datasets:

```
using ScikitLearn.CrossValidation: train_test_split
Random.seed!(0)
X_train, X_test, y_train, y_test =
    train_test_split(X, y,test_size=0.3,random_state=0,stratify=y);
```

5. The next step is scaling the data (that is, removing the mean and scaling to unit variance; this is not required in our example, but it might change the efficiency of some other machine learning methods):

```
@sk_import preprocessing : StandardScaler
stdsc = StandardScaler();
X_train_std = stdsc[:fit_transform](X_train)
X_test_std = stdsc[:transform](X_test)
```

6. Once the datasets have been transformed, we build the models:

```
@sk_import linear_model: LogisticRegression
logreg = LogisticRegression(fit_intercept=true)
fit!(logreg,X_train_std, y_train)
y_pred = predict(logreg,X_test_std)
```

7. Let's estimate the model quality:

```
julia> @sk_import metrics : (accuracy_score,confusion_matrix);
julia> accuracy_score(y_test,y_pred)
0.8666666666666667
julia> confusion_matrix(y_test,y_pred)
3x3 Array{Int64,2}:
 15   0   0
  0  10   5
  0   1  14
```

8. Now, let's build a random forest classifier model and evaluate variable importance:

```
@sk_import ensemble : RandomForestClassifier
forest = RandomForestClassifier(n_estimators=100,  random_state=0)
fit!(forest,X_train, y_train)
y_pred = predict(forest,X_test)
importances = forest[:feature_importances_]
indices = sortperm(importances,rev=true)
```

9. Output the variable importance:

```
julia> DataFrame(Name=names(iris)[indices],
Importance=importances[indices])
4×2 DataFrame
| Row | Name           | Importance  |
|     | Symbol         | Float64     |
| ----- | -------------- | ------------ |
| 1   | PetalWidth     | 0.458133    |
| 2   | PetalLength    | 0.4064      |
| 3   | SepalLength    | 0.103548    |
| 4   | SepalWidth     | 0.0319198   |
```

10. We can assess the model quality by looking at the confusion matrix:

```
julia> confusion_matrix(y_test,y_pred)
3×3 Array{Int64,2}:
 15   0   0
  0  15   0
  0   1  14
```

11. The machine learning models are often easier to illustrate and understand when their response surface is plotted. Let's use the `mlxtend` library to show how our classifier works:

```
using PyPlot  #important!
@pyimport mlxtend.plotting as mlp
fill_vals=Dict{Int,Float64}()
fill_rngs=Dict{Int,Float64}()
for ind in indices[3:end]
    fill_vals[ind-1] = mean(iris[names(iris)[ind]])
    fill_rngs[ind-1] = std(iris[names(iris)[ind]])
end
mlp.plot_decision_regions(X,y,forest,X_highlight=X_test,
    feature_index=(indices[1:2].-1),
    filler_feature_values=fill_vals,filler_feature_ranges=fill_rngs)
xlabel(names(iris)[indices[1]])
ylabel(names(iris)[indices[2]])
```

Once the preceding code is run, you should see the following output (note that the test observations are highlighted by a circle):

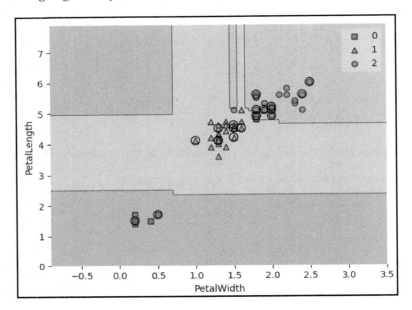

How it works...

We start by loading the dataset from the internet. The `CSV.read` method requires a stream of data, and we use `IOBuffer` to create one from the downloaded bytes. Since there is a trailing newline character at the end of the file that would cause `CSV.jl` to create a record consisting of only `missing`, we remove that character. Finally, the file at `https://archive.ics.uci.edu/ml/machine-learning-databases/iris/` does not contain column names, so we add them manually with the `names!` function.

`ScikitLearn` works on numerical arrays rather than on data frames or categorical values. Hence, we need to convert the data to an appropriate presentation. The `categorical` function can be used to convert an array of nominal values into a `CategoricalArray` object. The actual `UInt32` values of the `CategoricalArray` items are present in the `.level` field. The `mlxtend` library assumes that the classes are numbered starting from 0, so we subtract 1 from the `level` value.

Once the data is prepared, we split it into training and testing datasets. The CrossValidation module has been fully ported from Python to Julia (not the case for several other ScikitLearn.jl modules), and hence we can use the Julia version.

Many machine learning algorithms require scaling the data (that is, transforming the data in such a way that the mean is equal to 0 and the standard deviation is equal to 1; see http://scikit-learn.org/stable/modules/generated/sklearn.preprocessing.Standard Scaler.html. For this data scaling, we use the StandardScaler object from the preprocessing module, which needs to be imported with the @sk_import macro (since it only has a Python implementation). Similarly, the ScikitLearn model quality metrics functions are also imported via the same macro.

Please compare the code for creating a logistic regression and a random forest model. The big advantage of ScikitLearn.jl is in having a homogenous usage pattern across machine learning modules. They always follow these five steps:

1. Use the @sk_import macro to import an appropriate machine learning method
2. Create an object representing the model
3. Run the fit! function on the training dataset
4. Run the predict function to calculate predictions on the test dataset
5. Use functions available with the metrics module to evaluate model quality

Lastly, we plot decision regions for our random forest. For that purpose, we use the mlxtend library. Please note that the PyPlot module **must** be imported **before** any calls to actual plotting functions are made; otherwise, the Julia interpreter will crash. Note also that mlxtend makes only two-dimensional plots. Since we have four dimensions, we choose the two most significant variables. However, in order to estimate the decision area, we need to have all four dimensions. Consequently, we use average values for the other variables (features). For the decision region plot, we have selected only those observations whose visualized features are not more than one standard deviation from the mean values. Documentation and more samples of decision regions for various machine learning algorithms are available at
https://rasbt.github.io/mlxtend/user_guide/plotting/plot_decision_regions/.

There's more...

The ScikitLearn.jl package provides the full functionality of the Python ScikitLearn library, which means that all the machine learning options from ScikitLearn are also available in Julia. We recommend looking at the documentation of ScikitLearn at http://scikit-learn.org/stable/.

There are also pure Julia packages for some of the machine learning algorithms, but they are not yet as mature as ScikitLearn. For instance, to create a random forest you could use the RandomForest.jl package, available at https://github.com/bicycle1885/RandomForests.jl.

See also

For a great tutorial on machine learning and the Python ScikitLearn library, we strongly recommend *Python Machine Learning - Second Edition* by S. Raschka and V. Mirjalili (https://www.packtpub.com/big-data-and-business-intelligence/python-machine-learning-second-edition). Using this recipe as an example, you can very easily translate every example from the Raschka and Mirjalili book into Julia code. In particular, all the ScikitLearn examples in this book are available in the form of Jupyter Notebooks, which can be explored at https://github.com/rasbt/python-machine-learning-book-2nd-edition.

10
Distributed Computing

In this chapter, we present the following recipes:

- Multiprocessing in Julia
- Sending parameters to remote Julia processes
- Multithreading in Julia
- Distributed computing with Julia

Introduction

The goal of this chapter is to present how to use Julia for parallel and distributed computing tasks. An important feature of Julia is the ability to scale up computations across many processes, threads, and distributed computational clusters. We show how to scale Julia by presenting multiprocessing, data communication issues across processes, multithreading, and distributed computing.

Multiprocessing in Julia

Julia provides efficient mechanisms for writing programs that spawn across many processes. This mechanism is called **multiprocessing**. In this recipe, we show how to use Julia's multiprocessing mechanism to spawn a worker process that is killed when it takes too long to respond.

Getting ready

Mechanisms for distributed computing are built into the Julia language. Thanks to this, our recipe does not require the installation of any Julia packages. Simply start the Julia REPL.

In the GitHub repository for this recipe, you will find the `commands.txt` file, which contains the presented sequence of Julia commands.

How to do it...

In this example, we consider a scenario where a user wants to start up computations that take up a significant amount of time. Such computations arise for two reasons:

- Firstly, one might want to dynamically collect information on their state
- Secondly, a computation might be stalled, and hence it might turn out to be necessary to terminate it

Start the Julia command line by typing `julia` in the OS shell command line. We start by loading the `Distributed` module:

```
julia> using Distributed
```

We currently have only Julia master process running. Therefore, add a worker (remote) process to Julia:

```
julia> addprocs(1)
```

Let's check the ID numbers of the master and worker processes:

```
julia> Distributed.myid()
1

julia> workers()
1-element Array{Int64,1}:
 2
```

Since the remote worker has the ID of 2, the value that the `myid()` command ran on that worker should return is 2:

```
julia> res = @spawnat 2 myid()
Future(2, 1, 3, nothing)

julia> fetch(res)
2
```

Now, we create an anonymous function, `remote_f`, which will be used to run a job on a remote process.

In our example, it is simply a function that sleeps for a given number of seconds and then returns a random value. We add the `println` function calls for debugging purposes:

```
remote_f = function(s::Int=3)
    println("Worker $(myid()) will sleep for $s seconds")
    sleep(s)
    val=rand(1:1000)
    println("Completed worker $(myid()) - return $val")
    return val
end
```

Now, let's test the function (we assume that the 2 worker is present; you can use the `workers()` command to display the list of available workers):

```
julia> @fetchfrom 2 remote_f(4)
        From worker 2:    Worker 2 will sleep for 4 seconds
        From worker 2:    Completed worker 2 - return 466
466
```

Now, let's define a function that runs a remote process, waits a given time, and collects the results:

```
function run_timeout(timeout::Int, f::Function, params...)
    wid = addprocs(1)[1]
    result = RemoteChannel(()->Channel{Tuple}(1));
    @spawnat wid put!(result, (f(params...), myid()))
    res = nothing
    time_elapsed = 0.0
    while time_elapsed < timeout && !isready(result)
        sleep(0.25)
        time_elapsed += 0.25
    end
    if !isready(result)
        println("Not completed! Computation at $wid will be
        terminated!")
    else
        res = take!(result)
    end
    rmprocs(wid);
    return res
end
```

Now, let's use the `run_timeout` function to run the `remote_f` function remotely; we start by assigning an amount of time that a job can complete:

```
julia> run_timeout(3, remote_f, 2)
        From worker 3:    Worker 3 will sleep for 2 seconds
        From worker 3:    Completed worker 3 - return 335
(335, 3)
```

Then, run a job that lasts longer than an actual computation:

```
julia> run_timeout(3, remote_f, 10)
        From worker 4:    Worker 4 will sleep for 10 seconds
Not completed! Computation at 4 will be terminated!
```

We can see that this job has spawned a new process with an ID equal to 4, and this process terminated after three seconds (when the timeout was reached). Let's check what jobs are still running:

```
julia> workers()
1-element Array{Int64,1}:
 2
```

We can see that only the remote worker initially added at the beginning of this recipe is present.

How it works...

Multiprocessing in Julia gives us the ability to spawn a single running program across many processes. The processes are identified by their process IDs. The originally launched process (master) always has an ID equal to one. The slave processes can be added in various ways. In this recipe, we used the `addprocs` function; another alternative is to use the `-p` option when launching Julia (for example, `julia -p 2` will launch Julia with one master process and two slave processes).

Please note that if you pass a function as a parameter, it needs to be either locally scoped or be a lambda function. Additionally, the same rule applies to all functions that are being called from the created function:

```julia
julia> using Distributed

julia> @everywhere function myF2(); println("myF2 ", myid()); end;

julia> @spawnat workers()[end] myF2();

        From worker 3:    myF2 3
```

The `run_timeout` function creates a new process that is used to handle a site job. For this process, a `Channel` object is created; channels enable inter-process communication. The process waits for a given amount of time, constantly checking whether new data has appeared in the created `Channel`. If the data appears, it will be returned as a result. The process for running the side job is killed regardless of whether or not the job completed within the maximum time allotted.

There's more...

One thing to be aware of is that passing a function as a parameter to the `@spawnat` or `@fetchform` macro normally requires that the function is defined on the remote process. However, in the case of anonymous functions, they can be passed as parameters to the preceding macros. Still, if a function uses a method not defined on a remote process then it will fail:

```julia
julia> hello() = println("hello");

julia> @fetchfrom 2 hello()
ERROR: On worker 2:
UndefVarError: #hello not defined

julia> f_lambda = () -> hello();

julia> f_lambda()
hello

julia> @fetchfrom 2 f_lambda()
ERROR: On worker 2:
UndefVarError: #hello not defined
```

In both of the preceding cases, we got an identical error—the `hello` function is not defined on the remote processes. The solution to the preceding problem is to use the `@everywhere` macro to define any function across all remote processes:

```julia
julia> @everywhere hello() = println("hello")

julia> @fetchfrom 2 f_lambda()
        From worker 2:    hello
```

See also

The documentation for distributed computing in Julia can be found at `https://docs.julialang.org/en/v1/manual/parallel-computing/`. Please also see subsequent recipes in this chapter.

Sending parameters to remote Julia processes

In this recipe, we examine a distributed computation scenario running across many workers, where each worker process needs to communicate with other processes. Examples include running complex analytical jobs or large simulation/computational models.

In the recipe, we use a simplified example of how to run a distributed cellular automaton using Julia's `Distributed` module and the `ParallelDataTransfer.jl` package. Cellular automaton is a type of discrete model consisting of a number of cells with a finite set of possible states and a deterministic rule for transforming one state to another (see `http://mathworld.wolfram.com/CellularAutomaton.html` or `https://en.wikipedia.org/wiki/Cellular_automaton`). There are many possible rules for describing how subsequent states are calculated.

In this recipe, we will construct a one-dimensional binary cellular automaton, based on what is known as Rule 30 (see `http://mathworld.wolfram.com/Rule30.html` or `https://en.wikipedia.org/wiki/Rule_30`). It is defined on an infinite one-dimensional vector that can hold `false` or `true` in each entry. The automaton evolves in discrete time. Initially, only one cell is set to `true` and all other cells are set to `false`. Denote by `s[i,t]` the state of cell `i` at time `t`. The rule of evolution of the Rule 30 automaton is given by the formula `s[i,t+1] = xor(s[i-1,t], s[i,t] || x[i,t])`.

In our recipe, in order to explain how inter-process communication works in Julia, we implement this automaton not on an infinite vector, but on a finite ring.

Getting ready

For this recipe, you need the `ParallelDataTransfer.jl` package. It can be installed with the Julia package manager. In the Julia command line (REPL), press the] key and run this command:

```
(v1.0) pkg> add ParallelDataTransfer
```

This will install the `ParallelDataTransfer.jl` package and all its dependencies.

Additionally, we will run Julia with 4 worker processes. When launching Julia from the command line, type this:

```
$ julia -p 4
```

Once started, check your configuration:

```
julia> using Distributed

julia> nworkers()
4
```

In the GitHub repository for this recipe, you will find the `commands.txt` file, which contains the presented sequence of shell and Julia commands.

How to do it...

In this example, we will create a distributed version of Rule 30 cellular automaton.

Let's start by loading the required modules across all processes (we assume that there are 4 workers; however, the code in this recipe can be run with an any even number of worker processes):

```
using Distributed
@everywhere using ParallelDataTransfer
```

Now, we define Rule 30 (note that the border data for the first and last bit will come from a different worker process, and hence we iterate over elements from 2 up to end−1):

```
@everywhere function rule30(ca::Array{Bool})
    lastv = ca[1]
    for i in 2:(length(ca)-1)
        current = ca[i]
        ca[i] = xor(lastv, ca[i] || ca[i+1])
        lastv = current
    end
end
```

The next step is defining the function that can be used by an individual worker to acquire data from its neighbors:

```
@everywhere function getsetborder(ca::Array{Bool},
                                  neighbours::Tuple{Int64,Int64})
    ca[1] = (@fetchfrom neighbours[1] caa[end-1])
    ca[end] = (@fetchfrom neighbours[2] caa[2])
end
```

We also need a function to visualize the cellular automaton state:

```
function printsimdist(workers::Array{Int})
    for w in workers
        dat = @fetchfrom w caa
        for b in dat[2:end-1]
            print(b ? "#" : " ")
        end
    end
    println()
end
```

The next function is for iterating over the cellular automaton state:

```
function runca(steps::Int, visualize::Bool)
    @sync for w in workers()
        @async @fetchfrom w fill!(caa, false)
    end
    @fetchfrom wks[Int(nwks/2)+1] caa[2]=true
    visualize && printsimdist(workers())
    for i in 1:steps
        @sync for w in workers()
            @async @fetchfrom w getsetborder(caa, neighbours)
        end
        @sync for w in workers()
            @async @fetchfrom w rule30(caa)
        end
```

```
        visualize && printsimdist(workers())
    end
end
```

At this point, we are ready to define the simulation state variables for each worker node, along with information about its neighbors:

```
wks = workers()
nwks = length(wks)
for i in 1:nwks
    sendto(wks[i],neighbours=(i==1 ? wks[nwks] : wks[i-1],
                              i==nwks ? wks[1] : wks[i+1]))
    fetch(@defineat wks[i] const caa = zeros(Bool,15+2));
end
```

Finally, we can run the distributed cellular automaton:

```
julia> runca(20,true)
```

You should see the following output:

How it works...

We start by loading `ParallelDataTransfer.jl` across all modules. Next, we define the `rule30` function that implements the algorithm. Please be aware that this function does not operate on the border cells of the data. The border data is actually acquired by each worker from its neighbors, using the `getsetborder` function. Please see the following diagram for an explanation as to how the data is shared among the processes:

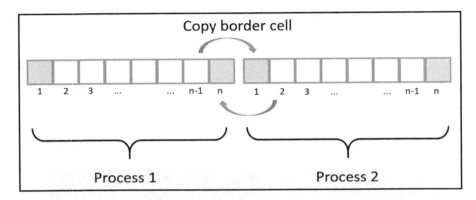

Note that in our example, each worker processes 17 cells (15 internal plus 2 border cells), which is set up by the `@defineat wks[i] const caa = zeros(Bool,15+2)` statement. As we have mentioned before, our simulation works on a ring; this means that the first and the last workers are neighbors, which is set up by the following code in the recipe:

```
neighbours=(i==1 ? wks[nwks] : wks[i-1],
            i==nwks ? wks[1] : wks[i+1])
```

The core of the simulation is the `runca` function. In the first loop, the state of the cellular automaton is reset across all worker processes. Each function call is asynchronous across all processes. Once the data has been reset, we set one cell's value to `true`. Finally, the main loop asynchronously invokes border cell copying across the workers (see the preceding diagram), and once the border cells have been copied, the `rule30` function is called asynchronously on each worker node. The `@sync` keyword in front of each loop makes sure that all asynchronous computational processes started within the loop have completed before program execution continues.

Before the `runca` function can be started, each worker needs to have information concerning its neighbors; we use the `sendto` function to pass information about the left and right neighbors of each worker.

There's more...

In this recipe, we described a basic pattern for running distributed computations. In our case, the processes share only a single data cell. However, note that the approach discussed here could easily be extended into multidimensional shared data.

Distributed computing does not come without a cost. In the simulation presented earlier, the time required for inter-process communication is around two milliseconds per single step. Hence, running distributed scenarios only makes sense for cases where each step for a single worker takes a reasonable amount of time to complete.

Additionally, you should also know that the @defineat macro always defines global variables. Therefore, those variables in remote processes should always be used within functions.

See also

Documentation for the ParallelDataTransfer.jl package is available at https://github.com/ChrisRackauckas/ParallelDataTransfer.jl.

Multithreading in Julia

In this recipe, we use Julia's multithreading mechanism to speed up computations of statistics over a large DataFrame.

Getting ready

For this recipe, you need to use the DataFrames.jl and BenchmarkTools.jl packages, which can be installed with the Julia package manager. If you need to add them then in the Julia command line, press the *]* key and run these commands:

```
(v1.0) pkg> add DataFrames
(v1.0) pkg> add BenchmarkTools
```

This will install the DataFrames.jl and BenchmarkTools.jl packages and all their dependencies.

In this recipe, we use Julia's threading mechanism. The number of threads is controlled via the JULIA_NUM_THREADS system variable, which needs to be assigned before starting the julia process. In order to set the variable, start a new command-line console and execute this command (Windows version):

```
C:\ set JULIA_NUM_THREADS=4
```

In a Linux console, run this:

```
$ export JULIA_NUM_THREADS=4
```

Now, start Julia:

```
$ julia
```

You can check whether the number of threads has been properly allocated:

```
julia> Threads.nthreads()
4
```

Please note that if you are running Julia inside Juno, then the number of threads is set by default to the number of cores. On most laptops, this will amount to 2 or 4, and with the default setting, you will observe performance gains in the example presented in this recipe. The number of threads in Juno can be changed by selecting **Packages** | **Julia** | **Settings...** in the Juno menu bar (note that since Juno uses a cycler boot mode by default for Julia processes, you will need to restart the Julia command line twice for this setting to take effect).

 In the GitHub repository for this recipe, you will find the commands.txt file, which contains the presented sequence of shell and Julia commands.

How to do it...

In order to parallelize computations over DataFrame, follow these steps:

1. In the first step, we import the Julia packages required for the computation:

    ```
    using DataFrames, BenchmarkTools, Random, Statistics
    ```

2. This recipe will be illustrated by an artificial dataset with $100,000$ rows filled with random values:

```
Random.seed!(0);
N = 100_000;
const data = DataFrame(rowtype = rand(1:12, N));
data.x1 = data.rowtype .* randn(N);
```

3. Let's examine the beginning of the data (since we use `Random.seed!(0)`, you should see an identical output):

```
julia> head(data, 5)
5×2 DataFrame
| Row    | rowtype   | x1        |
|        | Int64     | Float64   |
|--------|-----------|-----------|
| 1      | 1         | -0.298115 |
| 2      | 3         | -2.71766  |
| 3      | 10        | -28.0064  |
| 4      | 6         | 4.39991   |
| 5      | 1         | 0.809952  |
```

4. Our goal in this example is to perform some statistical calculations for values in the `x1` column, grouped by the value of `rowtype`. A sample function that performs computations could look like the one shown here (for illustrative purposes, we calculate the mean of 100 medians of bootstrap samples of our data):

```
function stats(df)
    m = MersenneTwister()
    median_val = 0
    for i in 1:100
        median_val += median(rand(m, df.x1, nrow(df)))
    end
    return (rowtype=df.rowtype[1], n=nrow(df),
            tid=Threads.threadid(), median=median_val / 100)
end
```

5. Now, let's test the performance of the created function:

```
julia> @time by(data, :rowtype, stats)
  6.007125 seconds (15.10 M allocations: 1.024 GiB, 9.05% gc time)
12×2 DataFrame
| Row | rowtype | x1                                                    |
|     | Int64   | NamedTup...                                           |
|-----|---------|-------------------------------------------------------|
| 1   | 1       | (rowtype = 1,n = 8384,tid = 1, median = -0.0186428)   |
```

```
          .
          .
          .
| 12 |  7    | (rowtype = 7,n = 8327,tid = 1,median = 0.129859)    |


julia> @time by(data, :rowtype, stats);
 0.693117 seconds (12.92 k allocations: 234.419 MiB, 3.51% gc time)
```

6. Now, consider a scenario that uses Julia's threading mechanism to parallelize the preceding computation:

```
function threaded_by(df::DataFrame, groupcol::Symbol, f::Function)
    groups = groupby(df, groupcol)
    f(view(groups[1], 1:2, :)); #needed for precompilation!
    res = Vector{NamedTuple}(undef, length(groups))
    Threads.@threads for g in 1:length(groups)
        rv = f(groups[g])
        res[g] = rv
    end
    DataFrame(rowtype=getfield.(res, groupcol), x1=res)
end
```

7. We can then use `threaded_by` to run the `stats` function in a multithreaded fashion:

```
julia> @time threaded_by(data, :rowtype, stats)
 0.711555 seconds (746.21 k allocations: 271.676 MiB, 5.07% gc time)
12×2 DataFrame
| Row | rowtype | x1                                                  |
|     | Int64   | NamedTup...                                         |
| --- | ------- | --------------------------------------------------- |
|  1  |  1      | (rowtype = 1,n = 8384,tid = 1,median = -0.0186428)  |
.
.
.
| 12 |  7      | (rowtype = 7, n = 8327, tid = 4, median = 0.129859) |

julia> @time threaded_by(data, :rowtype, stats);
 0.236068 seconds (12.94 k allocations: 233.531 MiB, 11.25% gc time)
```

We can see that the running time has reduced from around 0.69 seconds in the single-threaded version to 0.23 second in the multithreaded version.

How it works...

In this recipe, we explained how to write a simplified multithreaded equivalent of the by function present in the DataFrames.jl package. The Threads.@threads macro provides an easy and simple mechanism for loop parallelization. Since the data for computation is divided by the DataFrame columns, we use the groupby function to partition the data. In the loop within the threaded_by() function, we use a typical pattern with an array that contains a number of slots equal to the number of computations to be run (another possible approach for partitioning is to use Threads.threadid() for identifying the slot to store the results). The results are finally collected as DataFrame of NumedTuple; it is possible to extend NumedTuple into a set of DataFrame columns, but we wanted to keep the recipe simple.

The last important thing to note is that when several threads are being run in parallel, each thread should have its own MersenneTwister pseudo-random number generator object. In particular, calling the rand function without the rng parameter would cause all threads to use the same global random state and hence it would not be thread-safe.

The approach presented resulted in a nearly 60% speed-up of the computational process. However, there are many factors that need to be considered in parallelizing the code; see the following *There's more...* section.

There's more...

If your threads modify some variables that exist outside a multithreaded loop, you need to make sure that two threads do not write simultaneously to the same memory address. Consider the following example:

```julia
julia> Threads.nthreads()
4

julia> total = 0;
julia> Threads.@threads for i in 1:1_000_000
           global total = total + 1
       end

julia> total
264595
```

Since many threads are trying to modify the same `total` variable, they are using outdated values to calculate its increments. The correct way to handle such computation is by using a locking mechanism (we still use the same Julia session with 4 threads):

```julia
julia> total2 = 0;

julia> s = Threads.SpinLock()
Base.Threads.TatasLock(Base.Threads.Atomic{Int64}(0))

julia> Threads.@threads for i in 1:1_000_000
           Threads.lock(s)
           global total2 = total2 + 1
           Threads.unlock(s)
       end

julia> total2
1000000
```

You can see that when locking is employed the total value is correct. The loop shown can easily be extended by other operations; all operations changing the shared external state should be within the block from `Threads.lock` to `Threads.unlock`. Note that for this concise example, an `Atomic{Int64}` type for the `total` value could merely have been used. However, we wanted this code snippet to be more general.

It's important to be aware that the support for multithreading in Julia is still experimental and sometimes unexpected behavior can be observed. One example of such behavior is that occasionally Julia can crash when a function is being compiled within a `@threads` loop. Yet another source of instability could result from the extensive use of a garbage collector among many threads competing for system memory.

See also

The documentation for the Julia threading API is available at
`https://docs.julialang.org/en/v1/base/multi-threading/index.html`.

Distributed computing with Julia

Julia provides built-in language functionality to run a program across many processes that can run locally, across a distributed network, or in a computational cluster. In the *Multiprocessing with Julia* and *Sending parameters to remote Julia processes* recipes, we saw how can you run data and exchange data between Julia processes.

A typical scenario for distributed computing is running a parameter sweep over a significantly large set of computations. In this recipe, we will show how to create a distributed cluster that performs a parameter sweep over a numerical simulation model.

We explain how to use the `--machine-file` Julia options to run Julia workers across many nodes. However, the computational example can also be run on a single machine using the multiprocessing mode (for example, in Julia launched with the `julia -p 4` command).

Getting ready

In this example, we will run a distributed cluster in Julia. You can run the cluster on a single laptop or across a cluster of machines. We assume that Linux Ubuntu 18.04.1 LTS is used and the username for the computations is `ubuntu`. However, after minor modifications, the following instructions can be applied to a Linux-based system.

 In the GitHub repository for this recipe, you will find the `commands.txt` file, which contains the presented sequence of shell and Julia commands; the `config` file that should be placed in the `~/.ssh/` folder on cluster nodes; and a sample Julia machine file, `machinefile.txt`.

In order to build a distributed cluster, we need to configure passwordless SSH. Julia uses SSH connections to spawn workers on remote nodes. For passwordless SSH, we will configure key-based authentication. In order for passwordless SSH to work, the master node needs to have the private key, while each slave node needs to have the public key in the `~/.ssh/authorized_users` file.

We start by creating the key. You will find the command and a sample output, as follows:

```
$ ssh-keygen -P "" -t rsa -f ~/.ssh/cluster
Generating public/private rsa key pair.
Your identification has been saved in /home/ubuntu/.ssh/cluster.
Your public key has been saved in /home/ubuntu/.ssh/cluster.pub.
The key fingerprint is:
SHA256:ssxPaYN2OfBsogwSK47s47Scsj3l3kBtwq1k+u6ggNg ubuntu@ip-172-31-5-210
The key's randomart image is:
+---[RSA 2048]----+
|                 |
|                 |
|                 |
|    . o          |
|.    * * S        |
|o+ =.* B o       |
```

```
|B.Eoo B %          |
|X=+=.= B o         |
|BXo=B . .          |
+----[SHA256]-----+
```

The next step is to edit the `~/.ssh/config` file. Ensure that the following lines are present:

```
User ubuntu
PubKeyAuthentication yes
StrictHostKeyChecking no
IdentityFile ~/.ssh/cluster
```

Now, we need to add the contents of the public key to the `~/.ssh/authorized_keys` file. Please note that the contents of `~/.ssh/cluster.pub` should be copied to `~/.ssh/authorized_keys` on every node in the cluster:

```
$ cat ~/.ssh/cluster.pub >> ~/.ssh/authorized_keys
```

Now, we can test our configuration on a local machine:

```
$ ssh ubuntu@localhost
Warning: Permanently added 'localhost' (ECDSA) to the list of known hosts.
Welcome to Ubuntu 18.04.1 LTS (GNU/Linux 4.15.0-1023-aws x86_64)
[welcome messages omitted]

$
```

Notice that the `StrictHostKeyChecking no` option caused the remote machine to be accepted even on the first connection (see the preceding `Warning` message). When you build a computational cluster, normally all machines are within a private network and you use private IPs, and hence such SSH client configuration is recommended. However, if you decide to open an SSH connection to a remote host over a public network, this configuration will be prone to a spoofing attack (in such scenarios, you would rather add fingerprints of all remote servers to the SSH `known_hosts` file).

Please also note that TCP/IP network connectivity among all computers forming the cluster should be open, preferably on all ports. For example, in the case of the AWS cloud computing service, you need to create a `SecurityGroup` that allows unlimited connections to itself (for more details, check the AWS documentation).

Distributed multiprocessing in Julia is achieved using the `--machine-file` launch option of the `julia` command. The functionality is similar to the `-p` option but much more powerful since you can distribute Julia over any cluster size. Sample `machinefile.txt` content is presented in the following code snippet. The first number in each line provides the number of worker processes that should be started on the remote host. It is followed by an asterisk `*` character and the username on the remote host. In a production environment, you would provide IP addresses of the remote host rather than `127.0.0.1`:

```
2*ubuntu@127.0.0.1
1*ubuntu@127.0.0.1
1*ubuntu@127.0.0.1
```

The preceding options will allow you to use Julia's distributed cluster mechanism on just a single local machine. We recommend that you also try adding the IP addresses of the remote machines to the preceding file.

Once you have the `machinefile.txt` file ready, you can tell Julia to load it by running the following command:

```
$ julia --machine-file machinefile.txt
```

This will launch the Julia master process and a number of Julia slave processes, according to the definitions given in the `machinefile.txt` file. For the preceding example, you should see 4 workers:

```
julia> using Distributed

julia> nworkers()
4
```

Additionally, for this recipe, you will need the `Distributions` and `DataFrames` packages, which can be installed with the Julia package manager. In the Julia command line, press the *]* key and run this command:

```
(v1.0) pkg> add Distributions
(v1.0) pkg> add DataFrames
```

The preceding packages should be installed on every worker node within the cluster.

How to do it...

In this recipe, we assume that you have created a Julia cluster following the instructions in the *Getting ready* section. However, if you do not have the cluster, the recipe can also be run with Julia in multiprocessing mode (for example, you can run the recipe using Julia started with the `julia -p 4` command). This is the simplest approach to run this recipe if you are working on Windows.

We start by loading the required modules across all nodes within the cluster:

```
using Distributed
@everywhere using Distributed, Distributions, DataFrames, Random
```

In this recipe, we will run a distributed parameter sweep of a multiparameter function. We consider an inventory simulation model representing the average daily profits of a retailer that earns a fixed commission by selling each product. In the simulation model, we assume that the daily demand for the product fluctuates around the average value of 20. Each unit sold yields some predefined profit, though there are two costs involved: a daily storage cost and a delivery cost. In this setting, the retailer needs to decide on the optimal stock reordering strategy.

We define a function that simulates a retailer's average daily profit over a given time span:

```
@everywhere function sim_inventory(reorder_q::Int64,
                                    reorder_point::Int64;
    days = 100,
    sd = Normal(20,20^0.5), #daily sales distribution
    wh = 0.1,   #warehousing costs
    p = 4.0,  #unit profit (when sold)
    d_prob = 0.50, #probability of delivery at given day
    k = 60.0, # fixed delivery cost
    rng = MersenneTwister(0))
    profit = 0.0 # Cumulated profit
    stock = reorder_q
    for  day in 1:days
        if stock < reorder_point && rand(rng)< d_prob # an order
                                                      # arrives
            profit -= k # we pay for the delivery
            stock += reorder_q
        end
        sale = max(0, min(Int(round(rand(rng, sd))), stock))
        stock -= sale # decrease stock
        profit += p*sale - wh*stock # gain profit
    end
    return profit / days
end
```

Now, we define a parameter, sweep, for the computation. Suppose we want to run the simulation for different values of reordering quantity (from 10 to 250), and reordering point (from 10 to 250), and with different decision time horizons (from 20 to 60):

```julia
julia> sweep = vec(collect(Base.product(10:10:250,10:10:250,20:5:60)))
5625-element Array{Tuple{Int64,Int64,Int64},1}:
 (10, 10, 20)
 (20, 10, 20)
 .
 .
 .
 (250, 250, 60)

julia> Random.seed!(0);
julia> Random.shuffle!(sweep);
```

Now, let's create random number generators that will be used on each worker:

```julia
const rngs = Dict(i=>MersenneTwister(i) for i in workers());
```

The next step is to construct the loop:

```julia
res = @distributed (append!) for s in sweep
    rng = deepcopy(rngs[myid()])
    profit = 0.0
    for sim in 1:10000
        profit += sim_inventory(s[1],s[2],days=s[3], rng=rng)
    end
    DataFrame(worker=myid(), reorder_q=s[1], reorder_point=s[2],
              days=s[3], profit=profit/10000)
end
```

Let's take a look at the results:

```julia
julia> res
5625×5 DataFrame
```

Row	worker	reorder_q	reorder_point	days	profit
	Int64	Int64	Int64	Int64	Float64
1	2	160	30	35	61.3314
2	2	190	160	25	51.4862
.					
.					
.					
5624	5	220	120	25	56.2689
5625	5	80	40	20	57.0728

Suppose that we want to find out which decision yields the highest expected profit, depending on the time horizon. This can be achieved with the following single command:

```julia
julia> sort!(vcat(view.(sort!.(DataFrame.(groupby(res, :days)),
                              :profit, rev=true), 1)...),
           :days)
```

```
9×5 DataFrame
| Row | worker | reorder_q | reorder_point | days  | profit  |
|     | Int64  | Int64     | Int64         | Int64 | Float64 |
|-----|--------|-----------|---------------|-------|---------|
| 1   | 3      | 210       | 30            | 20    | 63.8009 |
| 2   | 3      | 180       | 40            | 25    | 62.8532 |
| 3   | 3      | 210       | 40            | 30    | 62.4882 |
| 4   | 5      | 180       | 40            | 35    | 62.2812 |
| 5   | 4      | 200       | 40            | 40    | 61.9419 |
| 6   | 2      | 180       | 40            | 45    | 61.8942 |
| 7   | 5      | 170       | 40            | 50    | 61.7305 |
| 8   | 5      | 180       | 40            | 55    | 61.6626 |
| 9   | 3      | 200       | 40            | 60    | 61.5916 |
```

How it works...

In this recipe, we ran a distributed parameter, `sweep`, in Julia. We started by loading the required libraries and the function performing the computation across all workers in the cluster, using the `@everywhere` macro.

The `sim_inventory` function simulates sales and deliveries for a given number of days of warehouse operation and calculates the resulting profit. Note that when the `stock` level is below `reorder_point`, there is only a 50% chance that the stock will get refilled. Also, note that the `rng` random number generator is present among the arguments of the `sim_inventory` function so we can control random number generation across the workers.

The `sweep` variable contains all combinations of the reorder quantity (`reorder_q`), the level when an order is placed (`reorder_point`), and all values for the simulation time span (`days`). Since the time required for the computation depends on the number of days, and we want to have similar workloads for each worker, we randomly shuffle the `sweep` parameter array.

We create an array of random number generators that are copied across workers. This array can be parameterized differently, depending on the parameter sweep scenario.

Finally, a distributed loop is run across the array of parameter values. For each point along the parameter sweep, we repeat the simulation 10,000 times and we average the result. The last instruction in the loop creates DataFrame, presenting the simulation results for the given sweep item. We provide the append! function as the parameter to the @distributed macro, in order to aggregate the results across simulation sweep runs and workers within the cluster.

There's more...

If you use a **High Performance Computing (HPC)** system such as Cray, the passwordless SSH mechanism might not be available. However, such systems usually contain some form of cluster job management software, such as SLURM, SGE, or PBS. These job managers can be used from within Julia via the ClusterManagers.jl package. A sample command on a Cray supercomputer running a Scientific Linux installation and SLURM could look like this:

```
using ClusterManagers
n_workers = 100
addprocs_slurm(n_workers,job_name="myjobname", account="cray_account_name",
time="01:00:00",
exename="/path/to/julia/executable/compiled/for/worker/nodes/julia")
```

Note that the time parameter will be used to provide the maximum worker lifespan (after the allocated time elapses, the worker will be killed by the SLURM cluster manager). Once the preceding commands have been successfully executed and the worker processes have been added to the cluster, you can run the distributed computation in an identical way to using the --machinefile Julia command-line parameter.

It is also important to note that in some HPC clusters you may find out that you need to build Julia separately for the access and worker nodes because of different hardware architectures; see the recipes in Chapter 1, *Installing and Setting Up Julia*, for Julia build and installation instructions. We have found out that Julia parallelization works without any problems across a heterogeneous set of compiled versions on different Intel platforms.

The cloud provider **Amazon Web Services** (**AWS**) provides a set of scripts called **CfnCluster** (short for **Cloud Formation Cluster**—`https://github.com/awslabs/cfncluster`), which provides tools for cluster creation and automation mechanisms for installing and configuring cluster managers, such as SLURM or SGE, across cluster nodes. The main issue with installing CfnCluster is the long bootstrap time; it takes around 15 minutes to bring it into operation. Therefore, if you run a cluster in a public cloud, such as AWS or Azure, we definitely recommend configuring passwordless SSH and using the `--machinefile` option.

For easy configuration of clusters in the AWS cloud, we recommend KissCluster (`https://github.com/pszufe/KissCluster`), developed by one of the authors of this book. KissCluster runs a distributed loop across any number of processes, running across any number of servers. It is worth noting that within KissCluster the computation state is stored on serverless cloud services (DynamoDB and S3) rather than on the master node. For more details, see the project's documentation.

Last but not least, when running computational clusters in the cloud, consider the AWS EC2 Spot Fleet mechanism. AWS EC2 Spot instances allow you to buy computing power very cheaply, at around 0.01-0.02 USD per vCPU core per hour (the actual price depends on the AWS region selection and the time of purchase). The configuration of AWS EC2 Spot Fleet is usually achieved by making a custom **Amazon Machine Image** (**AMI**) along with a `cloud-init` script. The previously mentioned KissCluster can automatically generate such scripts; on the other hand, EC2 Spot Fleets are not supported by CfnCluster (and hence it costs you more).

See also

The documentation for parallel and distributed computing in Julia is available at `https://docs.julialang.org/en/v1/manual/parallel-computing/index.html`. Once you have read it, we also recommend looking at the documentation of the `Distributed` module at `https://docs.julialang.org/en/v1/stdlib/Distributed/index.html`.

Other Books You May Enjoy

If you enjoyed this book, you may be interested in these other books by Packt:

Julia 1.0 Programming - Second Edition
Ivo Balbaert

ISBN: 9781788999090

- Set up your Julia environment to achieve high productivity
- Create your own types to extend the built-in type system
- Visualize your data in Julia with plotting packages
- Explore the use of built-in macros for testing and debugging, among other uses
- Apply Julia to tackle problems concurrently
- Integrate Julia with other languages such as C, Python, and MATLAB

Hands-On Computer Vision with Julia
Dmitrijs Cudihins

ISBN: 9781788998796

- Analyze image metadata and identify critical data using JuliaImages
- Apply filters and improve image quality and color schemes
- Extract 2D features for image comparison using JuliaFeatures
- Cluster and classify images with KNN/SVM machine learning algorithms
- Recognize text in an image using the Tesseract library
- Use OpenCV to recognize specific objects or faces in images and videos
- Build neural network and classify images with MXNet

Leave a review - let other readers know what you think

Please share your thoughts on this book with others by leaving a review on the site that you bought it from. If you purchased the book from Amazon, please leave us an honest review on this book's Amazon page. This is vital so that other potential readers can see and use your unbiased opinion to make purchasing decisions, we can understand what our customers think about our products, and our authors can see your feedback on the title that they have worked with Packt to create. It will only take a few minutes of your time, but is valuable to other potential customers, our authors, and Packt. Thank you!

Index

used, for detecting problems 285, 289
types
  reference 47

U

UTF-8 strings
  working with 93, 95, 97, 98

V

Vim
  used, for configuring Julia 19

W

web services 115

wide format 316
Windows
  Julia, installing 14

X

xlrd package
  reference 146
XLSX.jl documentation
  reference 146
XPath language
  reference 357

Z

ZMQ.jl package
  reference 122

Made in the USA
Middletown, DE
24 May 2019